MW01620277

+++++

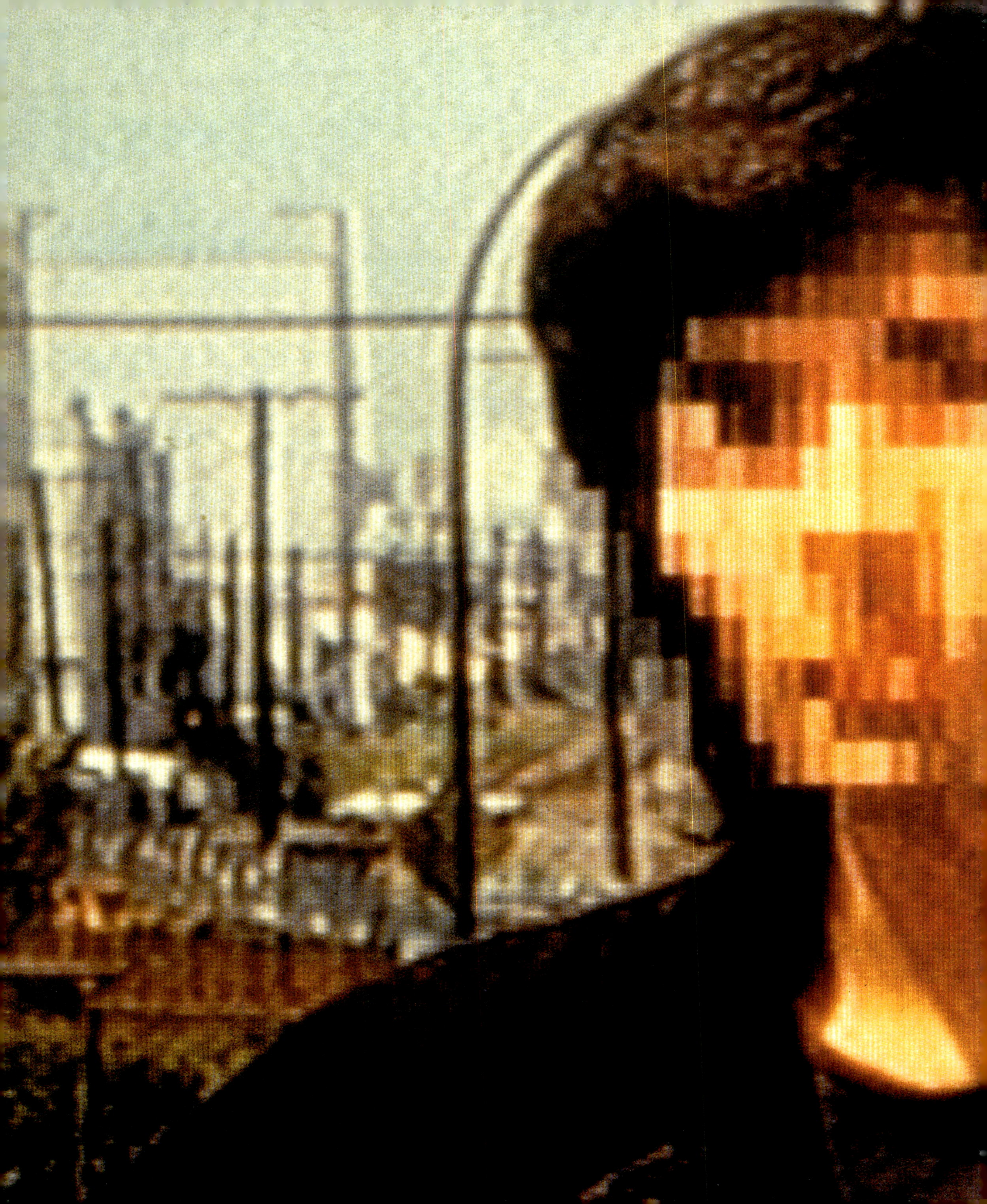

SEEING TIME

SELECTIONS FROM THE PAMELA AND RICHARD KRAMLICH COLLECTION OF MEDIA ART

DAVID A. ROSS

ROBERT R. RILEY

MARITA STURKEN

CHRISSIE ILES

THEA WESTREICH

SAN FRANCISCO MUSEUM OF MODERN ART

SEEING TIME: SELECTIONS FROM THE PAMELA AND RICHARD KRAMLICH COLLECTION OF MEDIA ART is organized by the San Francisco Museum of Modern Art with special cooperation from Thea Westreich Art Advisory Services, New York. Exhibition dates: October 15, 1999, to January 9, 2000.

This exhibition is sponsored by Credit Suisse First Boston and New Enterprise Associates. Additional support provided by Thomas Weisel Partners LLC.

Generous underwriting is provided by Diane and Scott Heldfond.

PUBLICATIONS DIRECTOR
Kara Kirk

PUBLICATIONS MANAGER
Chad Coerver

EDITOR
Karen Jacobson

DESIGNERS
Appetite Engineers:
Martin Venezky + Sara Cambridge

PUBLICATIONS COORDINATOR
Alexandra Chappell

PRINTER
Dr. Cantz'sche Druckerei

PHOTOGRAPHY CREDITS: Unless indicated below, all photographs are courtesy of Thea Westreich Art Advisory Services. COVER: photo by Ian Reeves (front); video still by San Francisco Museum of Modern art (back). FIGURES: figs. 1–2: ©1999 Bruce Nauman/Artists Rights Society (ARS), New York; fig. 3: video still by San Francisco Museum of Modern Art; fig. 5: ©1994 Mathew Barney, photo by Michael James O'Brien; figs. 7–8: video stills by San Francisco Museum of Modern Art; fig. 12: photo by Kira Pirov; fig. 14: courtesy 303 Gallery, New York; fig. 15: courtesy Galerie Max Hetzler, Berlin; fig 17: courtesy Lothar Baumgarten and Marian Goodman Gallery, New York; fig. 18: photo by Thomas Struth, courtesy Marian Goodman Gallery, New York; figs. 19–23: photos by Ben Blackwell, courtesy Thea Westreich Art Advisory Services. PLATES: pls. 1–10: photos by Ian Reeves; pls. 17–20: video stills by San Francisco Museum of Modern Art; pl. 22: courtesy 303 Gallery, New York; pls. 30–32: courtesy Lothar Baumgarten and Marian Goodman Gallery, New York; pls. 35–38: courtesy Galerie Max Hetzler, Berlin; pl. 49: courtesy Jay Jopling, White Cube, London; pls. 53–54: photos by Kira Pirov; pl. 55: courtesy James Coleman and Marian Goodman Gallery, New York; pls. 56–59: ©1999 Bruce Nauman/Artists Rights Society (ARS), New York; pls. 70–74 and 76–77, video stills by San Francisco Museum of Modern Art.

Front Cover:
MARCEL BROODTHAERS,
Fig. 0, Fig. 1, Fig. 2, Fig. A, 1971, detail of film still from *Une discussion inaugurale* (1968).

Back Cover:
LARRY CLARK,
Nate, G-Street Live, 1992,
video still (detail).

Frontispiece:
STAN DOUGLAS,
Monodramas, 1991,
detail of video still from "Guilty I."

LIBRARY OF CONGRESS CATALOGING-IN-PUBLICATION DATA:
Riley, Robert R.
Seeing time: selections from the Pamela and Richard Kramlich collection of media art / Robert R. Riley, Marita Sturken, Chrissie Iles.
p. cm.
Published on the occasion of an exhibition held at the San Francisco Museum of Modern Art, Oct. 15, 1999 to Jan. 9, 2000.
ISBN 0-918471-55-9 (softcover)
ISBN 0-918471-57-5 (hardcover)
1. Technology and the arts Exhibitions. 2. Arts and electronics Exhibitions. 3. Postmodernism Exhibitions. 4. Kramlich, Pamela—Art collections Exhibitions. 5. Kramlich, Richard—Art collections Exhibitions. 6. Arts—Private collections Exhibitions. I. Sturken, Marita, 1957– . II. Iles, Chrissie. III. San Francisco Museum of Modern Art. IV. Title.
NX180. T4R55 1999
770–dc21 99-36661
CIP

+++++

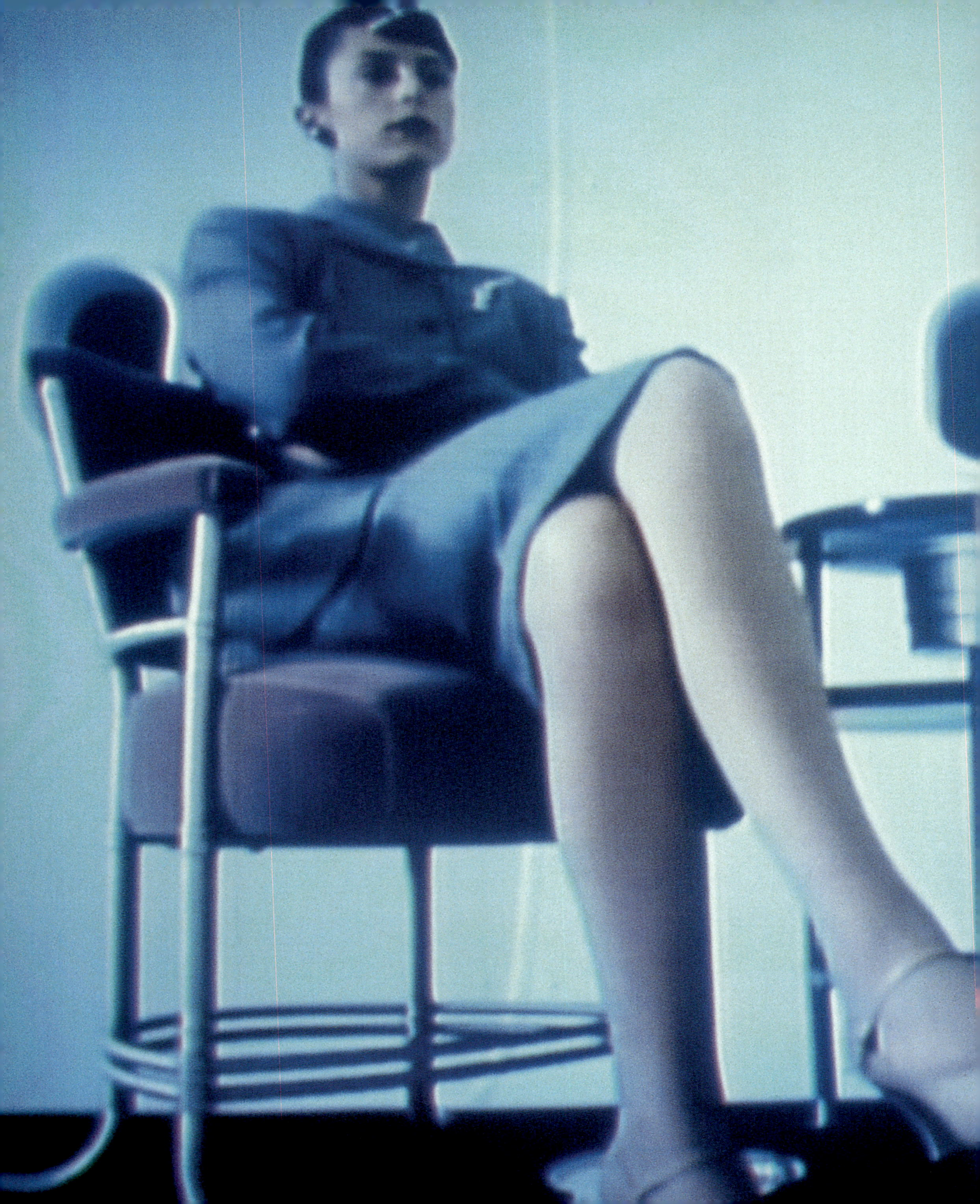

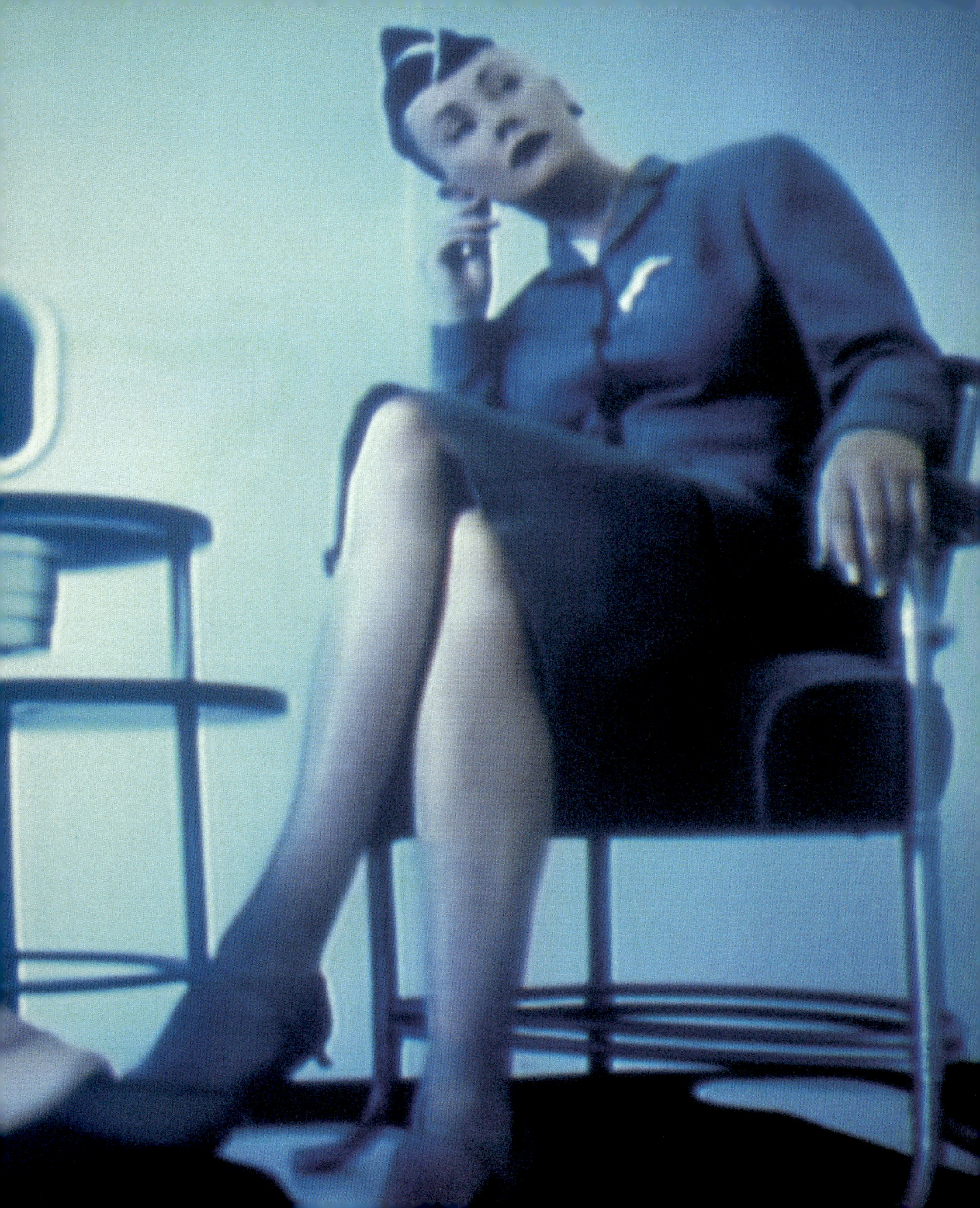

SEEING IN REAL TIME

DIRECTOR'S FOREWORD

DAVID A. ROSS

Perhaps it's obvious that inherently complicated activities resist simple definitions. On the surface, some complex things may seem easily categorized and understood, yet the very attempt to define them inadvertently exposes our ignorance, as well as the poverty of our assumptions. One can say without fear of overstatement that contemporary art collecting is one of these things.

Defined as the act of selecting, acquiring, holding, and giving at least provisional order to a group of disparate works of art, art collecting is more than just the accumulation of material things produced by artists. In an era of extreme self-consciousness, collectors of contemporary art are often discussed as if they were mere speculators or unintentional products of the marketplace. But contemporary art collectors are a misunderstood lot. Unable to rely upon historical evidence or resolved critical reception to guide their acquisitions, the best of them rely upon a sense of the moment—an instinct—developed from direct engagement with the art and ideas of our times.

At its best, collecting is both a manifestation of creative intelligence and an act of active patronage. Not merely the result of some natural accretion running parallel to the accumulation of wealth, serious contemporary art collecting requires the development of a carefully considered point of view and the conscious construction of what might best be called a text.

In this regard, art collecting is uniquely challenging and particularly fascinating. A resolutely complex activity, it is essentially an experimental, epistemological process: a radical form of lifelong learning. In a real sense, then, the effort to locate, acquire, preserve, and exhibit a thoughtfully assembled art collection is a process of cultural construction. The act of collecting the art of one's time generates a secondary layer of meaning, resulting from the juxtaposition of the works to form a collection. Great art collections are capable of conveying meaning richer and far more complex than that of any individual work of art. That is why we value them so dearly.

Since our understanding of works of art shifts in relation to context and the ways in which they are exhibited, the practice of collecting demands a continuing focus. As meaning flows from the collecting process, a unique learning experience informs and directs the collection's growth and refinement. This activity is similar to what takes place within public art collections—though free of the particular social dynamic of art museum acquisition practices—so that private collectors can take the kinds of risks that even the most adventurous contemporary art museums rarely take.

Previous pages:

MATTHEW BARNEY,
Cremaster I,
1995–96, video still (detail).

When passion, courage, and genuine curiosity propel the collecting process, the results can be extraordinary. And that is precisely what we find when we encounter the collection of Pamela and Richard Kramlich. In only slightly more than a decade, the Kramlichs have assembled the most important private collection of time-based video and film installation works in the United States. Beginning from the premise that during the past twenty-five years new technologies have transformed social and intellectual life (including art practice), Pam and Dick Kramlich have built a collection that manages to represent the aesthetic transformation of our era. Many of the challenges confronting artists of our moment—including the shifting understanding of how time and temporal experience can be manipulated and represented—are embedded in the works the Kramlichs have acquired.

The first major exhibition of the Kramlich Collection provides an opportunity to explore aspects of recent contemporary art and an important contemporary collection. When the Kramlichs decided to focus on acquiring video art, the impetus was more than the desire to collect in an area where few other serious collectors were working. Theirs was an almost immediate understanding—evident in their systematic and intense collecting style as well as in the seriousness of their response to works of art that many other collectors found either aesthetically incomprehensible or too technically complex to risk owning and to enjoy living with.

To collect video, the Kramlichs began by developing a fine "library" of single-channel artist's videotapes. This enabled them to study the various directions in which artists were taking the still relatively young medium. As their confidence and understanding grew, they became increasingly active collectors of video installations—room-sized audiovisual sculptural works constructed around or activated by projected video images or video monitors.

Ignoring the perhaps-obvious fact that these works could not be easily installed in a domestic setting, the Kramlichs pushed ahead, transforming their San Francisco home into a virtual museum for media art. As of this writing, they have begun building a second home in Napa County expressly to house the collection.

All of this would be of minor interest if it were not for the fact that the works that have become part of the Kramlich Collection are uniformly first-rate examples of video art at its most sophisticated. That is to say, the works are not about video per se; they use video technology not primarily for its formal qualities, but rather to examine issues of far greater consequence.

In this exhibition, *Seeing Time*, complex and contradictory notions of temporality—ranging from existential musings to the social, political, and psychosexual ramifications of time—are expressed and explored. Drawn entirely from the Kramlich Collection, the exhibition makes it clear that the collection is demonstrably rich in works of this particularly philosophical orientation. What both the exhibition and this catalogue also make abundantly clear is that video installation works—as well as various other audiovisual installation variants—continue to serve as examples of some of the most advanced sculptural practice of our time.

An exhibition of this scope and complexity could not have been undertaken without the skill and acumen of Robert R. Riley, curator of media arts at SFMOMA. His tremendous enthusiasm for the artworks in this collection as well as the close relationships he has with so many of the artists are manifest in both the elegant installation of the exhibition and the striking and substantive publication that accompanies it.

Thea Westreich has also played an instrumental role in all aspects of this undertaking. Her tireless efforts to build this unique collection with the Kramlichs were directed with equal gusto to bringing it to the public eye at SFMOMA. Christopher Eamon, her associate at Thea Westreich Art Advisory Services, provided invaluable counsel throughout this process, and we thank him for his patience and good humor.

Chrissie Iles and Marita Sturken joined Robert Riley and Thea Westreich in writing texts for this catalogue, and we are grateful to both of them for their outstanding contributions. Karen Jacobson edited the texts with the sensitivity and attention to detail they required. Martin Venezky and Sara Cambridge of Appetite Engineers brought great creativity and enthusiasm to the design of this publication, and we offer them express thanks for their efforts. We are indebted to Museum staff members Kara Kirk, publications and graphic design director, and Chad Coerver, publications manager, who oversaw all aspects of the editing, production, and design of this book; they were assisted in their efforts by Publications Coordinator Alexandra Chappell and intern Pilar Rubin.

At SFMOMA, this project received particular care from staff members Matt Biederman, exhibitions technological manager; Olga Charyshyn, registrar, exhibitions; Steve Dye, exhibitions technical assistant; Evan Forfar, chief preparator; Ruth Keffer, curatorial associate; Barbara Levine, exhibitions director; Carol Nakaso, film program coordinator and administrative assistant, Media Arts; Jeff Richards, preparator; Kent Roberts, exhibition design manager; Marcelene Trujillo, assistant exhibitions director; Polly Winograd, communications manager.

In addition, we have received invaluable help from our colleagues at the following galleries: Roland Augustine, Lawrence Luhring, and Michelle Maccarone, Luhring Augustine, New York; Lisa Spellman and Kurt Brondo, 303 Gallery, New York; Barbara Gladstone, Barbara Gladstone Gallery, New York; Catherine Belloy, Elaine Budin, and Marian Goodman, Marian Goodman Gallery, New York; Jeffrey Deitch, Jeffrey Deitch Projects, New York; Marie Gillisen, estate of Marcel Broodthaers, Brussels; Tanja Grunert, Klemens Gasser and Tanja Grunert, Inc., New York; Jay Jopling, White Cube, London; Max Hetzler and Caroline Käding, Galerie Max Hetzler, Berlin; Anthony Reynolds and Tristram Pye, Anthony Reynolds Gallery, London; Anthony d'Offay and Robin Vousden, Anthony d'Offay Gallery, London; Nicholas Logsdail and Michelle D'Souza, Lisson Gallery, London.

The presentation of this exhibition would not have been possible without the generous sponsorship of Credit Suisse First Boston and New Enterprise Associates, the additional support of Thomas Weisel Partners LLC, and the generous underwriting provided by Diane and Scott Heldfond. Media sponsorship has been provided by the San Jose Mercury News and Silicon Valley.com, with product support by Metreon—A Sony Entertainment Center.

Great thanks are due to the twenty-seven artists, many of whom have provided invaluable assistance in making the presentation of their works possible. The works by this diverse group—from the early pioneers of media art to the younger artists whose work builds on the groundwork of their predecessors—are a lasting contribution to our understanding of perception and time.

Most importantly, this exhibition tells us a great deal about a private collection of contemporary art that displays a focus and intelligence that set it apart from all others. In a modest way, it also tells us a great deal about the passion and daring of Richard and Pamela Kramlich, two collectors who continue to redefine our idea of the art of collecting.

STEPHANIE SMITH AND EDWARD STEWART, *Sustain*, 1995, video still.

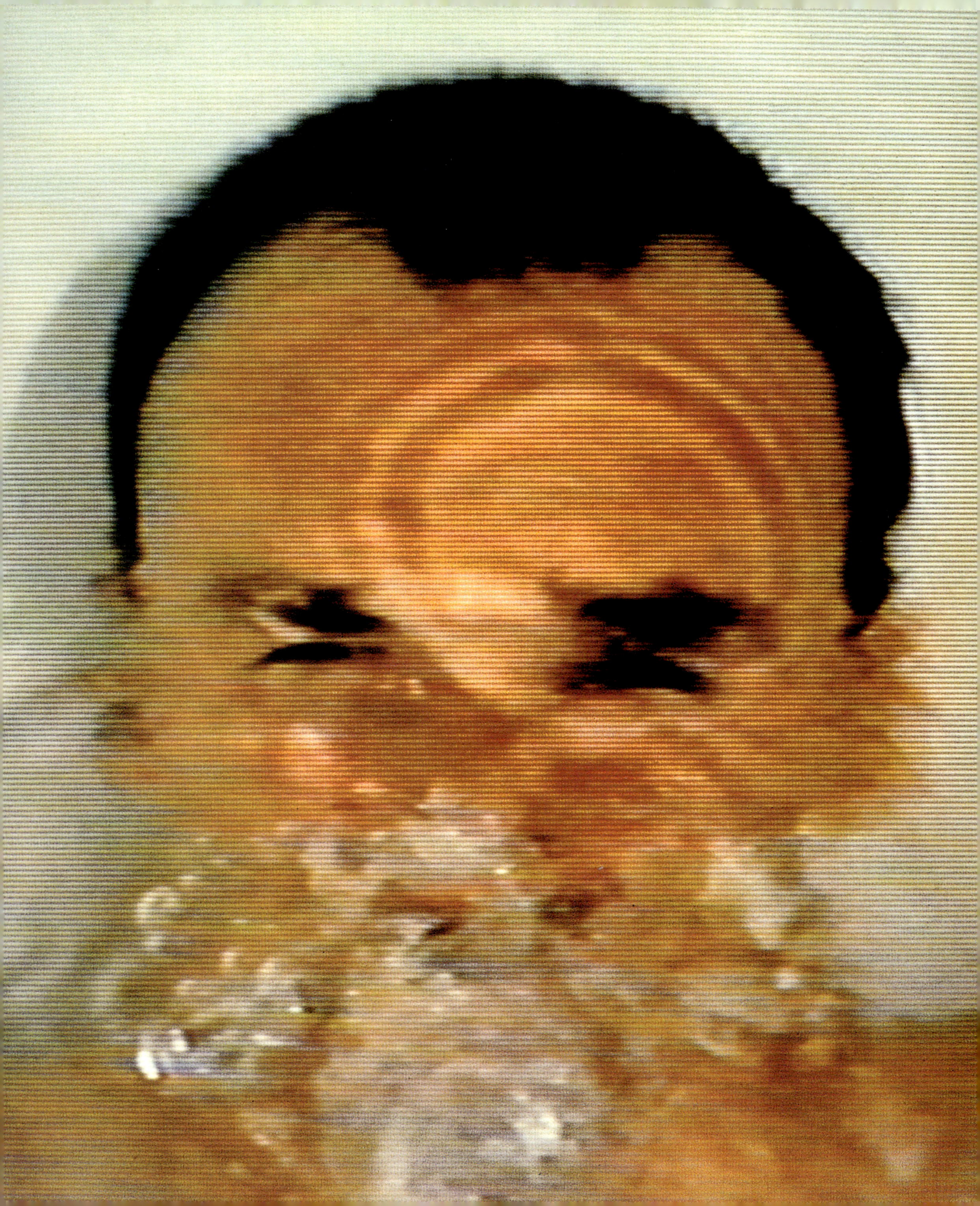

TIME, PERCEPTION, AND SIGHT 15

ROBERT R. RILEY

Perception as a philosophical question has been pursued in a broad array of artistic inquiries throughout art history and has been a significant focus of contemporary forms of media art. The video installations and multimedia environments in *Seeing Time* explore aspects of perception, beginning with the principle that vision is shaped by the time in which we live and the idea that life today can no longer be distinguished from the influences of mechanical and technological devices of perception. *Seeing Time* engages the relationship of sight to knowledge. The visual artists represented in the exhibition examine the dilemma of perception, reflecting on the particular emotional states and ways of thinking that result from the influences of technological media on contemporary life.

The artists in *Seeing Time* condition visibility by posing vision as a modern philosophical question through their installations of still, moving, and projected images. Mechanical and technological forms of art—from works investigating the science of perspective to photographic images, cinematic forms, and video environments—have inspired the philosophical discussion of perception as defined in this century. The notion of perception reflected in current art practices differs in fundamental ways from that of earlier eras because of the technology employed. The formation of vision in contemporary media art is both figurative and technical: instrumentation, ways of seeing through visual technology, and media as material for art are the unifying concerns of the work in this exhibition.[1]

The parameters of media art are defined by its relationships to technical instrumentation, mechanical reproducibility, and each medium's time-based properties. Traditionally the history of media art has been understood in terms of the spatial construction of information (the physical components of video and image apparatuses as elements of the artwork) and the temporal organization of data in each photographic medium (the rapidly obsolete, fugitive materials of film, video, and, most recently, digital media and interactive networks). The artworks in *Seeing Time* materialize and demonstrate the ambitions of three generations of artists who have addressed, or provoked, a revolution in perception through their emphasis on prescient content and their innovative presentation methods, each relevant to its time of production. The installation form contains within it the history of media art, through which the relationship of the viewer to the artwork and that of art to perception have been consistently reworked and redefined.

1. The relationship between optics, perception, and instrumentation is examined in PETER GALISON, "Judgment against Objectivity," in *Picturing Science Producing Art*, ed. Caroline Jones and Peter Galison (New York and London: Routledge, 1998).

Overleaf:

Figure 1 (left)
BRUCE NAUMAN, *Raw Material—OK, OK, OK*, 1990, video still (detail)

Figure 2 (right)
BRUCE NAUMAN, *Raw Material—OK, OK, OK*, 1990, video still (detail).

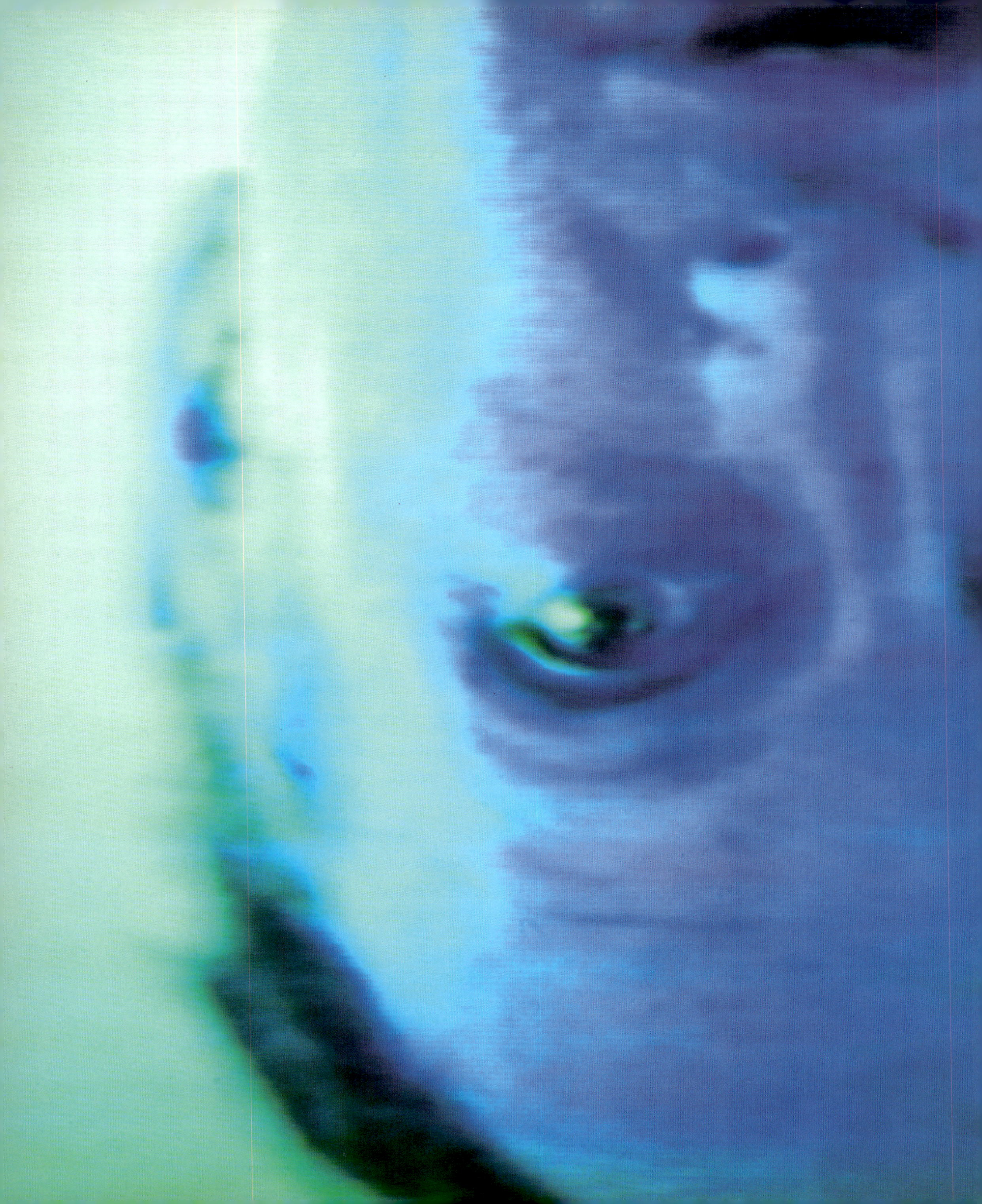

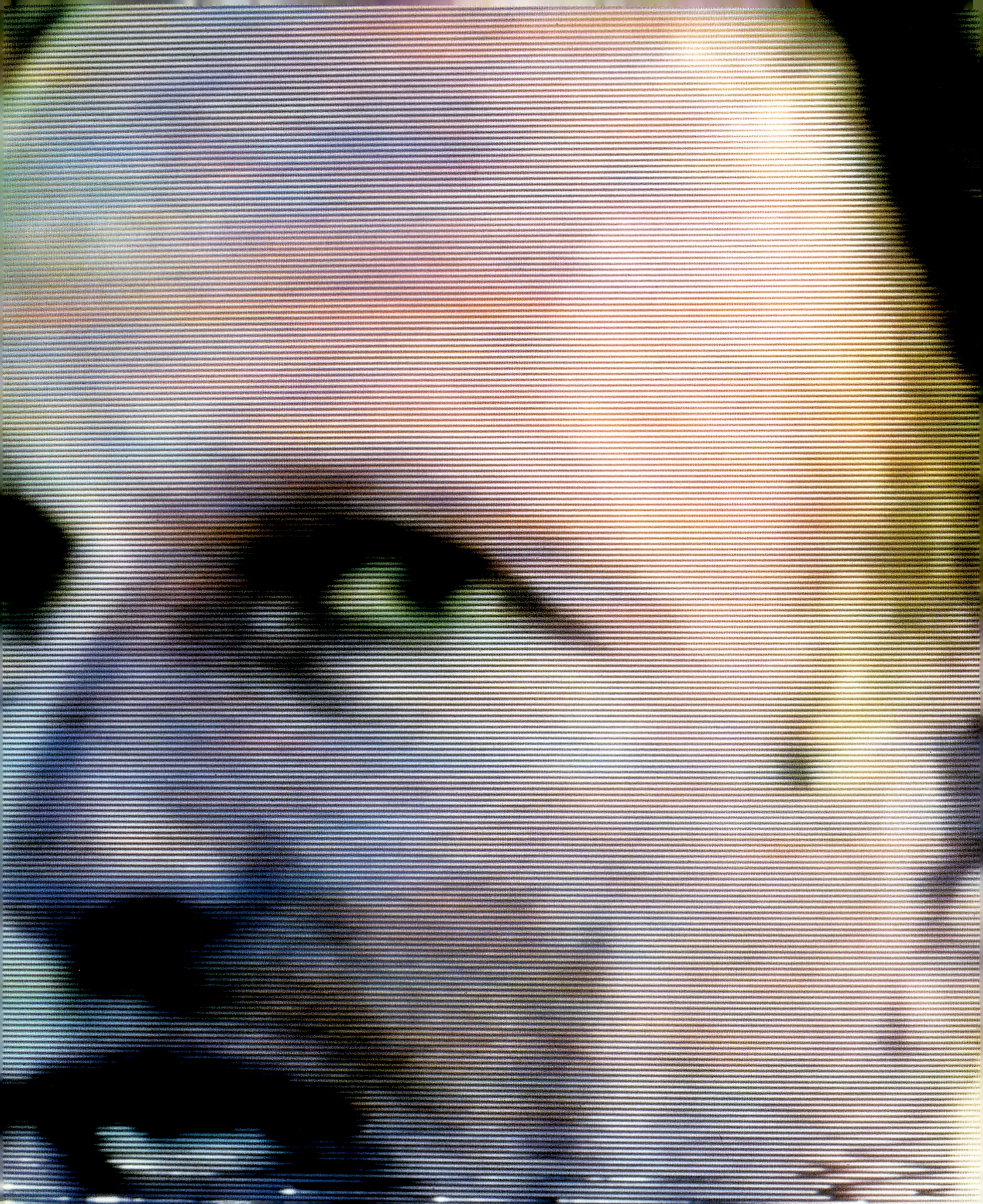

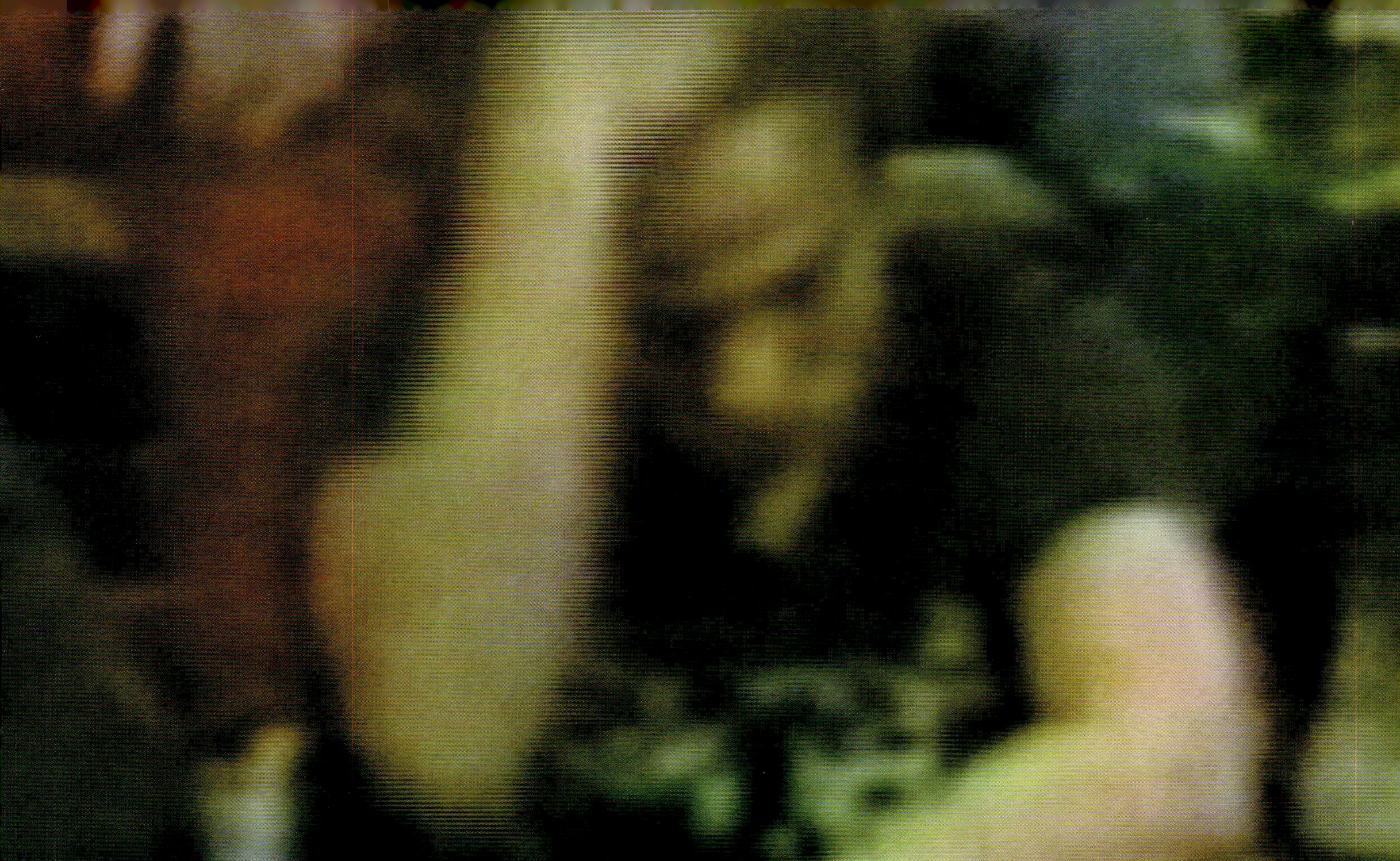

Figure 3
LARRY CLARK,
Nate, G-Street Live, 1992,
video still (detail).

REPETITION AND PRESENCE

Many of the works in the exhibition focus specifically, and self-consciously, on the artists' common desire to shift the status of the artwork, defining it as an aspect of temporal human experience rather than as a discrete, tangible object. Earlier artists who worked with technology investigated the outer edges of ecstatic, optical, and auditory stimulation, opening the way for media art that shapes perception through nonabstract imagery in dialogue with its technical medium.[2] In contrast to works of art in moving-image media, which are based on a linear notion of perception in time, many artworks in the exhibition propose a vision of time that stands in opposition to the notion of episodic progression through narrative. These works introduce repetition as an expressive device that affords artists the chance to repeat actions, suspend and emphasize movements, and heighten perception of a specific moment.

The effects of repetition are realized to the fullest extent in Bruce Nauman's *Raw Material-OK, OK, OK* (1990; figs. 1–2), a sparse video installation that incorporates the undisguised components of media—the cathode ray tube video projector, videotape players, the screen, and video monitors—as dynamic sculptural materials. Here, as in his experimental video art of the late 1960s, Nauman uses his body as the vehicle through which his concepts for art are translated to form. His projects underscore his interest in expressing the body's confinement in relation to time. The figure, whose motion is contained

2. The value of art in reproducible media is discussed in WALTER BENJAMIN, "The Work of Art in the Age of Mechanical Reproduction," in *Illuminations*, trans. Harry Zohn (New York: Schocken, 1969).

in the fixed field of the video image and extended in time, is Nauman's enduring subject. Time is used to trap the figure within the frame, and video restricts action to an enclosed space. In *Raw Material* the four edges of the static video frame are accentuated by the obsessive motion it contains: the artist's head spinning in place. In his first work to use his own image since the 1970s, Nauman chose to portray only his head before a stationary video camera. The video images of his head alternate in right-side-up or upside-down orientation in repetitive sequences in which rudimentary special effects were used in postproduction to create image reversals and color changes. The artist's head spins in place, as if disembodied and suspended in time, shouting the often-heard phrase of despair or resignation: "Okay, okay, okay, okay. . . ."

Nauman's exploration of repetition through speech and gesture is concerned not with the futility of circular motion but rather with the conflict between vision and its consequential material production as art. The redirection of the body within the frame functions to question whether art is a durable form of labor and to measure its value in the age of information. *Raw Material* invokes the fusion of opposites, reconciling the states of motion and stasis in a single artwork. Repetition holds the viewer in time, just as Nauman's figure is suspended in video.

In its repetitive structure *Raw Material* displays affinities with Bill Viola's *The Greeting* (1995; pls. 53–54), with its slow-motion image that simultaneously repeats and appears to stand still, and with Larry Clark's *Nate, G-Street Live* (1992; fig. 3; pls. 70–73), in which repetitive video images offer a commentary on the experience of adolescence within a wider social context. Clark sketches a video portrait of passivity through his depiction of the aggression directed at the central figure by the voices of hostile off-screen callers. Similarly, in the large-scale projected video installation *Intercourse* (1993; pls. 78–79) and the individual video work *Sustain* (1995; pls. 80–82), by collaborators Stephanie Smith and Edward Stewart, the artists' intimate gestures of interdependence and aggression are reiterated. These works of video art resist narrative progression and reach outside the space they materially occupy to acquire, through repetition, a character of tension and suspense.

In philosophical terms, repetition forces a reexamination of time, particularly in relation to perception. Once repeated, an event is never again seen as it was the first time. In twentieth-century philosophy the concept of repetition has theological implications: consciousness of the self, within a set of socially imposed influences that condition self-perception, becomes pronounced through repetition.[3] Repetition draws attention to the self in order to effect projection of inner life or an emotional state to external manifestation as art. In media art, repetition resists reflection for the purpose of expression.

Whereas repetition calls into question the concept of a distinct moment in time, the realization of a moment, or the idea of the moment alone, is often discussed by philosophers and theologians as "presence." While repetition in art expresses the compulsion to resolve conflict, presence is the recognition of sensory and perceptual influences that define the self in relationship to the immediate visual, auditory, and temporal environment.[4] As a disquieting perceptual engagement with a moment that is infinite in its effects on consciousness, presence does not describe an awareness recovered from the past by memory, but rather a startling encounter with the present time and place.

3. SOREN KIERKEGAARD, *Repetition*, ed. and trans. Howard V. Hong and Edna H. Hong (Princeton, N.J.: Princeton University Press, 1983).

4. RALPH HARPER, *On Presence: Variations and Reflections* (Philadelphia: Trinity Press International, 1991).

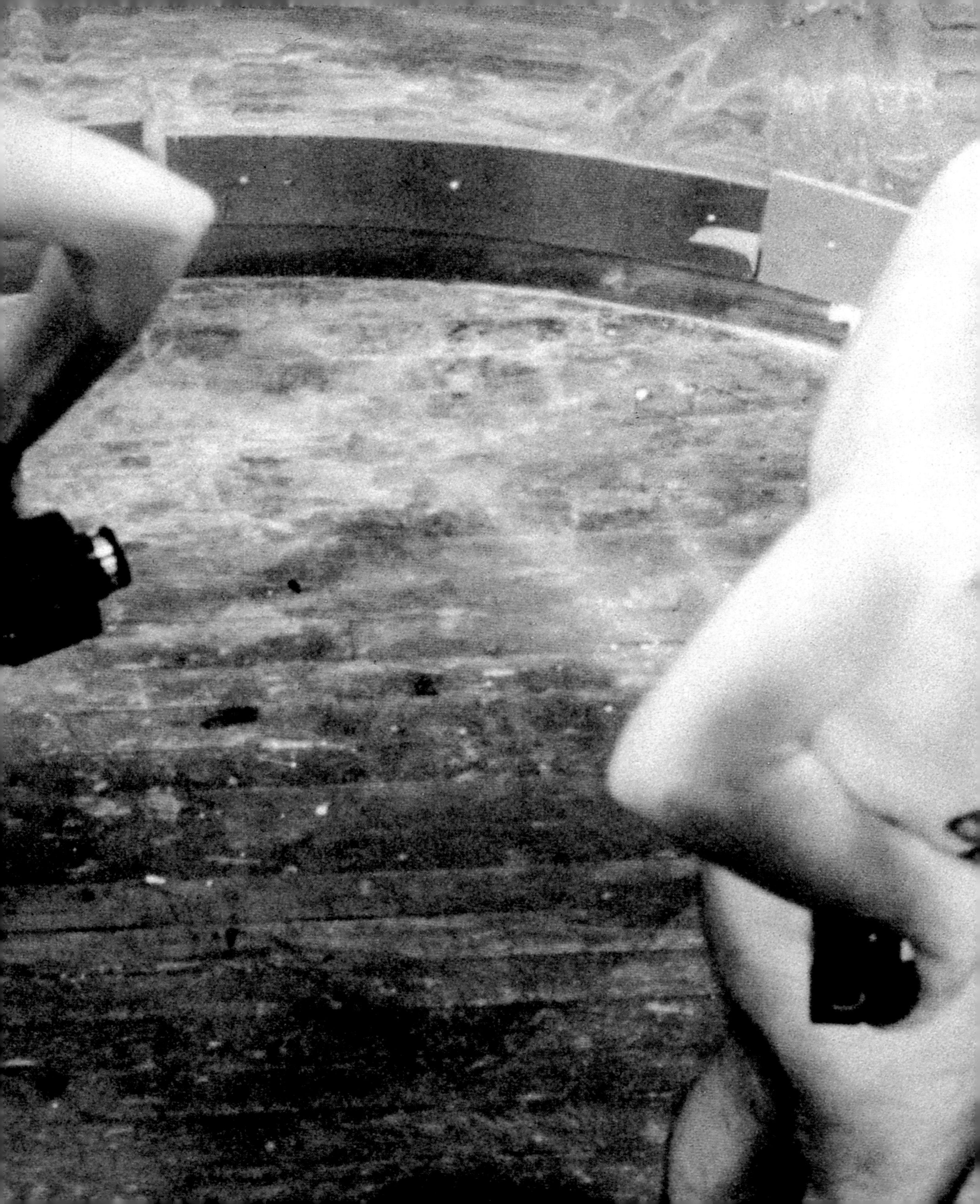

—Jeff Wall's large photographic images, back-lit as luminous screens, depict the condition of presence in their complexity of form, image, and social subject. Wall's work is concerned with the visibility of the unseen subject, returning to the tradition of the metaphysical image in art. He uses the presentation of the human figure under duress to detect illusion in real life,[5] to suggest a world behind appearances, and to reveal truths otherwise obscured. In such works as *The Quarrel* (1988; pl. 25) and *Untangling* (1994; pl. 26), he distills moments from a larger narrative to depict discordant conditions that might be attributed to the expanding role of technology in everyday life. The viewer's attention is drawn away from habitual modes of seeing, toward subtle provocations of cause and effect.—

—The tension between the still image and its moving-image component is realized in Steve McQueen's *Deadpan* (1997; pls. 66–67) as a performance of condition of presence. In *Deadpan* the collapse of a barn façade from background to foreground is repeated as a single action, yet the narrative is shifted by changes in camera angle to create multiple points of view. McQueen is framed within the falling building, which is framed within the video image and then within the installation form itself. From one camera angle he appears heroic, from another diminished. His figure remains stationary while the world around him collapses. McQueen's stationary presence creates a contained moment of time within a set of repeating moving-image sequences.

THE BODY AS A SITE OF KNOWLEDGE

—Depiction of the human figure in media installations positions the body as a field of meaning, a site of social knowledge and inscription. The mediating presence of the figure in *Seeing Time* accentuates its role in the process of perception. The range of engagement with the body in these media installations, in full figure or fragment, reveals its importance in contemporary artistic, philosophical, and technological discourses. Figuration is often a means to articulate the methods through which technology and instrumentation create new ways of being.—

—*Body Press* (1970–72; fig. 4), a projected-image installation by Dan Graham, places the body within the frame of the installation as a means to formulate vision through instrumentation. The installation is distinguished in its combination of image-making machinery and in its conceptual scheme: hand-held movie cameras are used in the artwork as navigational instruments to introduce change as a concept of space as mediated by technology. Graham combines in film the physical, three-dimensional ground of sculpture with a four-dimensional perception of time. The cameras in *Body Press* circumscribe the surface contours of two figures, mapping the body's physicality.[6] The mass of the body is captured on film through the press of the camera against it. A perception of infinite, regressive space and a feedback system of image and reflection are conveyed in the work's autographic form: the presence of the body infused to the camera simultaneously creates and defines space.—

5. See JEFF WALL, "Landscape Manual, 1969-1970," in *Information*, ed. Kynaston L. McShine (New York: Museum of Modern Art, 1970).

6. DAN GRAHAM, *Rock My Religion: Writings and Art Projects, 1965–1990*, ed. Brian Wallis (Cambridge: MIT Press, 1993), 138.

Figure 4
DAN GRAHAM,
Body Press, 1970–72,
detail of plate 24.

Whereas Graham models changes of perception through the fusion of the camera, the body, and its reflection in sculpture, the four-image installation *Stasi City* (1997; pls. 22–23), by Jane and Louise Wilson, constructs a contained space limited from within for the purposes of information collection and surveillance—the former headquarters of the secret police in East Berlin. The figure is used in these works to approach and translate to the viewer the condition of presence in media environments. Stasi was a state security agency deployed for the tracking of data about citizens through the surreptitious application and manufacture of sophisticated clandestine instruments. It was Stasi officials who designed and manufactured a full surveillance environment of image- and sound-recording devices originally for use in Cold War espionage and spy tactics: the cigarette lighter infitted with a camera lens, ventilation or plumbing utility repurposed as a covert communication system, and so on. Instruments were not only engineered to trace the movement of citizens but were also fused to appliances such as the telephone in order to translate ordinary conversation into data.

The Wilsons' mass of collected impressions of the abandoned Stasi headquarters appear to float freely, like the panoramic images in Graham's *Body Press*, but *Stasi City* also translates to video installation the material space of the abandoned headquarters to describe the invisible forces that shape perception. Fleeting images of figures in office interiors acquire a lyrical content. Images of open doors congesting hallways, of cabinets left ajar, revealing empty shelves, and of drawers pulled from desks imply a hasty evacuation. Furnishings once used by secret police to conceal their materials reveal here the subject of information. The refuse of information is transformed by time, which was arrested at the moment the space was left deserted. In their sculptural forms and figuration, *Stasi City* and *Body Press* reflect the ways in which spatial perception is conditioned through time and place.

In *Stasi City* and *Body Press*, as in McQueen's *Deadpan*, the figure is defined through its relationship to space. Other works in the exhibition focus on the body's fusion with technology and loss of autonomy through it. The title of Smith and Stewart's *Intercourse* evokes a passage from Leo Tolstoy's 1930 essay "What Is Art?" in which the writer defines the qualities that distinguish a work of art, qualities that are relevant to media art today: "Beyond a discussion of form, art is found in intercourse, its capacity to translate experience, through its materials, from one [person] to another." A work of art, he claims, "destroys in the consciousness of the recipient the separation between himself and the artist, and not that alone, but also between himself and all whose minds receive this work of art." He argues that the art object affects the process of perception between its source as image and its reception as knowledge; in doing so, art goes beyond the superficial conveyance of information.[7]

7. LEO TOLSTOY, "What Is Art?" (1930) in *Art and Philosophy: Readings in Aesthetics*, ed. W. E. Kennick (New York: St. Martins Press, 1964), 7–18.

Smith and Stewart address the physicality of their relationship as collaborators in video through obsessive actions and symbolic gestures staged for the camera. They express their codependence through the exchange of air or body fluids in repetitive sequences. Here the body is used symbolically to convey the complexity of interdependence and empathy. The viewer is held in suspense as the gestures of breathing and spitting are repeated. Thus, repetition has the effect of provoking empathy in the viewer. In contrast to the observed figures of *Body Press* and *Stasi City*, here the body is presented in all its unadorned morphology. In Smith and Stewart's *Intercourse* and *Sustain*, the body is constructed as a site of knowledge through its most intimate functions. Fluidity is the aspect of the body that most calls into question its permanence and autonomy. Similarly, in relation to other camera media, video can be seen as a fluid medium.

Figure 5
MATTHEW BARNEY, *Cremaster IV: The Loughton Candidate*, 1994, color photo produced in conjunction with the video *Cremaster IV*, 14 x 12 in. (detail).

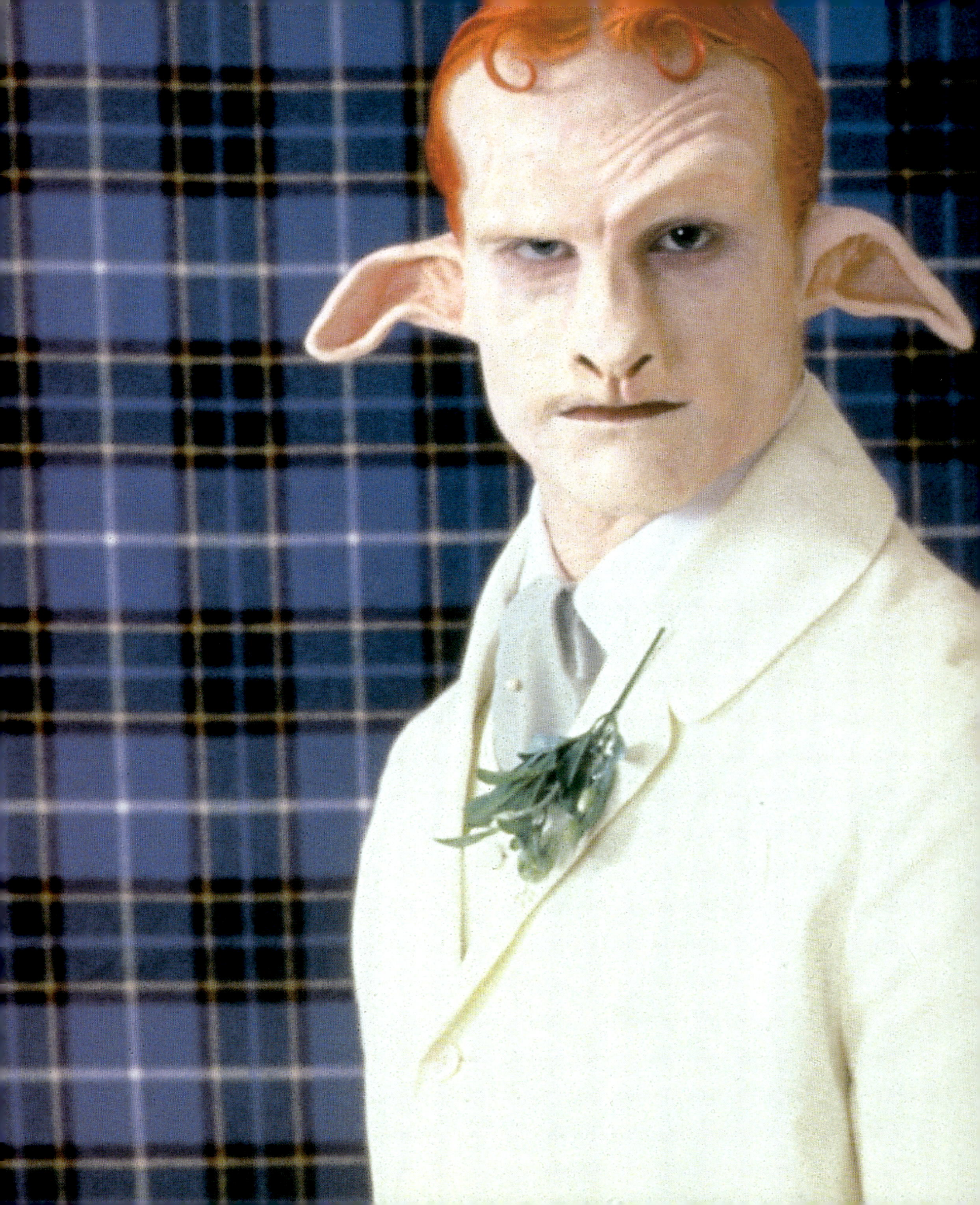

The fluidity of the video image is exploited in Matthew Barney's works to present the body as a transformative site of knowledge. In *Scabaction* (1988; pls. 83–88) and the *Cremaster* series (1994–97; fig. 5; pls. 89–94), Barney deploys video in conjunction with a larger palette of materials (latex, petroleum jelly, prosthetic plastic) that evoke flesh and bone and the substance of cellular matter. His work is about the process of transformation through the body: Barney sees his own body as a site of metamorphosis, always in transition between inside and outside and between surface and structure. The orifices of the body are symbolic of the exchange between inside and outside, the liminal site at which the physical boundaries of the body are overcome. Barney is using these materials and technologies in order to express the difference between being and becoming.

Japanese artist Mariko Mori, like Barney, transfigures her identity through the metamorphosis of physical materials. In works involving chameleon-like adaptations, she allows the technological tools of industrial design, automation, and electronic media to influence her identity; she becomes the subject of technology through a process of osmosis, of assimilation through absorption. In *Miko no inori* (1996; pls. 64–65), she appears with digitally altered eyes, portraying a body that is adapted rather than resistant to a technological mode of being. Through technological effects, she turns the video screen into a liquid surface, emphasizing its fluidity and, by extension, her own transformative state. Whereas Barney's body is an ecstatic expansion through the skin and beyond the surface, in Mori's body the pleasure is in being contained within the technological frame.

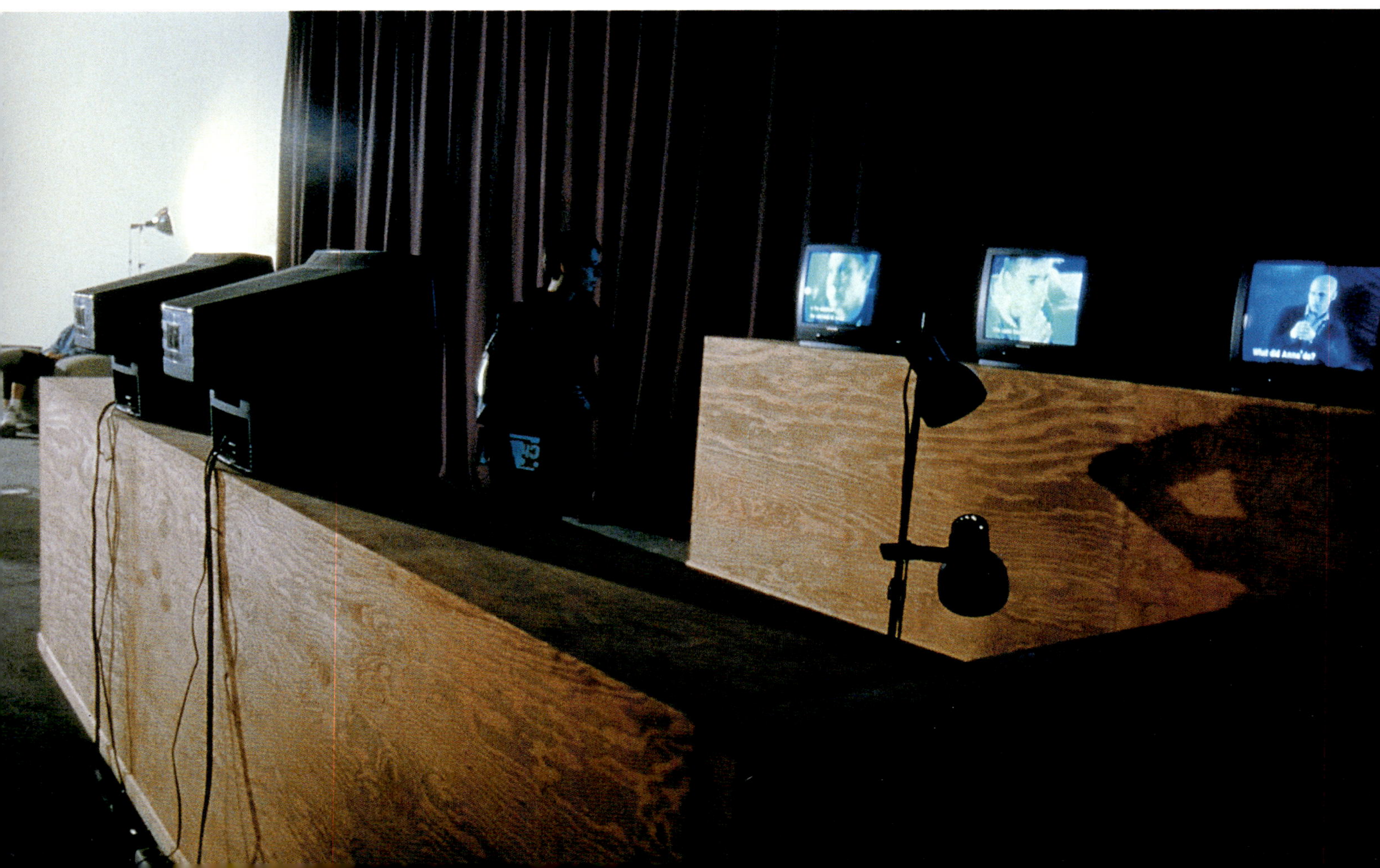

Figure 6
EIJA-LIISA AHTILA,
Anne, Aki, and God, 1998,
installation view.

The degree to which we understand the world around us is largely conditioned by camera images, photographic reproduction, and the widespread distribution of visual information. For example, one photograph now serves as a substitute for headline text on the front page of daily newspapers, condensing the complexities of historical events into a single frame. Several works in the exhibition foreground the ways in which perception is influenced by the mass media. Their goal is to disrupt the viewer's relationship to media images, to transform the viewer's attitude from one of receptivity to one of engagement.

In Vito Acconci's *Pornography in the Classroom* (1975; figs. 7–9; pls. 74–77), the body is already inscribed with social meaning before the viewer encounters its representation. The notion of embodied knowledge identifies the body as a container of social conventions and expectations. The work emphasizes the value of the body as a screen through the eroticization of the media apparatus. In Acconci's evocation of the protruding lens or the image inserted into the corner of the wall, he visualizes an ontology of reception and projection in order to address as his subject the power of desire over sight. Abstracting pornographic images in close-up, the work reveals the impossibility of defining pornography. Projected on the opposite wall, Acconci's handwritten scripts read as slogans: "public issues and private troubles," "system and structure," "theory and praxis," and "will," among many others. These texts are projected in sequence against repetitive images of the human figure to suggest the interchangeability of body parts as objects of desire. The language of controversy conditions the viewer's reception of this figurative imagery. *Pornography in the Classroom* challenges the rhetoric of classification and pedagogy by transforming familiar tools of instruction—the audiovisual elements of the illustrated lecture, the carousel slide projector, the television, and the filmstrip—into sculptural materials in order to direct their expository function to questions of desire and obscenity.

This recoding of the media apparatus through the installation form is also a fundamental aspect of Dara Birnbaum's *Tiananmen Square: Break-in Transmission* (1988–90; pls. 45–48). Birnbaum's placement of hardware and video monitors forms a graphic exposition on the crisis of social division in modern China through the same communication devices that inspired, and documented, the insurgence. The 1989 student uprising broke government-imposed silence through the use of communications networks. Birnbaum's installation articulates, through its changes in technological scale and reorganization of video imagery, the movement of information from its original subjective source to its so-called objective forms in news journalism. In the installation's sculptural form, the mass-media images of the student rebellion are only one of many narratives of what took place. *Tiananmen Square* argues that there is not one dominant story that forms the historical record, but that the memory of an event is composed of multiple and often contradictory perceptions.

The convention of social commentary in media installation is also employed by Eija-Liisa Ahtila in the multimedia installation *Anne, Aki, and God* (1998; fig. 6; pls. 68–69) to express how the complexities of inner life are affected by popular media. Based on real events, Ahtila's seven-channel video installation portrays the

Overleaf:

Figures 7–8 (left)
VITO ACCONCI,
Pornography in the Classroom, 1975,
video stills.

Figure 9 (right)
VITO ACCONCI,
Pornography in the Classroom, 1975,
installation view.

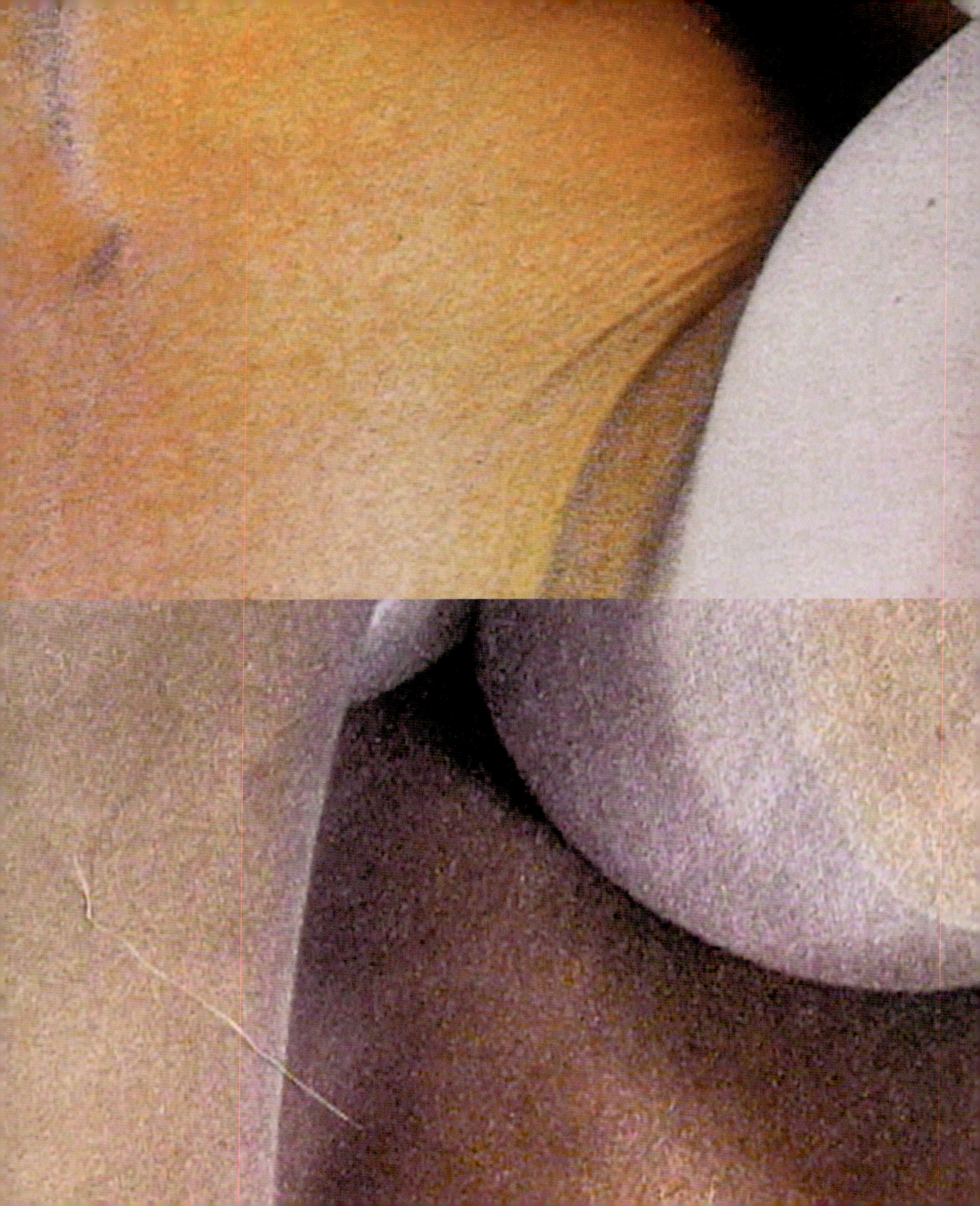

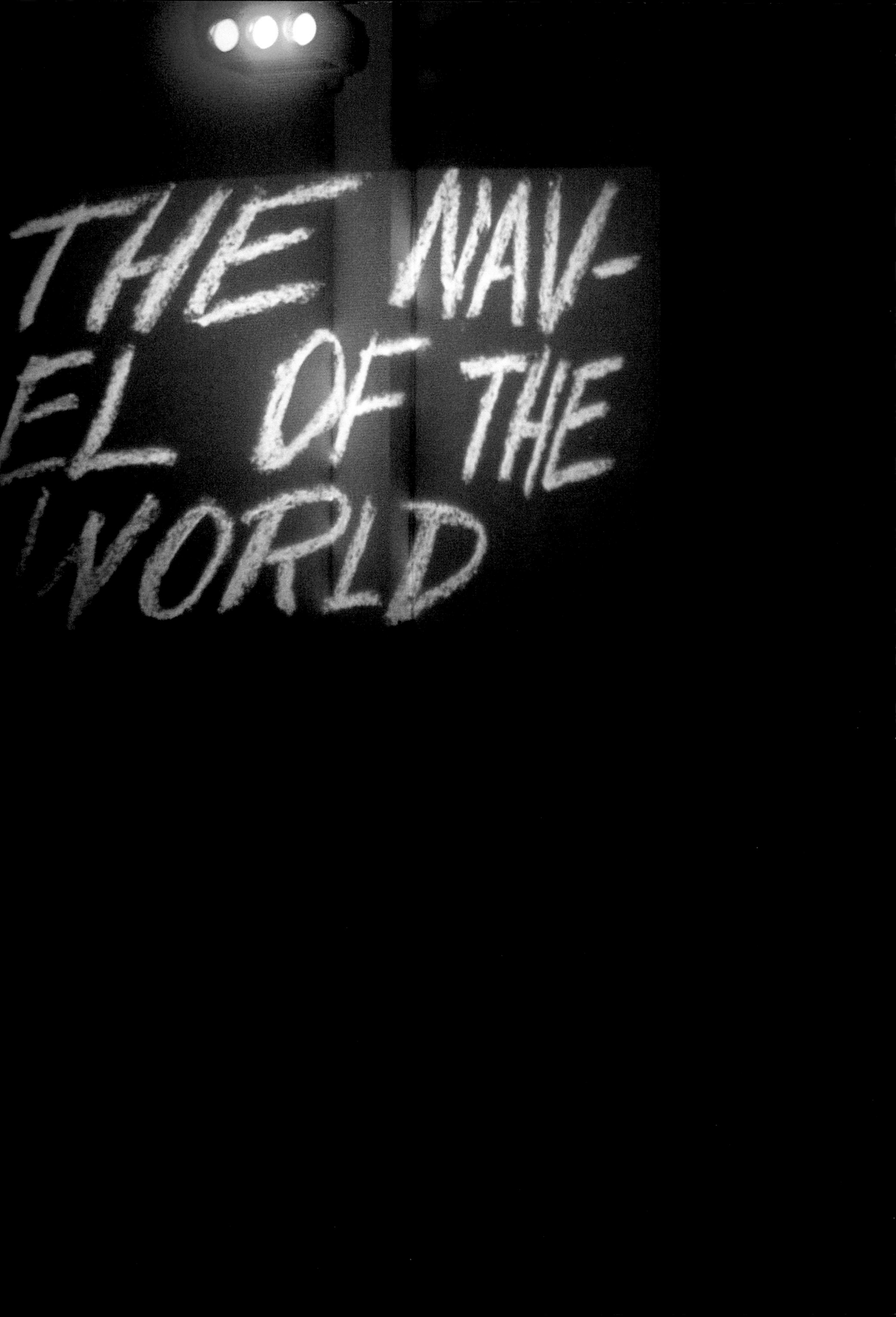

THE NAV-
EL OF THE
WORLD

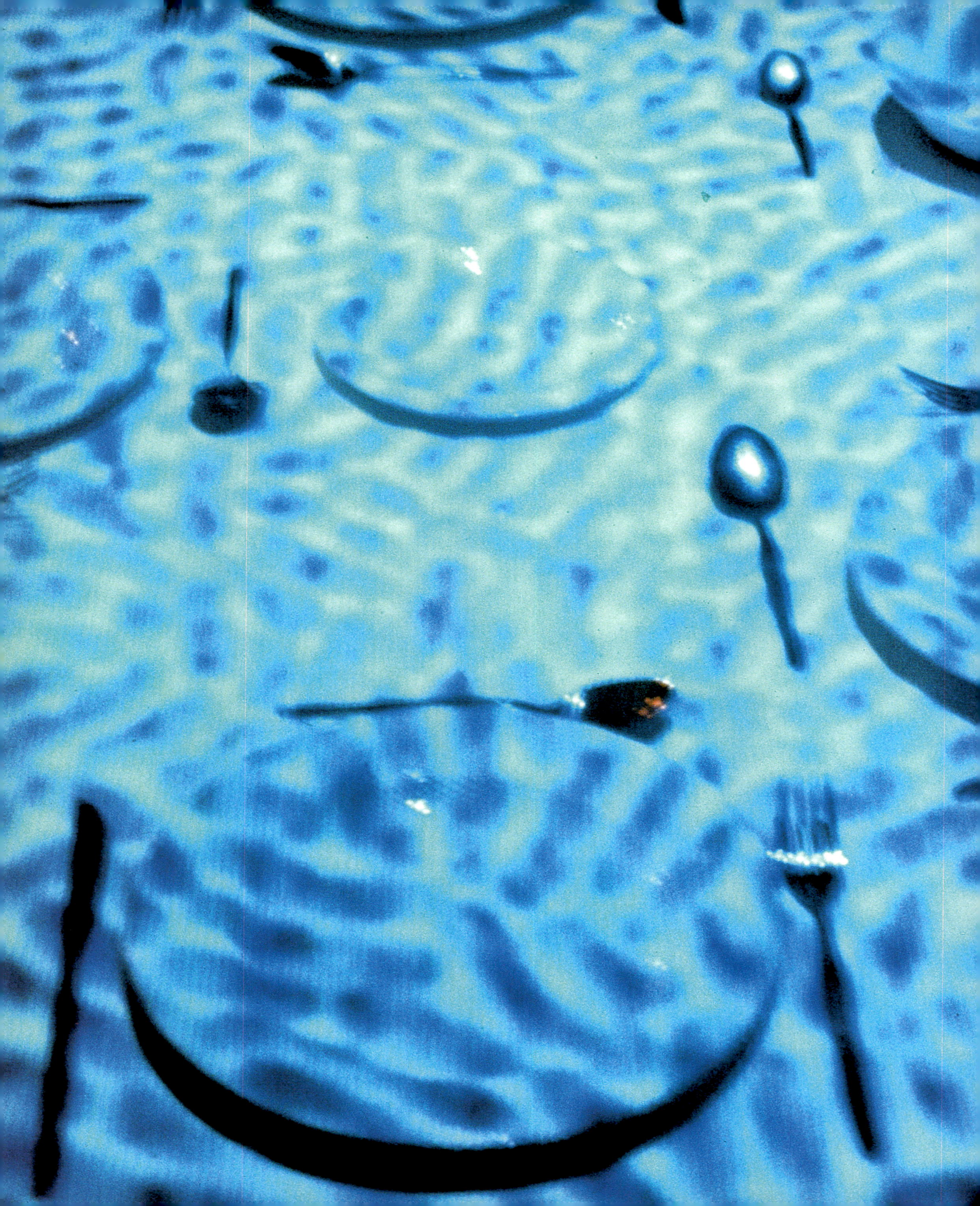

role of the imagination in perception and in delusion. *Anne, Aki, and God* tells the story of a man who descends to lunacy and becomes obsessed with finding the perfect woman to fulfill his fantasy. In Ahtila's set of video portraits, put into play by the disclosure of an erotic fantasy, she explores the ways in which we are at some level merely a construction of the multiple meanings and identities that others project upon us.

ART AND THE DISAPPEARANCE OF THE BODY

Society's habituated manner of seeing through established forms of technology is made obsolete once new technologies and advancements of vision are offered.[8] Artists respond to the conditions of living in their time. Many of them have subsequently introduced new concepts drawn from scientific discovery in the related fields of physics, biology, and psychology. The inventions and instrumentation of physics and engineering, including the computer, have produced new forms through which life can be envisioned and represented. In the context of scientific discovery that values objectivity, creativity can be related to concepts of cosmology. These artists are creating works at the axis of different bodies of thought: psychology, theology, biology, philosophy, and so on. They are the cultural figures through whom these fields of thought converge. Through the subjective response of artists to the world of information, art comes to symbolize the meaning of our existence.[9]

Keith Tyson's *Artmachine Iteration AMCHII-XLII: Angelmaker Part II Quadruped* (1995; fig. 10; pls. 27–29) synthesizes ideas from scientific invention, mass media, information distribution and data, statistics, and theological inquiry. Tyson creates a system that has a cosmology unto itself, one that confounds genre in both its sensibility and its investigation of data and statistics. In Tyson's work, the disappearance of the body in the "artmachine" takes place in cataclysmic episodes.

Tyson's "Angelmaker" is based on four probable causes of death, presented in tableau environments: Titanic, Auto-asphyxiation, Bacteria, and Earthquake. His "death-recording machines" are built from calculations that originate in his use of the computer as a source of art-making instruction. The computer functions as Tyson's "artmachine iterative" device, operating as a labor-generating machine, not a labor-saving instrument. Tyson strips the artistic project down to its bare essentials, allowing the technology to act as his collaborator.

Artmachine Iteration AMCHII-XLII takes the exhibition full circle in its reiteration of materiality in relation to the photographic and video image. Tyson points to the stationary quality of material things, through which our perception is constantly changing. Materials remain, yet our experience of them is temporary. His tableau engages data to re-create effects of both endangerment and transformation out of the material world; it is an "angel maker." In this work, fittingly, Tyson effects hazards and scintillation—the final moment of material existence, translated to light.

8. MARSHALL MCLUHAN, "The Agenbite of Outwit," *Location* 1 (spring 1963).

9. ANDREY TARKOVSKY, "The Artist's Responsibility," in *Sculpting in Time: Reflections on the Cinema*, trans. Kitty Hunter-Blair (Austin: University of Texas Press, 1986), 176.

Figure 10
KEITH TYSON, *Artmachine Iteration AMCHII-XLII: Angelmaker Part II Quadruped*, 1995, installation view.

RECLAIMING THE ARCHIVE

ART, TECHNOLOGY, AND CULTURAL MEMORY

MARITA STURKEN

At the cusp of the millennium, the world looks not so much forward as indirectly toward the past. Despite proclamations that postmodernism negates the past, it seems increasingly that history and memory are one of its primary subjects. The past circulates in the present through both declarative artifacts and unspoken absences. Memorials and monuments continue to be built, and postmodern pastiche remains fixed on a kind of pilfering and reworking of the past. While this irreverent mixing of styles of previous eras has often been seen as an ahistorical move, it can also be understood as a drive to reconfigure the past and to look in new ways at the history of images. Out of this framework come new forms of looking and seeing, reflexive and self-aware engagements with the question of what it is that we do when we look at something. The installations and photographs in *Seeing Time* can be understood in terms of their engagement with these issues of perception and consciousness of time, in particular, the use of technological media both to explore the assumptions of visual perception and to excavate the past, be it the past of social history or that of art and image making.

Postmodernism in art is often thought of as a questioning of basic tenets of modern art, such as authorship, creativity, the distinction between the original and the copy, linearity and progress, and the possibility of narrativizing the past. But it can also be seen as an emphasis on the formative role of memory, both individual and cultural, with all its nuances, absences, rescriptings, fantasies, and reconfigurings, as opposed to modern views of the inviolability of historical narrative. What does it mean, then, to look at the archive of art through the lens of memory? In what ways are new art technologies not expressively about the new per se, but about looking toward the future through the archives of the past?

Throughout history the archive has been understood both literally and metaphorically as the legitimated site of a culture's history. As French philosopher Michel Foucault once wrote, the archive is the "system of enunciability" through which a culture speaks of and through its past.[1] At the same time, the postmodern excavation of the archive is about resorting its contents and dismantling its structures. In this sense, much contemporary art can be seen as a deliberate undoing of the archives—institutional, authoritarian, colonial—that were taken for granted under modernism.

The works in this exhibition deploy technological art media in strategies that move beyond modernist notions of media specificity. In modernism the focus was often on the particular properties of a given medium, its form and its uniqueness. Hence, photography and cinema were understood to be significantly distinct in

Thanks to Dana Polan for suggestions on an earlier draft.

1. MICHEL FOUCAULT, *The Archaeology of Knowledge* (New York: Pantheon, 1972), 129.

terms of their inherent properties, such as the still image versus the moving image. Yet the works in this exhibition defy the reductive simplicity of medium categories. Here the video camera, the photograph, the cinematic and video screen, and the slide projector are not presented as pure and distinct media forms so much as means to investigate other media, to brush one medium up against another.—

—Modernism embraced the idea that technology would succeed in extending human perception to new, uncharted terrain. The photograph, as the quintessential modern medium, was understood as a means to see beyond the limitations of the human frame—to see from the air, to see through a microscope, to see things as they really were, and to see into the human soul. It was the technology of photography that promoted this notion of a new perception, one seemingly unfettered by human uncertainty. Emile Zola reportedly declared, "We cannot claim to have really seen anything before having photographed it."[2] Hence, technological media—in particular the photographic, cinematic, and video cameras—were understood in modernism as carrying the burden of a positivist legacy: the belief that the camera could provide proof and evidence of the real. The merging of art and technology thus carried with it this belief in the capacity of the camera to render a new vision of the world. The belief that art's function is both to entice and to demand of us a new way of seeing was a primary tenet of modernism, one that comes under scrutiny in postmodernism.—

—As recent investigations in the media of video, cinema, photography, and installation, the works in this exhibition represent the range of contemporary explorations of the camera as a means of perceptual expansion. At the same time, these installation works also represent a rethinking of the modernist creed that the camera simply offers a means to see further, to see beyond the human eye, functioning as an extension of the human senses. Rather, these works demand a reconsideration of the very basic concept of perception and the idea of seeing better. They can be regarded, in a certain sense, as works that investigate meta-perception, or the idea that what we are looking at is the process of looking itself.—

—Hence, the technological aspects of this exhibition can be regarded as indicating the important ways in which contemporary engagements of art and technology have moved beyond the modernist concept of technology as a means of expanding perception. These works are technologically engaged yet are not reductively or simply about the technological. As such, one could say that they defy traditional engagements with the idea of technology in art and indicate the ways in which new image technologies can be said to have transformed the terrain of art.—

—Yet it is precisely the technological medium and imaging-making machine of the camera—whether photographic, cinematic, or video—that enables an excavation of the image archive. From Marcel Broodthaers's deconstruction of a painting in *Bateau tableau* (1973; fig. 11; pls. 11–12), to Jeff Wall's elaborate photographic stagings of painterly composition, to the Wilson Twins' haunting images of the deserted space of Stasi headquarters in *Stasi City*, these installations return again and again to the past through their restaging of the present. They deploy contemporary media—photography, video, film, installation—as a means of reperceiving technology and its future through the lens of the past.

2. Quoted in GEORGES DIDI-HUBERMAN, "Photography—Scientific and Pseudo-scientific," in *A History of Photography: Social and Cultural Perspectives*, ed. Jean-Claude Lemagny and André Rouille, trans. Janet Lloyd (New York: Cambridge University Press, 1987), 71.

Narratives of technology have often understood progress in terms of the evolution from the still to movement. Modernism, for instance, was fascinated by motion, preoccupied with concepts of mobility, and fascinated by the idea of both representing movement and stopping it in an instant. The photograph was thus understood as a more realistic medium than painting, and cinema as an improvement on the still image in terms of its capacity to render a kinetic experience of the real. In the works in *Seeing Time*, this progressive narrative of the moving image is reexamined through a focus on the tension between still and moving image—in reasserting, one could say, the moment of the instant or the glance.

Broodthaers's *Bateau tableau* uses the mechanical apparatus of the slide projector to deconstruct, indeed to take apart, the representational image of a painting of a boat. The small painting, literally titled *Un Tableau representant le retour d'un bateau de pêche* (A painting representing the return of a fishing boat), is depicted through eighty slides of its details. As the sequence moves beyond the gold frame and further into the painting, these fragmented details form a kind of dissection. The representational image of the boat disappears, and we see instead the minutia of a brush stroke, the texture of the canvas, and small swatches of color. What emerges is an experience of painting not as a system of representation or reading, but as a mechanical process—*Bateau tableau* reveals to us the technology of painting. How, we begin to wonder, do these small fragments converge to create an

Figure 11
MARCEL BROODTHAERS,
Bateau tableau, 1973,
projected image (detail).

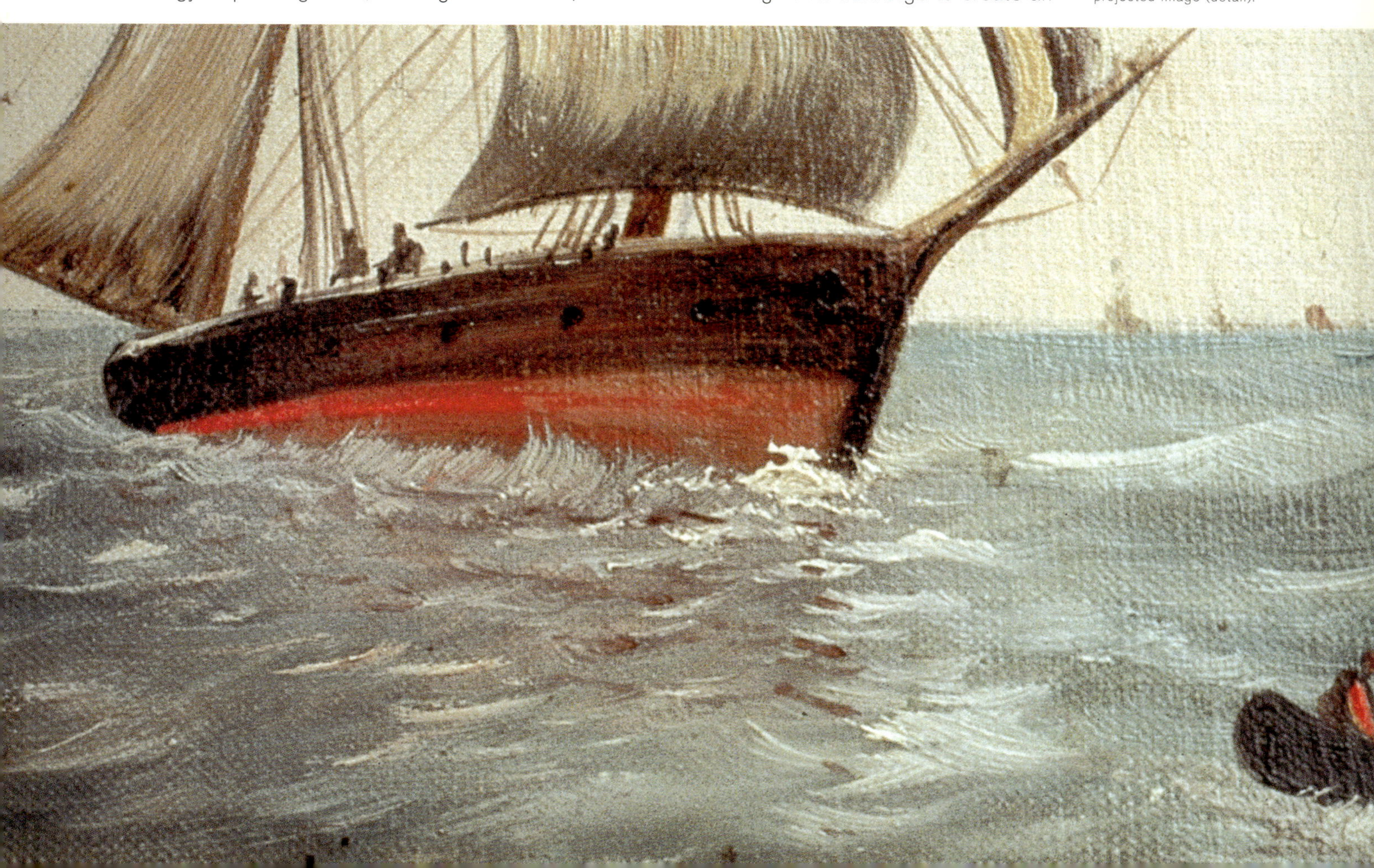

image of the real? How could these little bits of painting, these small brush strokes, accomplish such a representation? How could this blotch of paint denote a sail, and that a person? As the images detail the edge of the tattered canvas and the faded texture of the paint, they reveal further the materiality of the paint, canvas, and frame.

Broodthaers referred to slide projection as a "photo-film" or "reading system." It is significant, however, that he specifically chose to produce this reading with a slide projector, precisely because the clunky sound of the projector is a constant reminder of the mechanical. Indeed, the churning sounds of the projector induce a kind of nostalgia for the simplicity of the mechanical machine. Broodthaers's reading system thus demands a series of still images, rather than the continuity of the cinematic image. It also cleverly makes reference to the academic tradition of using slide projectors to look at art images—in an art history class, for instance. Yet here it is as if the explication system of art pedagogy has gone wrong, as the image becomes less and less clear and its representational form more abstract. Broodthaers accomplishes this by setting the still images in motion and obscuring the frame of the painting form. Similarly, he titles his work to demonstrate the capacity of language not to explicate, but to confound, as the words *bateau* and *tableau* echo each other and become indistinguishable if repeated quickly.

The photographic still is thus used as a means to dissect painting itself. Whereas the development of photography is understood historically to have dramatically changed the role of painting as a representational medium, in these works, photography is used as a means of both reframing painting as a technology and of reconfiguring the pictorial through a new medium. What does it mean, in the late twentieth century, to deploy photography as an artistic medium? In what sense is the photograph irrevocably modern? Does it always carry its positivist legacy within it?

In the work of Jeff Wall and Thomas Struth, this rediscovery of the photograph takes place through its reanimation. Both Wall and Struth situate photography in the context of nineteenth-century visual media such as the diorama and the panorama (which aimed to expand the modernist view of the world), as well as that of painting, cinema, and contemporary advertising. Distinctly photographic, yet also painterly and cinematic, these works demand an engagement with media that negates the possibility of media specificity. With their large format and Wall's back-lit framing, these images become more than photographs.

Wall's images combine the theatrical and the mundane, each tugging at the viewer as if to tell a different story. In *Untangling* (1994; fig. 13), the supposedly banal setting of a workshop takes on several layers of complexity, in which each detail, as in *Bateau tableau,* seems to demand scrutiny. A worker sits with a massive tangle of rope, his brow furrowed with the task, in a room stacked with equipment and deep with shelves. The illuminated surface of Wall's work, which provides a sensation of depth, if not realism, also functions to bring the image forward, referencing both the diorama format and the movie screen. Yet *Untangling* is deliberately pictorial, evoking classical painting in its elaborate staging and creating a tension between its seeming documentary effect and its studied composition. Similarly, *The Quarrel* (1988; pl. 25) engages us through its apparent intimate glimpse of a quotidian setting, a quarreling couple in bed, as he turns his back, hunching away, and she sits dejectedly by the harsh bedside lamp. The tension of the scene is rendered at once mundane and complex; the folds of the bedsheets seem both classically staged and haphazardly arranged.

Wall's deployment of the photographic medium creates this tension between the pictorial and the documentary precisely in its postmodern staging of the modern. Similarly Struth's *Louvre 1* (1989; pl. 33) does not merely document a group of visitors looking at art but reflects upon the activity of art viewing itself. The size of the image pulls the viewer into the scene of the gallery, where the enormous classical paintings seem almost incidental to the crowds of people congregating on the benches and floors. Art, the work seems to imply, is a means of socialization, an incitement to discourse, yet the artwork is ultimately itself beside the point. Struth's image both evokes the classical and deploys the photographic to contain it.

While these are *still* images, they create a tension between stillness and movement specifically in the self-consciousness of their painterly immobility. Each is emphatically static and, in the case of Wall, deliberately cinematic as well. In Bill Viola's *The Greeting* (1995; fig. 12; pls. 53–54), this tension between the still and the moving image is also restaged through references to classical painting. Here the work references a Renaissance painting by Pontormo of the pregnant Virgin Mary greeting her cousin Elizabeth. Hence, a rethinking of the modern understanding of the still and moving image is staged, as in Wall's work, ironically through a reconfiguration of classical art.

In *The Greeting* the tension between still and moving image is created through extended use of slow motion. The painterly image of the women greeting, as they speak and then embrace while another woman watches, is staged in eerily slow, hauntingly drawn-out movement. The biblical narrative recedes as the tension of movement emerges—the way in which the folds of the women's clothing move slowly in the breeze, the complexity of their expressions and gestures as they interact, each unsure of the other. Every little gesture is exaggerated, and every detail becomes important. Watching this work, one begins to consider just how complex the activity of greeting is—the layers of emotions, hesitancies, and signals—and all the ways in which the strange and the familiar are inseparably a part of this action. The history of art is not simply referenced in Viola's restaging, it is the means through which the capacity of contemporary media to change our frame of perception, here embodied in the technique of slow motion, is demonstrated. The slow-motion image is neither still nor moving, but is a continuous extension of stillness into movement. It is thus in a certain way emphatically a video image, not the sequence of still images that constitute film, but the elongated frame of the video image, stretching into movement.

What then of the legacy of cinema? The examination of the relationship of the still and the moving image seems in these works to reject the cultural impact of cinematic illusion. Broodthaers does this most emphatically in *Fig. 0, Fig. 1, Fig. 2, Fig. A* (1971; pls. 1–10), in which films are projected upon a screen marked by figure numbers. The branding of the screen with "fig. 1," "fig. 2," and so on references both the practice in art history books of assigning figure numbers to images and the scientific use of diagrams as a means of explication. The images of the films—visiting the site of Waterloo, mundane scenes of everyday life—are thus transformed into particular kinds of texts, codified and numbered. Broodthaers's very simple gesture of numbering the screen playfully intercedes in the cinematic

Overleaf:

Figure 12 (left)
BILL VIOLA,
The Greeting, 1995,
production still (detail).

Figure 13 (right)
JEFF WALL,
The Untangling, 1994,
detail of plate 26.

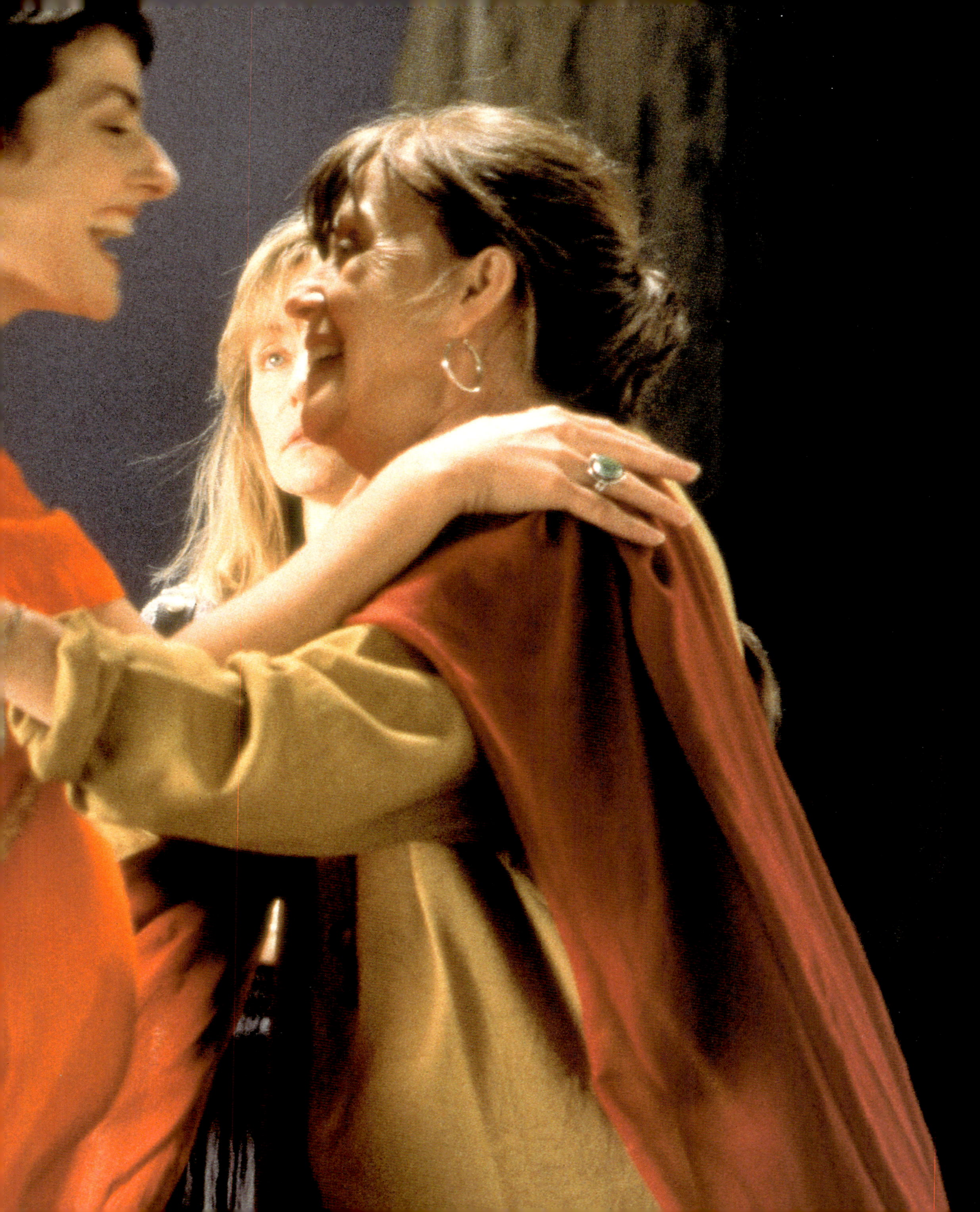

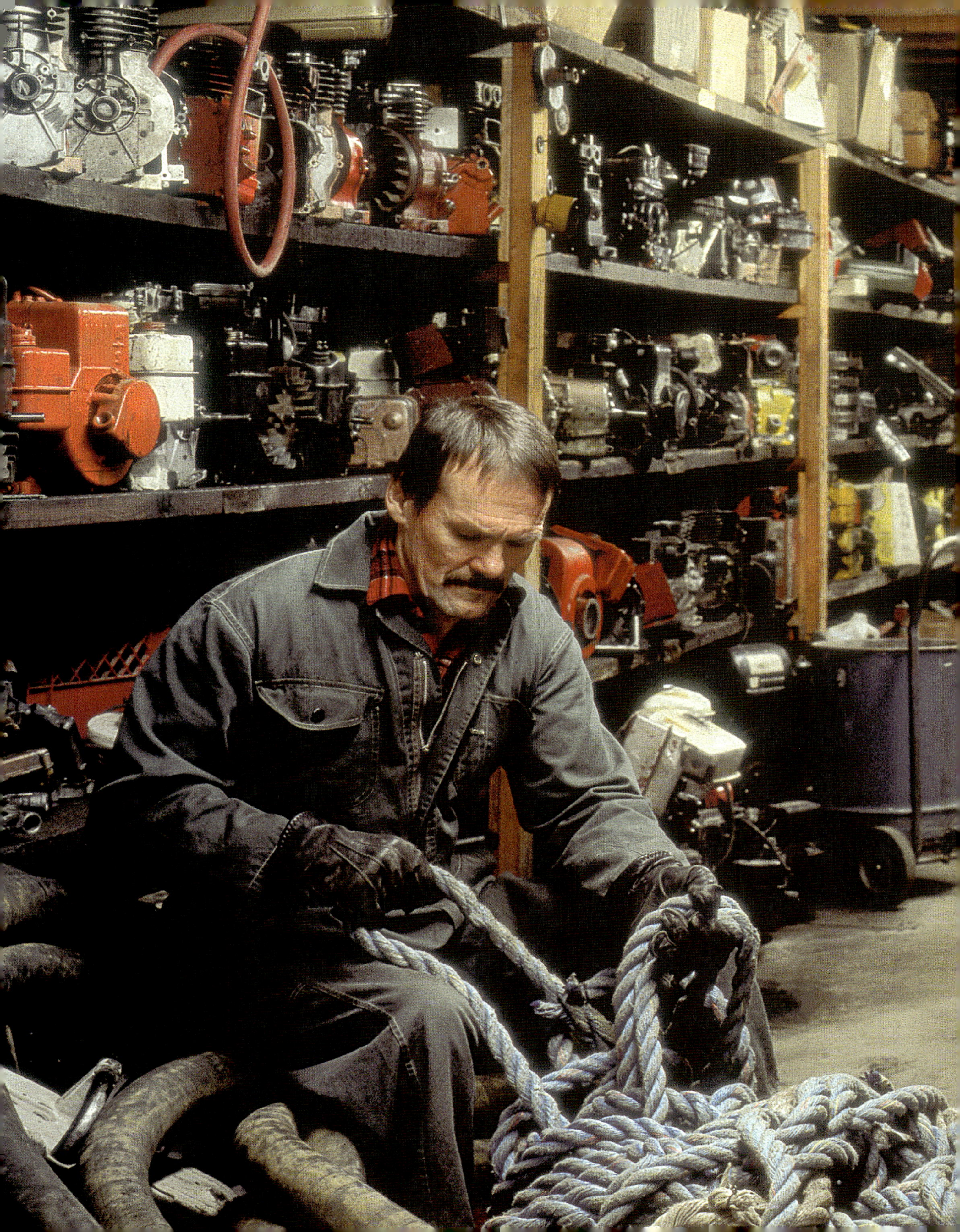

illusion of the films to create a third image, one that exposes the tension between the realism of the photographic screen image and the numbers themselves. Here Broodthaers plays against the codes of cinematic movement. Whereas in *Bateau tableau* he deliberately set still images into motion, here he attempted to stop the movement of the cinematic image by disturbing the screen on which it exists. The numbers thus begin to act as a kind of catalogue, one that codifies the images as forms of nostalgia, as if the elements of the screen have been tagged and marked for the archive of history.

What then are these works saying about the relationship of technology to time? History is evoked here as a means through which meaning is circulated in the present. Interestingly, at a time when the postmodern sense of rapid change and time out of control can be read as an extension of modernist fears of time moving forward too quickly, these works envision time in an increasingly slowed form. They slow it to a halt, render it static, and demand a scrutiny of the instant, the moment, or the stilled image.

In Reinhard Mucha's *Auto Reverse* (1994–95; pls. 51–52), this scrutiny of the past image within the present is presented in the biographical context of Mucha's childhood. The work consists of two images—Mucha as a child riding a scooter and an image of his son Roman sitting on a child's seat attached to his father's bicycle—which are connected through a complex technological mechanism of a 16mm film projector and a photographic light box. The young boy's voice is continuously heard saying "auto" as his image is projected next to that of his father as a child. The work is thus presented as a deliberately constructed contraption, one that expresses a love of technological complexity and mechanical gadgetry. The drawing together of different elements, each evoking personal and cultural history—in addition to the two photos, two scooters like the one Mucha is riding in the photograph, an image of the industrial pipe that was made in the factory where Mucha now has his studio, and a mirror—has the effect of creating a circuit of history and memory, in which each circles back into the other. The formal elements of the work, which present various technologies as artifacts of the past and present, are thus deployed in a cycle of personal references. With the image loop of the 16mm film and the constant repetition of the word "auto," the work appears deliberately to be stuck in the present, unable to move forward. Yet it is in constant motion in that moment, reiterating the past again and again, in "reverse." In Mucha's contraption of history, technology is deployed as a kind of animated creature, through which the passage of time is realized, re-realized, and reconfigured. His is, in fact, a kind of memory machine, which depicts both the mechanical and technological embodiment of memory in the image and its elusive presence.

UNDOING THE ARCHIVE OF HISTORY

What are the spaces of the past that these technological media are spatializing anew? Where, we might ask, are the ruins of twentieth-century history? In *Stasi City* (1997; fig. 14; pls. 22–23), Jane and Louise Wilson use a camera to rescript the now empty spaces of the buildings that once housed the Staatsicherheit—the intelligence police of the former East Germany—in an area of East Berlin now unofficially called Stasi City. Here, history and its archive are embodied in the deserted rooms, each of which seems to speak many stories within its emptiness. Because these now empty rooms are known to have housed the activities that defined in a certain sense the nation of East Germany, its political system, and the broader context of the Cold War, their vacancy is packed with meaning. What is left behind when an entire system is rejected and abandoned? What is the refuse of the late twentieth-century political upheavals? Small details conjure up the tyranny not only of interrogation or investigation but also of bureaucracy—scattered scraps of paper, an old rotary phone, its cord wrapped around it, sitting alone on the floor. History inhabits the rooms themselves yet is hidden in the stories they now refuse to tell. These spaces embody memories within them.

At the same time, the Wilsons' camera is used to evoke the very processes that it sees in the cracks of these deserted spaces. It invades and surveys the space, it investigates, and it relentlessly observes and records. In a sense, the space is set into motion by the camera. Doors open and close, an elevator rides up and down, the legs of an anonymous figure come into view, and the sound of steps echoes in the halls. The camera seems to continue to search further and comes upon a figure who appears to hang in the air, unexplained and haunting. Here, as in Mucha's image and sound loop, Viola's repeating slow motion, or the held moments of Wall's images, this figure evokes the suspension of the past in the present, the continuous repetition and recirculation of the past into new forms—suspended because the future is always elusive, gone the moment we reach it. In *Stasi City,* the doubling of the projected image thus evokes the doubling of Mucha's images and hence the constant reflection between two mirrored images—as the twins mirror each other and as the two Germanys operated as a strange Cold War doubling of the nation. This doubling thus reflects finally on the question of the illusion of the individual and the whole—a dilemma as much for present-day Germany as for Mucha's father and child.

The spaces of *Stasi City* operate as a kind of theatrical set in which past dramas are imagined to have been played. Similarly, in James Coleman's *I N I T I A L S* (1993–94; pl. 55), the deserted space of an institutionalized past is used as a stage set for reflections on memory and history. Like Broodthaers, Coleman embraces the slide projector as a modern/postmodern medium. There is no attempt to disguise the technology, but rather, as with the work of Broodthaers and Mucha, the technology is presented as an art object in itself. Here then, the sound of the slide projector is integral to the viewer's experience of the tangled efforts at expression and communication in the work. The backdrop is a deserted hospital space, with a pile of now useless bed frames. As a group of "characters" who appear to be actors rehearse in the space, the voiceover of a young girl presents a narrative of communication and miscommunication. Through her emerges the voice of Irish literary figure W. B. Yeats and other references to Irish history such as the Autograph Tree, in County Galway, where well-known Irish poets and playwrights of the early twentieth century carved their initials.

The past is thus embodied in deserted spaces, carved into trees, and inscribed in the words that circulate in a culture. In *I N I T I A L S,* objects such as cloth are used to conjure national histories, and the painting and repainting of images evoke the rescripting of cultural memory. The actors change roles, as we do and as historical figures do over time; like us, they are never stable. *I N I T I A L S* thus refers both to the lasting marks of history—its initials—and the fleeting nature of our experience of the past and present. Coleman's pointed use of slide projection—evoking simultaneously the photographic and the cinematic, yet resisting the narrative pull of cinema—can be seen as a deconstructive

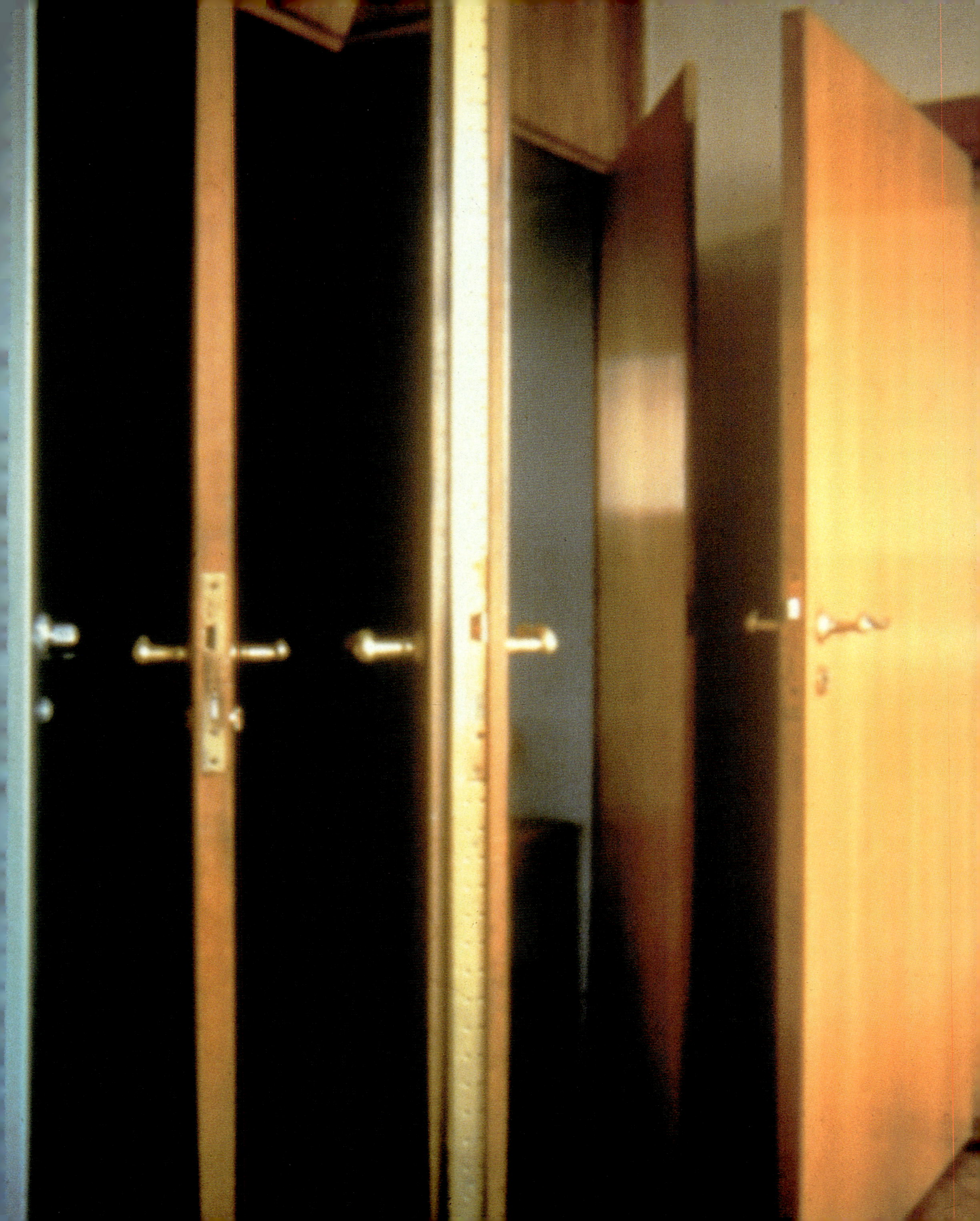

move. Like Broodthaers's *Bateau tableau,* in which the slide images fragment the image further and further, this work uses slides to deconstruct representation—to disconnect from the elusive voiceover, to suggest and not reveal.

In *Stasi City* and *I N I T I A L S,* history and memory are presented as entangled, each implicated within the other. These installations address the ways in which a postmodern excavation of the archives of history—literary, political, and cultural—is not ultimately about creating coherent narratives but about acknowledging the incommunicability of history, the many stories that will never be told. In the empty spaces of *Stasi City* or the deliberate fragmentation of historical narratives in *I N I T I A L S,* it is precisely the nontelling, the antinarrative, and the absence of the artifact that are revealed. This is where history resides, in the cracks between the stories, in the emptied spaces, in the unspoken, suspended in the present.

MOVING THROUGH VIDEO/ RECONFIGURING TELEVISION

The telling of stories in the late twentieth century takes place significantly and primarily through the mass media. While the photographic image—as image, projection, and sequence—circulates in this exhibition as a primary means of excavating the past, the television and video image is a constant reminder of the image world of the present. Video is deployed here as a medium of continuity and fragmentation, a storytelling medium through which a disruption of the narrative is inevitable. The relationship of and distinctions between the photograph and video echo again and again through these works.

Thomas Struth and Klaus vom Bruch's *Berlin-Project* (1997; fig. 15; pls. 34–38) exploits the tension between the photographic and the video image as a means of reflecting upon the ubiquitous presence of the television/video camera in contemporary life. At the same time, the convergence of images seems to evoke modernist views of travel within a postmodern critique of the notion of the foreign. Struth and vom Bruch juxtapose video images of people in public places around the world—such as the U.S., Germany, Italy, Switzerland, China, Japan, Cuba, Finland, Russia, and Tunisia—photographs of China by Struth, and a wall of video images. Here the modern notion of the image as a form of travel—the idea that, for instance, panoramic paintings, diorama displays of the "exotic," or photographic images from other places could be seen as a means of travel—is rethought. Juxtaposing the photographic document with the images on a video wall, which signifies a kind of postmodern fascination with spectacle and saturation with consumer culture, *Berlin-Project* reflects on what it means to update the modern sense of travel images in the contemporary global culture.

The images evoke constant movement and activity, in which passers-by are consistently defined as just that—people passing by. The video camera remains stationary as the movement is contained within the frame—traffic, pedestrians, cyclists, and cars. The effect is of a world moving in and out of view, at once decipherable yet elusive and uncontainable. People move into the image only to disappear beyond the frame. Linked by the video

Figure 14
JANE AND LOUISE WILSON
Stasi City (Eric Mielke's office, partial view), 1997, Cibachrome print on aluminum produced in conjunction with the video, 108 x 108 in.

camera, the apparatus of projection, and the multiple video wall, these images are connected through the technology yet also imply the ways in which their worlds are incommensurable. This is precisely because of the way in which the work rejects a modernist embrace of travel as self-knowledge and encourages a more complex and critical view of the connections and disconnections that distinguish contemporary worlds, nations, and cultures. These images tell us that these places and the people within them are essentially unknowable through the camera. Hence, we are not seduced here into conventional modernist ideas about the image connecting cultures and people. The juxtaposition of these images, reflected through these consumer forms of spectacle, establishes difference rather than the now defeated concept of universalism.

Thus, a critique of the idea of media as providing connections guides this work, allying it with Dara Birnbaum's *Tiananmen Square: Break-in Transmission* (1988–90; pls. 45–48). As Struth and vom Bruch intervene in the idea of media images as a global community, Birnbaum critiques contemporary concepts of media as information and history. The role of the media in "making history" is examined through a deconstruction of the media images generated about the uprising of Chinese students in Tiananmen Square in 1988.

The structure of *Tiananmen Square* forces the viewers to move through and beyond its images as they are shown on a sequence of monitors of varying sizes. The work thus situates the viewers as mobile, moving into and beyond the media images, in sharp contrast to the stereotype of the immobilized television viewer. The crisis of Tiananmen Square has been historicized as one of the first truly global media events of the late twentieth century, in which the new media of fax and satellite transmission were deployed by both the Western media and the student protesters. The images on the monitors range from the poignant to the chilling, from the intimate to the spectacular: students use fax machines to send messages out to the rest of the world, a group of singers rehearse a political song in a studio, news reporters set up their equipment, a policeman shoves a camera, Chinese citizens watch the events on their television sets. One comes away with an impression of complex media and communication vectors—television transmission and reception, messages sent and received, and the orchestration and production of media images.

Yet, at the same time, Birnbaum's reconfiguration of this event demonstrates its fragmented and incomplete effect. Ultimately, the viewer is left feeling that this barrage of information does not enlighten or aid in the production of knowledge; it simply complicates. Deeply moving images, such as the students singing their song "Wound of History," are interwoven with images of the news-making apparatus which define it as technologically allied with the authoritarian technologies of repression. There is no chance to stop and contemplate here. Just as we are compelled by the installation to move through, to be mobile spectators, the images also move through this event in such a way that the story remains elusive, its poignancy incommunicable, its history still untold.

It is precisely this thwarting of a story that compels Stan Douglas's video stories and antinarrative. Douglas takes television as his primary referent, creating works that can be seen both in the context of broadcast television and in a gallery setting. His brief interventions into the relentless stream of television flow are meant to act as glimpses of larger, real-life dramas, which can only be suggestions

Figure 15
THOMAS STRUTH AND KLAUS VOM BRUCH, *Berlin-Project*, 1997, video still (detail).

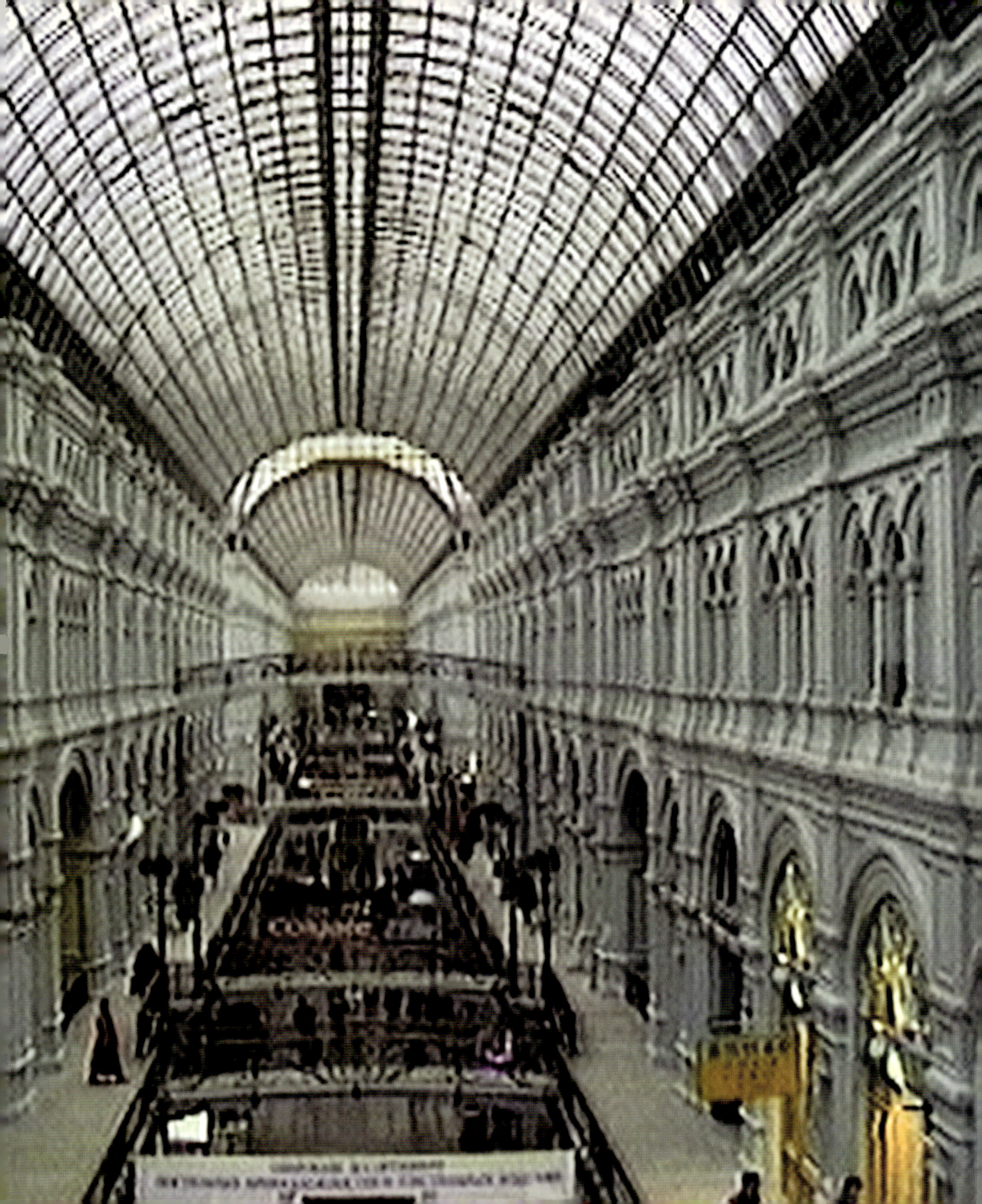

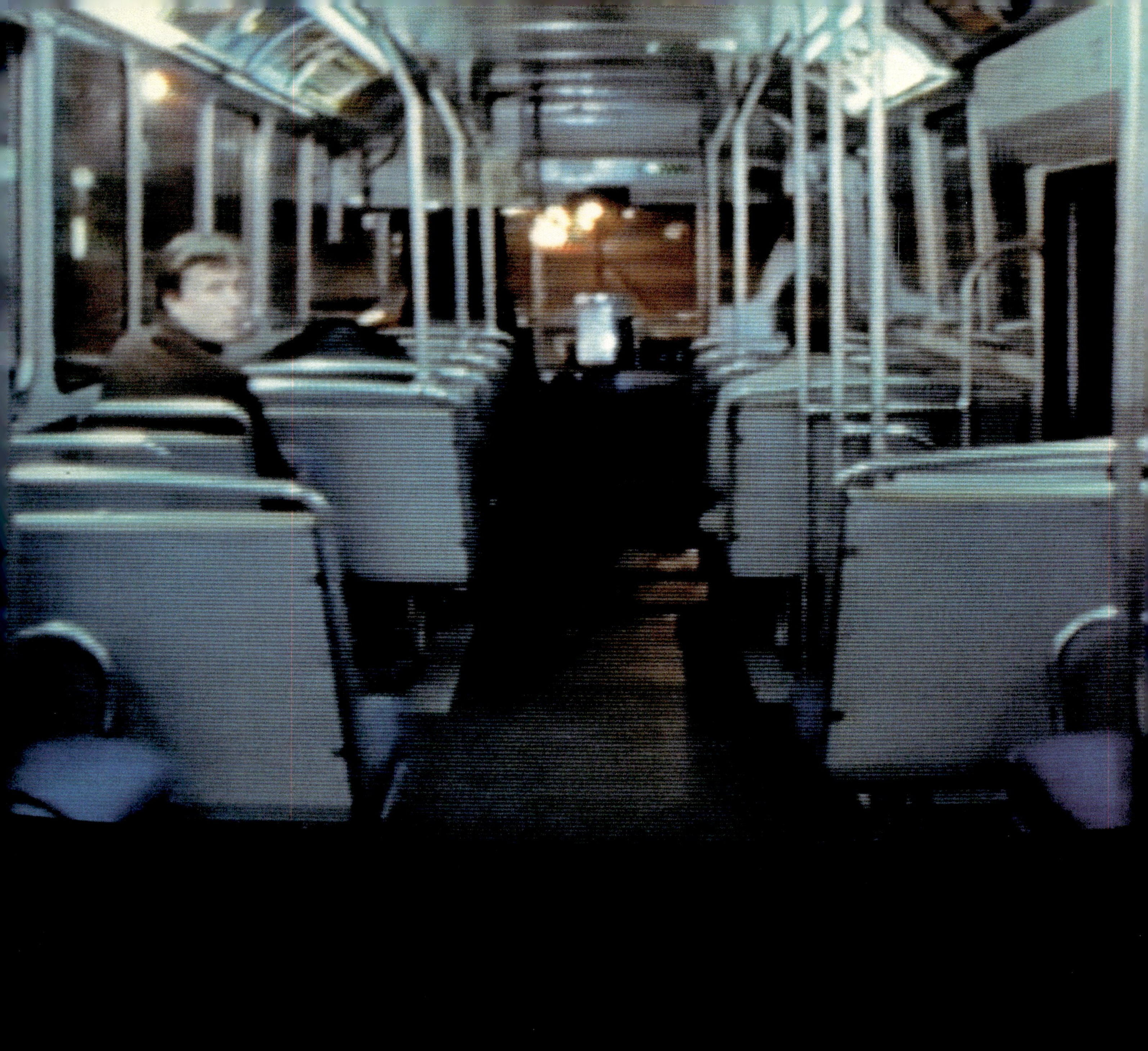

here. Deliberately elusive and purposefully unforthcoming, these images ask the viewer to create and/or complete the story they suggest beyond the frame.

Douglas's works are thus about intervening into the spectacular through a focus on the quotidian. In *Television Spots* (1987–88; fig. 16; pls. 39–41), brief scenes present fragments of the everyday that suggest larger, more complex stories: a woman sneezes while walking in a parking garage; a woman listens to someone talking, nodding her head in unconvincing agreement; a woman stands in a kitchen, smoking a cigarette while an answering machines answers in the background; as people sit on a bus, there is the sound of a woman laughing, and a man glances backward; four men walk down a street, and one shoves the other in a friendly way; and so on. One could see these images as those that are normally left out, unnoticed, or left, so to speak, on the cutting room floor. Yet their everydayness is riveting. In their focus on the ordinary, these glimpses seem freighted with meaning. One could see them as modern stories, through which the modern experience of the crowd of strangers is realized—what does it mean to have encounters with strangers on a daily basis? These images indicate the power of the moment and hence stand as a critique of the overdetermination of television style, in particular the general need in conventional television form to explain everything. Here the moment is suspended, as in *The Greeting* or *Stasi City;* one could say it is dangling in the present.

In Douglas's *Monodramas* (1991; pls. 42–44), the form is a longer segment, which approaches narrative cohesion only to withhold closure: A man stands on a balcony as the film *Cape Fear* plays on a television set. Then he is seen walking below, clearly suspicious of what he thought he saw or heard. Outside a motel two men pass each other. The first, who is white, says, "Hi Gary, how are you doing?" The other man, who is black, replies, "I'm not Gary." Three men sit on a bench; the hand of someone lying on the ground is visible within the frame. Someone says, "Get up, come on, get up," and the hand moves slowly, as if contemplating what to do next. A school bus and a car almost collide. Are stories being told here? We are privy to only the barest of details, all of which could be used to tell many different narratives. What happened before? What is going on here? While the fragmented quality of these dramas makes it possible for us to feel frustrated by their unresolved quality, their quotidian aspects allow us simply to notice the complexity of the unexplained moment.

This capacity in video for attention to detail and focus on the moment is reflected in Darren Almond's *H.M.P. Pentonville* (1997; pls. 49–50) to very different effect. Here the original transmission of the image, in this case between Pentonville Prison and the Institute of Contemporary Art in London in May 1997, demonstrates the capacity of the video medium through satellite technology to create connections between places and to effectively insert one place into another. The viewers see an image of an empty cell in the prison, its elements (a bunk bed, a table, a barred window) spare and stark, while they can hear the sound of the prison, voices, banging gates, the clang of keys, and someone humming. The sounds are resonantly alive, while the room is painfully bare. The stationary image demands a kind of scrutiny, because, like the view of the prisoner, it is all that one can see. The furniture remains stationary, yet the light from the window shifts slightly to indicate time passing. At the same time, the time code of the satellite transmission races forward in the corner of the image, indicating, on the one hand, time passing rapidly and, on the other, its slow crawl forward. The prison is the quintessential place where one does time, where time is strictly measured, where

Figure 16
STAN DOUGLAS,
Telelvision Spots, 1987–88,
video still (detail).

time is punishment. Here Almond is using the transmitted image to visualize time, yet to reflect ironically upon this contradiction of time, between the measured time of the disciplinary institution and the subtle, almost imperceptible changes in time indicated by the light from the window.

At some level, however, like *Tiananmen Square, Berlin-Project,* and *Television Spots, H.M.P. Pentonville* is reflecting through video on the incommunicability of modern and postmodern experience. The image of the prison is inserted through satellite technology into the art gallery itself, yet, as in these other works, video is used here not to tell a story so much as to indicate its inability to be told. Who are the people in these images, the people in these urban landscapes, in these quotidian scenes, beyond the image of this prison cell? Never are we allowed in these works to feel that the medium itself, the technology of imaging, allows us to know someone or to have the illusion of an experience.

PERCEIVING TIME/ TIMING PERCEPTION

In reconceiving vision against the modernist concept of using the camera to see further than the human eye, many of the works in *Seeing Time* examine the process of perception itself. What does it mean to look? What, as Gilbert & George ask, is the "nature of our looking"? If we reject the idea that technology will help us to see better, than what does it mean to create visual art with technological media?

In Gary Hill's work perception has always been tied to concerns with language. *Cut Pipe* (1992; pls. 62–63) addresses the contradiction of image and sound, of touch and technology. The cut pipe, which lies on the gallery floor, almost gives the impression that we are looking into a pipe of media, through which sounds and images are funneling. As images of hands touch the screen, creating a tactile surface at the place where the pipe has been "cut," a voice talks about skin, sound, and the image: "Give your skin to me, I want to put my finger on it . . . . I have my finger on my voice." Eventually the pipe, with its disembodied voice, seems both increasingly seductive and insistent, asking viewers to do more than look, demanding that they listen, that they imagine the touch.

Whereas *Cut Pipe* is precisely about the relationship of touch to the image, Hill's *Circular Breathing* (1994; pls. 60–61) is concerned with the ways in which time defines perception. Five bands of vertical video images are projected in a mathematical sequence in an elaborate circular framework. As images appear in sequence along these vertical bands, they are increasingly slowed as they grow in number, creating a sense of temporal suspension. Like *The Greeting* and *Stasi City, Circular Breathing* uses the video image to approach a state between the moving and the still image, one that suggests a possible threshold between the two.

Here, one could say, the viewer is being asked to see time, to read the image as time allows. One cannot look at these images without being aware of their temporal interplay. They seem to suggest stories, or multiple narratives, yet are replaced before we can begin to decipher them. At the same time, the constant movement of images seems to evoke a mechanical process, like the rhythmic movement of a train, as the images fill the full screen and then begin to empty from the opposite side in the same precisely timed fashion. It is as if the mechanical process suggested by the slide projectors of Lothar Baumgarten, Broodthaers, and Coleman is here deployed as an aesthetic for video. The rhythm of the images, rather than the images themselves, thus seduces viewers into suspending their desire to look with explicit meaning upon the individual image. The effect, rather, comes from the intervention of time into the process of seeing. The more images we see, the less they tell a story; rather, they seem to form an associative chain of memories, each sliding into the next. *Circular Breathing* thus says that perception never stands alone but is always caught in time.

What is it that *Circular Breathing* is "allowing" the viewer to see? The piece withholds its images and their potential narrative meaning so that we are left with the sensation of images passing, images breathing in and out, cycling around and back again. Perception then is presented here as a process of movement, change, and relentless recycling. This is not the static and wide reach of the photographic vision of modernism, where the camera allows us to see better and farther. Rather, it is a view of seeing through the continuous interchange and regeneration of many images in the contemporary imagescape in which we exist. Here we are allowed a glimpse of that which passes by quickly, that which is fleeting, ephemeral, and inarticulate.

This self-conscious view of perception, with its examination of what it is that we do when we perceive the world around us, is central to Gilbert & George's *A Portrait of the Artists as Young Men* (1972; pls. 17–20) and *The Nature of Our Looking* (1970; pls. 13–16, 21). Here, looking itself is the focus, in a style that veers between the comedic and the introspective. Gilbert & George present themselves as both lookers and those gazed upon, as both agents and objects, as both celebrities and mere props within the scene. In *A Portrait of the Artists as Young Men* they stand almost motionless, looking at the camera and, by extension, the viewer. Sounds of thunder and rain in the background invite the viewer to read their expressions as ones of anxiety and tension, to invest meaning in the slightest of gestures. While this work is a "portrait" that plays off the idea of revealing some "truth" about its subjects, it is also a study of the gaze upon, and returned by, the viewer. The viewer is thus gazed upon by the subjects themselves, compelling us to ask who the real subject is here.

In *The Nature of Our Looking*, Gilbert & George pose in two different scenes, sitting and standing almost motionless before the camera within lush landscapes. The viewer watches them looking offscreen. Whose look is the focus of the work's inquiry, their look upon a scene we cannot see or our look upon them looking? The black-and-white image, accompanied by silent film music, gives the artists a nineteenth-century air, as they pose stiffly, almost as if they were waiting for the long time exposure of an old camera. Presenting themselves as modern subjects, who sit in, yet are not part of, the natural landscape, the artists are also posing postmodern questions about the meaning of the look. It is our look upon their looking that is ultimately rendered most self-conscious.

The history of landscape painting that is invoked by Gilbert & George was steeped in codes of aristocratic privilege. The figure posed within the landscape was most often a landowner, who was shown surveying his property with an air of entitlement. Clearly, the "nature" of looking is a play on words, referring to the constructed and composed nature of both the landscape painting and this film image. Hence, the work reflects on the ways in which that history of imaging the landscape, of looking upon the world through the representational system of painting, has been more about the look and its meaning than about the land itself. Motionless within nature—except for an occasional, very human, shifting of position or the smoking of a cigarette—the two men draw attention to the pose itself as the object of an interested gaze.

This implicit critique of the practice of looking as a "natural" activity underscores all the works in this exhibition. This play on looking and nature, specifically looking at the question of nature in the history of the image, is achieved in Lothar Baumgarten's work *"Da gefällt's mir besser als in Westfalen" Eldorado 1968–1976* (1968–76; fig. 17; pls. 30–32) specifically through a deconstruction of the category of nature as nostalgia. Like Broodthaers and Coleman, Baumgarten uses the apparatus of the slide projector to both disassemble and reconfigure images of modernity. The trajectory of the images is orchestrated as a kind of ethnography of place, in this case the contained world of nature that exists within an urban environment. Here, at each moment when viewers are temporarily seduced into responding to an image of nature in an unexamined mode of viewing, they are reminded through textures of sound and small details that this is an urban environment. Lush images of the forest or lakes are interrupted by evidence of the refuse of inhabitation—a discarded map, a tire juxtaposed with a turtle's shell, a signpost, or a discarded potted plant. Hence, each desire to read these as images of nature within the history of the landscape, from painting to nature photography, is thwarted.

The work is thus a critique of nostalgia, both the nostalgic view of images of the past and the desire to see nature in terms of purity and authenticity. Nostalgia is, of course, the longing for that which never was. In the title, Baumgarten refers to a line from Voltaire's *Candide,* "I like it better there than in Westphalia," a reference to that work's questioning of nostalgia and the desire to return to another place, and to El Dorado, the always unfulfilled promise of an unattainable place. One could say that Baumgarten's title mocks the image of pristine landscape that the viewer keeps attempting to see within the images, the desire always to see nature as elsewhere. Instead, we are confronted not with nature but with culture—an airplane passing over, abandoned scraps of people's lives—with the refuse of the city enfolded within the landscape, which is in turn hemmed in by the urban. This then is the contradiction, the constant desire to do that which is impossible, to stand outside of culture.

Baumgarten refers to these works as "manipulated realities," precisely because the blurring of the boundary between nature and culture is an explicit part of his process. He finds debris and nature in these contexts yet also stages scenes within them and leaves his orchestrated debris behind. Some scenes that appear "natural" were orchestrated, and others that may read as staged were "found." Yet each is ephemeral, whether the changing context of found urban nature or the use of the landscape as a palette by the artist.

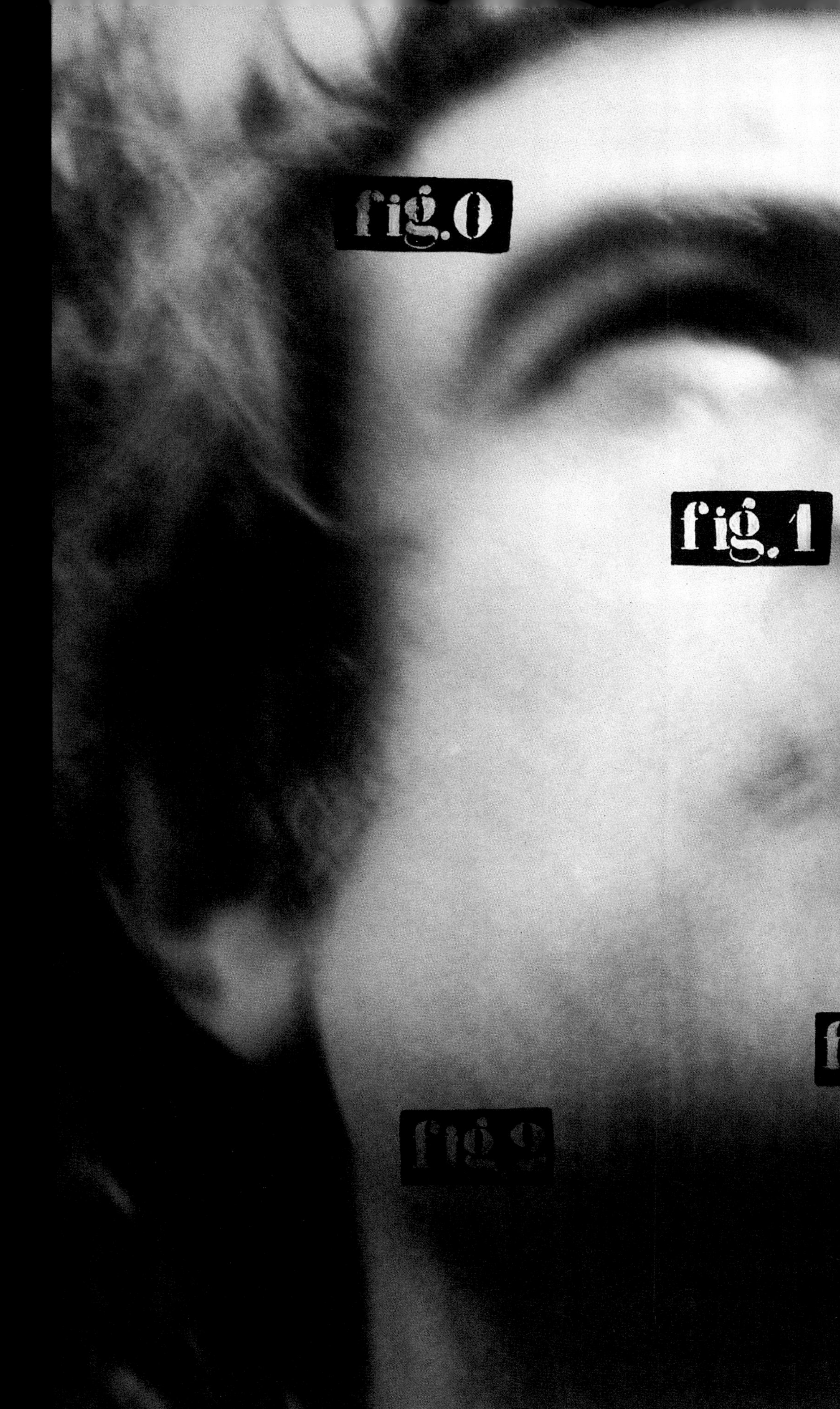
fig.0
fig.1

PLATES

ESSAYS BY CHRISSIE ILES

fig.2

fig.12

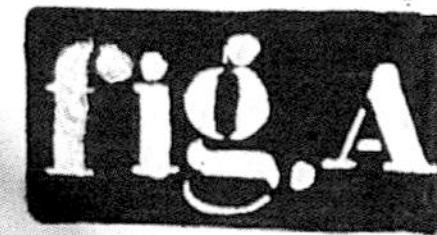

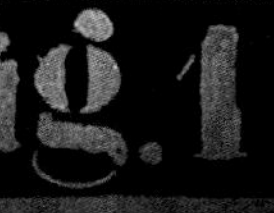

Finally, it is the return to the still image that is emphatically underscored in this work, the importance of the movement of the still image in a sequence that is deliberately about the threshold between the still photographic image and the moving image of cinema. Like Broodthaers, Baumgarten orchestrates the movement of still images as a form of deconstruction, one that demands a reconsideration of the modernist concept of perception. This work, like so many of the works in this exhibition, is a direct challenge to the modernist view that the camera provides the means to see beyond the human eye, to see further. It challenges us to see in a new way, to look critically with self-consciousness upon the process of looking itself. What is it that we see when we look at these images, and how do they at some profound level ask us to register the difference between what we see and what we want to see?

In the works in *Seeing Time,* the camera refuses to reveal neatly contained narratives, to tell coherent stories, or to give the viewer a simple sense of comfort and closure. These works reflect a deep engagement with the constructedness of the image and its inability to provide us, as modernism promised, with an expanded worldview or a new perspective on meaning. It is precisely the camera's capacity to withhold and thwart meaning that these works present to us, asking us to contemplate the elusive nature of communication itself. These works ask us to reflect in meaningful ways upon why it matters to look, why it matters to rethink the archive of images of the past, and why, ultimately, art matters.

Figure 17
LOTHAR BAUMGARTEN, *"Da gefällt's mir besser als in Westfalen" Eldorado 1968–1976,* 1968–76, image no. 31b (1968/69).

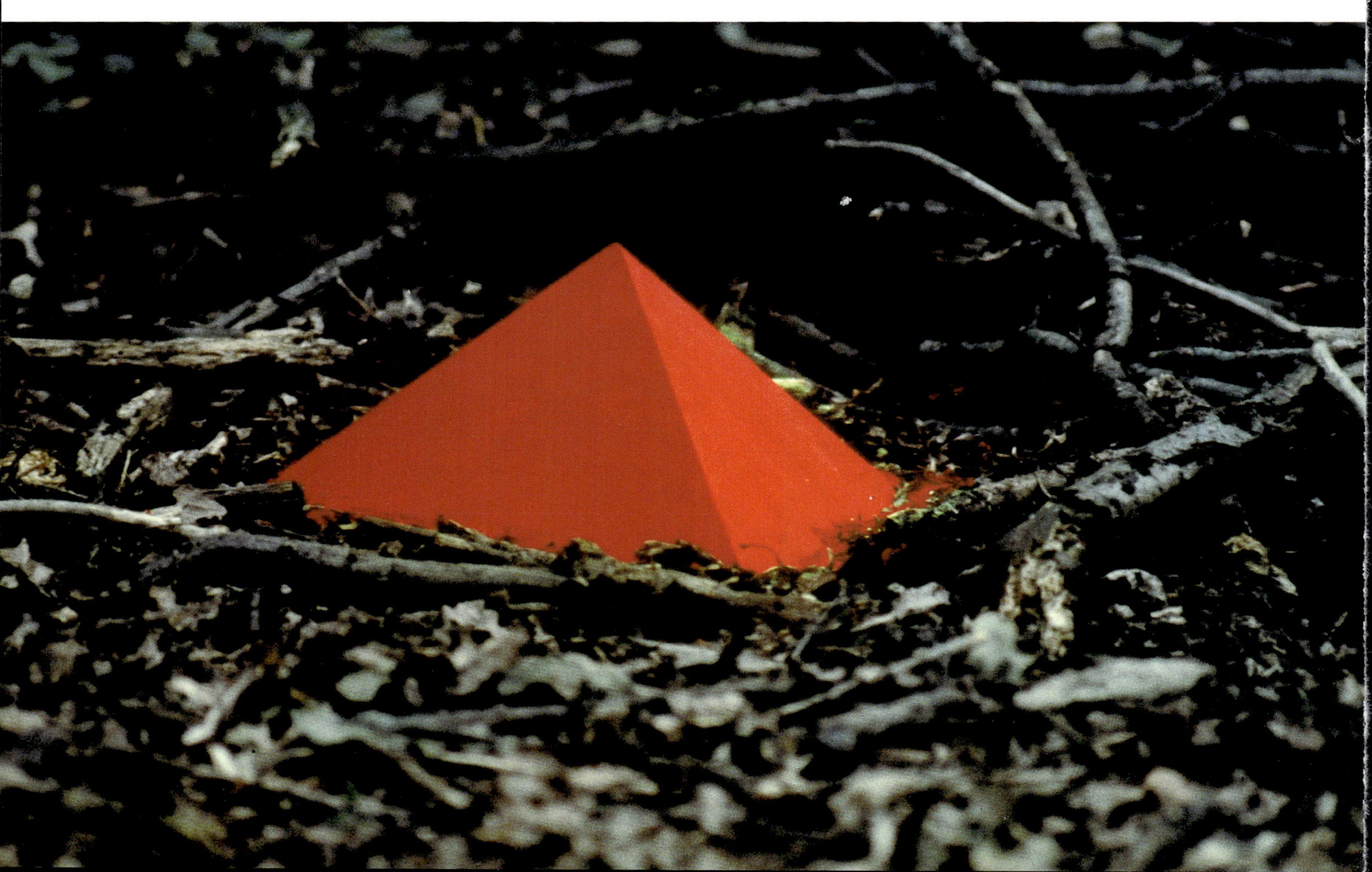

MARCEL BROODTHAERS

FIG. 0, FIG. 1, FIG. 2, FIG. A (1971)

+++++ In January 1971 Marcel Broodthaers created *Section cinéma*, a two-room installation in a basement in Düsseldorf, which transformed all subsequent presentations of his work and underlined the preeminence of film within his theoretical and aesthetic oeuvre. For Broodthaers, who began his career as a poet, film functioned as an extension of language. As Jean-Christophe Royoux has argued, the word *cinema* designated not film, but a new model of writing. This new model was deeply influenced by the radical poetry of the French writer Stephane Mallarmé, whom Broodthaers once described as "the source of contemporary art."[1] All the symbolic elements in *Section cinéma*'s elaborate composition refer to Mallarmé's ideas regarding time, whose march the poet sought to suspend in immobile eternity. The hour of midnight (indicated in Mallarmé's work by the number twelve, broken down into combinations of figures—fig. 1, fig. 2—in *Section cinéma*), that moment between the ending of one day and the beginning of another, became, for Mallarmé, the symbol of this suspension of time.

Mallarmé expressed his ideas about time by using radical typographic arrangements of words to create a new model of reading. In the two rooms of *Section cinéma* (itself a subset of the surreally titled *Département des aigles*, within a fictional Musée d'Art Moderne), Broodthaers developed Mallarmé's ideas of immobility and frozen time using a similar typographic method, creating a theory of time constructed by what could be termed a "Mallarméan" cinema. Onto each of the several large canvas film screens used in *Section Cinéma*, including *Fig. 0, Fig. 1, Fig. 2, Fig. A*, are printed several black rectangles showing stenciled numbers: "fig. 1," "fig. 2," "fig. 0," "fig. 12," and "fig A." Mallarmé's special number, twelve (midnight), is fragmented into a binary system of numbers, including twelve, all of which represent a fragment of time, frozen. These fragments arguably also represent individual film frames, which, projected at twenty-four frames per second (two times twelve, the total number of hours in a day), create the illusion of time passing. Broodthaers's screen subverts the linearity of time by symbolically isolating individual film frames, or "hours," and scattering them across the screen's surface, making visible, in concrete terms, the relationship between cinema and time.

As Broodthaers himself explained, the stenciled figures are also deliberately connected to the films projected onto the screen, which show the same typographic figures, in an attempt to integrate text and object. The film must therefore be, in Broodthaers words, "decipher[ed]. . . . It is an exercise in reading."[2] The space of the cinema screen, in other words, corresponds to the space of the page. This emphasis on language rather than image, and the bonding of each film to a particular group of screens, limiting their projection to the environment of *Section cinéma*, identifies them as part of a larger textual system, rather than as independent units operating within an open commercial or avant-garde film circuit. Broodthaers rejected the experimental film world—the influential New Wave European film, which

Plate 1

MARCEL BROODTHAERS, *Fig. 0, Fig. 1, Fig. 2, Fig. A*, 1971, film still from *Un voyage à Waterloo (Napoléon 1769–1969)* (1969).

had emerged during the 1960s, led by Jean-Luc Godard—and commercial Hollywood cinema, focusing instead on early silent cinema, to which all his films directly allude.

Part of a group of fifty film projects executed by Broodthaers, all silent and comedic, the five films projected in the black, outer room of *Section cinéma* parody a range of cinematic subjects, in an implicit critique of cinema. *Une discussion inaugurale* is constructed as a quasi-documentary, recording the beginnings of the fictitious Musée d'Art Moderne, of which *Section cinéma* is a part; *Voyage à Waterloo (Napoleon 1769–1969)* parodies historical drama; the re-presentation of a purchased classic silent film in *Charlie as Filmstar* brings an icon of mass culture into the museum. An ironic montage of purchased newsreel and documentary footage of dramatic events such as a volcanic eruption, a yacht race, and an air battle is interspersed with the 20th Century Fox logo in *Belga Vox—Mode—20th Century Fox; Brussel Teil II* challenges early film's claim to record and present the"truth."

Une discussion inaugurale most clearly demonstrates Broodthaers's challenge to the cinematic claim to documentary "truth." It also illustrates the completeness of the relationship between film, screen, viewing room, and the "museum" environment of *Section cinéma* as a whole. The film shows a series of sequences, including an art transport truck arriving at the basement, art crates, close-up shots of text stamped on the side of the crates, including "Fragile," "Section XIX Siècle/ Afdeeling XIX Eeuw" (nineteenth-century section), and "Museum." This lettering, when it appears on film, is directly juxtaposed with the figures painted onto the screen, uniting the two surfaces of film and screen and rendering the museum objects, to which both sets of numbers refer, illustrative. The invisible objects' illustrative status is further underlined by postcard images of famous paintings and drawings supposedly from the nineteenth-century collection, pinned onto the wall, which reveal the museum's contents to be imaginary. Broodthaers's antibourgeois critique of the institution of the museum is revealed in the deliberately constructed gap between the fantasy of the grand museum and the reality of the low-ceilinged, brick-walled basement.

The interchangeability of object and text suggested by the "figs." on both the screen and film is reiterated in the second room of *Section cinéma*, the "museum." Twelve everyday objects—including a clock stopped at midnight, a mirror, two wooden chairs, a gutted piano, and a chest—were strategically placed within this inner room, painted white. Inside the chest, a group of eleven small objects, combining with the chest to form twelve in total, completed an overall number of twenty-four objects, corresponding to the hours of the day, or number of film frames per second. As Royoux argues, these numerous references to Mallarméan time, echoing those in the adjacent room, state clearly the source of Broodthaers's cinematic model, through which he attempted to create a new framework for art. Echoing the figures on the film screen next door, each object was stenciled with "fig. 1," "fig. 2," "fig. 12," or "fig. A," shifting its status from object to illustration and unifying object, cinema screen, and film within what Royoux describes as an overall "expanded cinema of exhibition."[3]

As Royoux suggests, this "expanded cinema of exhibition"—*Section cinéma*—is a representation of a new theory, or system, of which the museum is a general image. At the base of its radical inquiry is a strong social critique. In making films that mimic the pre-corporate form of early slapstick silent films, looking back to a moment during the early 1920s when cinema was a vehicle for social transformation,[4] Broodthaers used cinema to comment on art's slide into commodity and its isolation from the "real" world. The answer to the questions "How can one be an integral part of society as an artist, without having to sacrifice the qualifier of 'art' to the overwhelming quantity of the commodity?" and "How can one make apparent that which is not the commodity in the artwork?"[5] appears, for Broodthaers, to lie in this cinematic model, through which he attempts to create a new space of representation.

1. JEAN-CHRISTOPHE ROYOUX, "Project pour un texte: The Cinematographic Model in the Work of Marcel Broodthaers," in *Marcel Broodthaers: Cinéma*, ed. Manuel J. Borja-Villel and Michael Compton (Barcelona: Fundació Antoni Tàpies, 1997), 297, 301.

2. MARCEL BROODTHAERS, interviewed in *Trépied* (*Tribune mensuelle de ciné-jeune*), no. 2 (February 1968): 4–5; reprinted in *Marcel Broodthaers: Cinéma*, 59.

3. ROYOUX, "Project pour un texte," 302.

4. As BRUCE JENKINS has argued, in "Un peu plus tard: Citation in the Cinema of Marcel Broodthaers," in *Marcel Broodthaers: Cinéma*, 290.

5. ROYOUX, "Project pour un texte," 303.

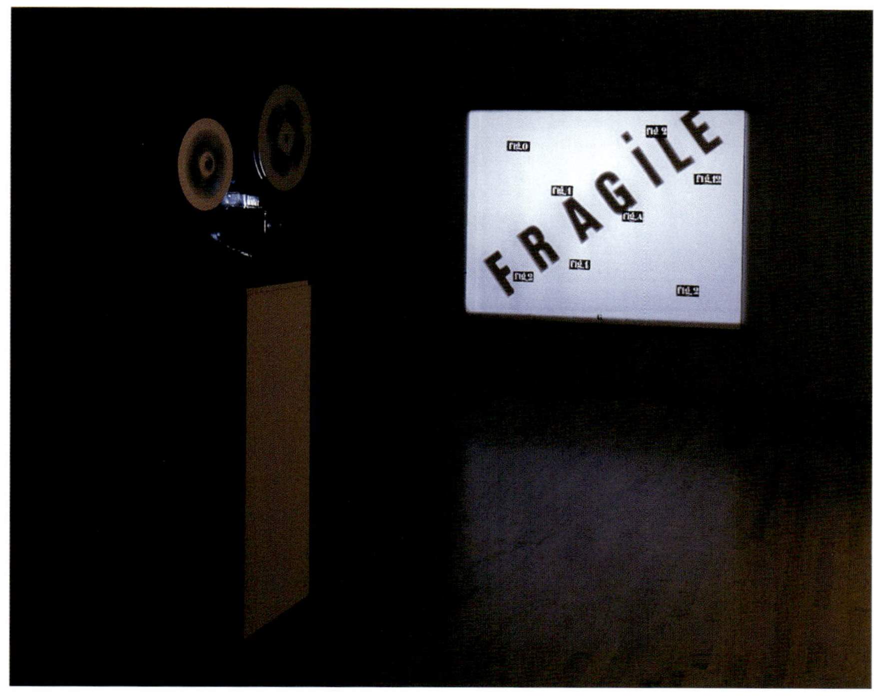

Plate 2

MARCEL BROODTHAERS, *Fig. 0, Fig. 1, Fig. 2, Fig. A*, 1971, installation view showing *Une discussion inaugurale* (1968).

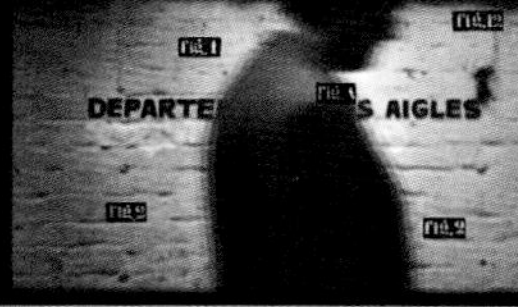
fig.1
fig.12
DEPARTE
S AIGLES
fig.2
fig.2

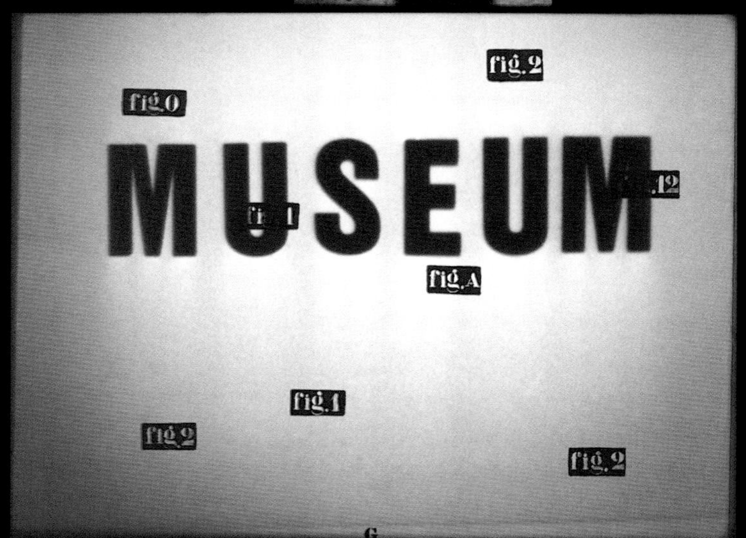
fig.2
fig.0
MUSEUM
fig.A
fig.1
fig.2
fig.2

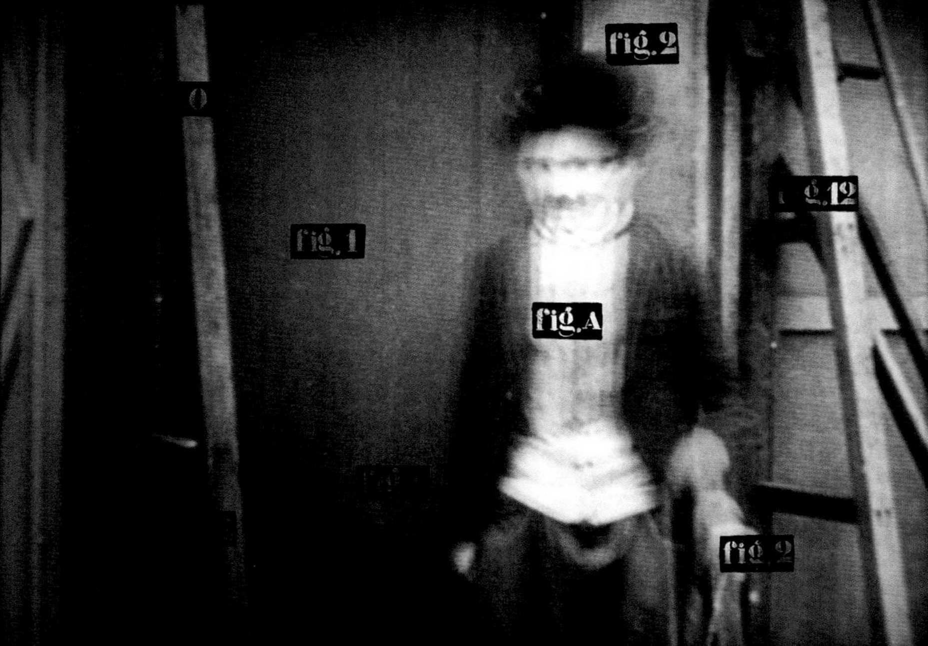
fig.2
fig.1
fig.A
fig.2

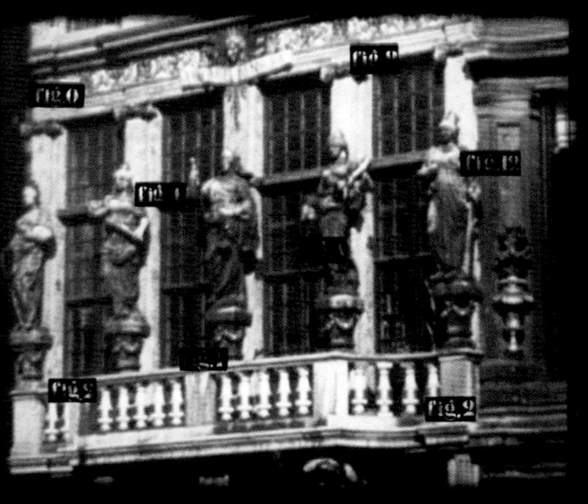
fig.0
fig.12
fig.2
fig.2

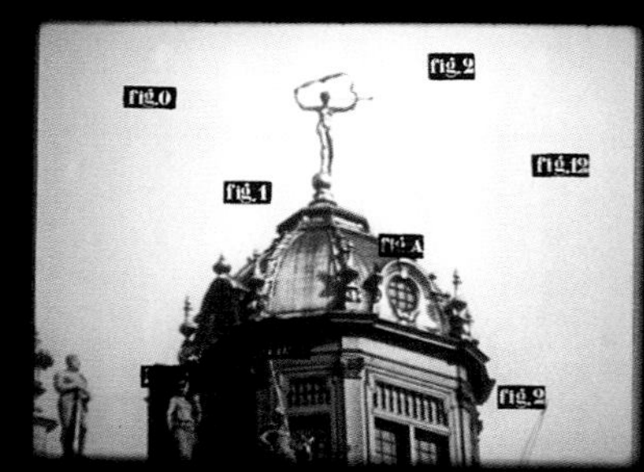

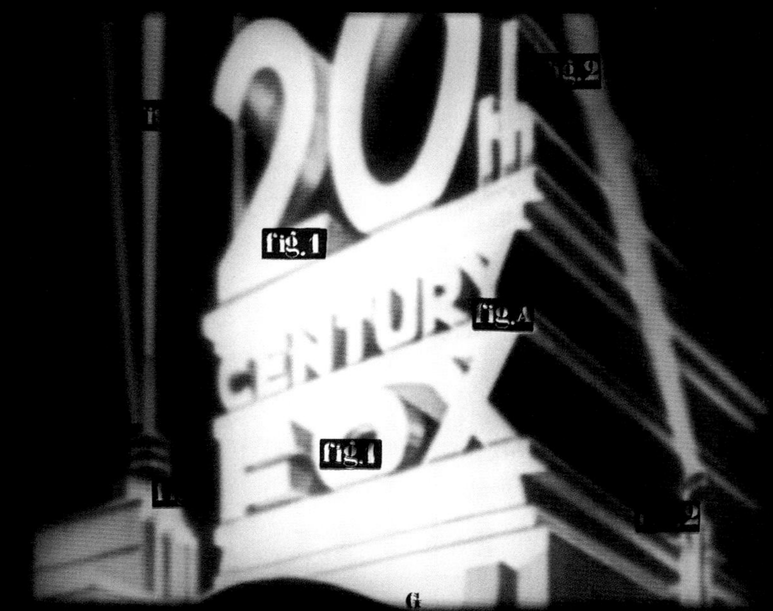

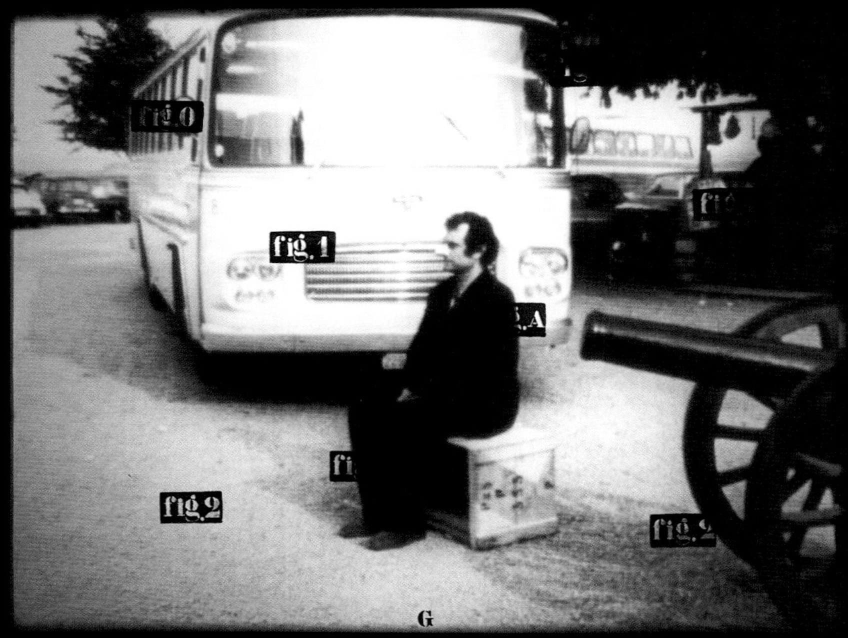

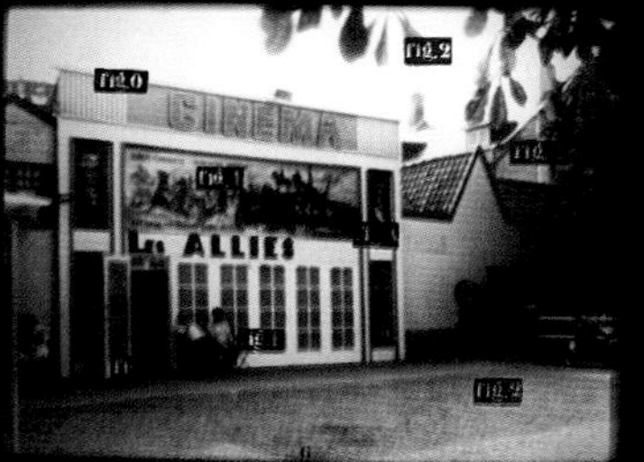

Plate 7

Brüssel Teil II

(1971).

Plate 8

Belga Vox-Mode-20th Century Fox (1971).

Plates 9-10

Un voyage à Waterloo (Napoléon 1769-1969) (1969).

MARCEL BROODTHAERS

BATEAU TABLEAU (1973)

+++++ The work of Marcel Broodthaers persistently questions the boundaries between different artistic disciplines, erasing the lines between poetry, photography, film, and painting in order to explore new forms of representation. *Bateau tableau* addresses the transition from modernism to postmodernism, setting up a tension between the older, nineteenth-century medium of painting and the newer, twentieth-century mechanical medium of photography.

The slide sequence of *Bateau tableau* occupies an ambiguous position somewhere between photography and film. Each still image combines with the next to create a progressive narrative while also forming a unique composition, related to, but separate from, the next. Eighty slides record different fragments of a small amateur painting of a fishing boat at sea, leading the eye to forgotten details and creating discrete, sometimes abstract compositions out of the original picture. In denying the persistent vision of a single complete image, the act of seeing is subverted, transformed into what Broodthaers refers to as a "reading system." As in *Fig. 0, Fig. 1, Fig. 2, Fig. A* (1971; pl. 1–10), the piece's structure renders it part of a larger textual dialogue, in which the artist constructs a critique of aesthetic and literary theory.

In a parody of traditional art historical academic analysis, the sequence moves from the whole to the fragment. The painting is first presented in its entirety, hung in a cheap gilt frame on the wall before the dissection begins, underlining its role as illustrative subject. As the sequence progresses, it is shown on another wall, then as an unframed canvas against a black background, and then in microscopic detail. A shot of the approaching boat is followed by close-ups of its sail and then of a buoy. Tiny details, such as a fisherman in a nearby rowboat, are blown up to become the central subject. The camera moves backward and forward between medium close-up and extreme close-up images, in a rhythmic series of shots that evoke Walter Benjamin's description of the film camera: "its lowerings and liftings, its interruptions and isolations, its extensions and accelerations, its enlargements and reductions."[1]

The sequential movement of the slides in *Bateau tableau* evokes the seriality of film frames viewed in extreme slow motion. The avant-garde filmmaker Maya Deren described slow motion in film as a "time microscope."[2] The photographic sequence of *Bateau tableau* illustrates Deren's emphasis on the photographic basis of film and on the conceptual function of the moving image: "Once we abandon the concept of the image as an end product of the creative process . . . we can . . . see that . . . the images' . . . individual reality is in no way dependent upon their sequence in actuality, and they can be assembled to compose any of several statements. In film, the image . . . should be only the beginning, the basic material of the creative action."[3]

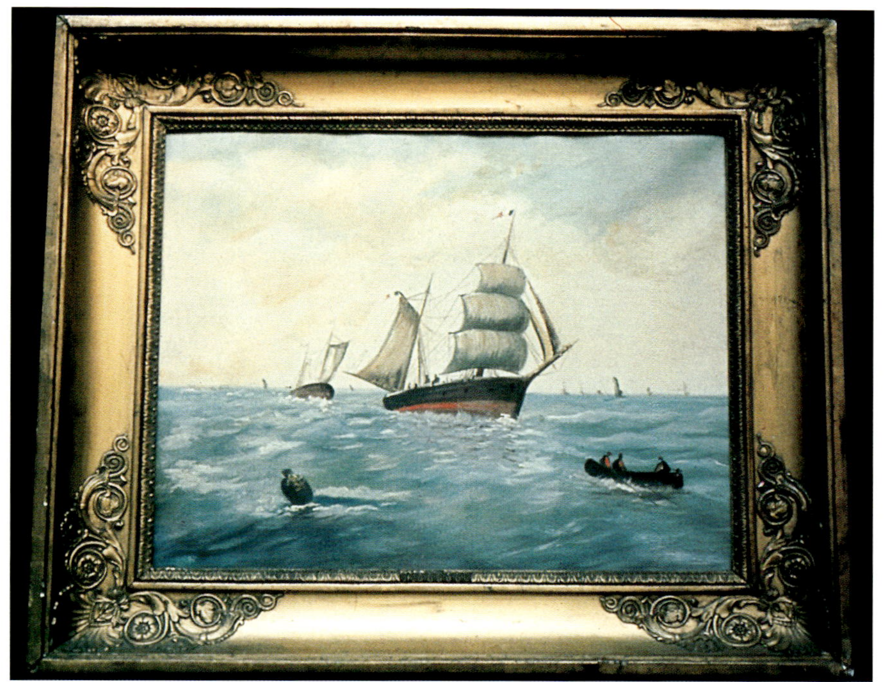

The connection between *Bateau tableau* and film is underlined by three films Broodthaers made in the same year as *Bateau tableau*, using the same painting: *A Voyage on the North Sea*, *Analyse d'une peinture*, and *Une peinture d'amateur découverte dans une boutique de curiosités*. The first film also appears as a book, whose black-and-white and color images of the painting recall *Bateau tableau*'s photographic analysis. The movement of the camera across the painting's surface evokes the figures scattered across the film screen in *Fig. 0, Fig. 1, Fig. 2, Fig. A*. In both cases, a unified image of time is replaced by a series of symbolic fragments, linking the object, photography, and language.

Broodthaers's method also makes evident the representational status of the painting itself, for, as Deren observes, a painting is a likeness, or image, not of a thing, but of a mental concept, which might resemble the subject directly or, in the case of abstract work, bear no visible relation to it. The difference between the physical presence of the painting and its representation in *Bateau tableau* echoes René Magritte's painting *The Treachery of Images (Ceci n'est pas une pipe)* (c. 1928–29), in which the gap between the physical object and its representation is stated directly through language. Broodthaers, by contrast, uses language within a temporally based structure to present his challenge to both traditional art historical representation and, on a deeper level, the basic tenets of modernism itself. His use of appropriation, evident in his first films of the 1950s and demonstrated in his numerous re-presentations of ignored and discarded objects, such as the amateur painting in *Bateau tableau*, prefigures the postmodernist era of simultaneity and fragmentation, raising fundamental questions regarding our perception of the artwork in the new, mechanical age. - - - - -

1. WALTER BENJAMIN, "The Work of Art in the Age of Mechanical Reproduction," quoted by Bruce Jenkins in "Un peu [plus] tard: Citation in the Cinema of Marcel Broodthaers," in *Marcel Broodthaers: Cinéma*, ed. Manuel J. Borja-Villel and Michael Compton (Barcelona: Fundació Antoni Tàpies, 1997), 290.
2. MAYA DEREN, "Cinematography: The Creative Use of Reality," reprinted in *The Avant Garde Film: A Reader of Theory and Criticism*, ed. P. Adams Sitney, Anthology Film Archives Series, no. 3 (New York: New York University Press, 1978), 67.
3. Ibid., 69.

Plate 11
MARCEL BROODTHAERS,
Bateau tableau,
1973, projected image (detail).

Overleaf:

Plate 12
MARCEL BROODTHAERS,
Bateau tableau,
1973, full sequence of 80 projected images, proceeding from top to bottom and from left to right.

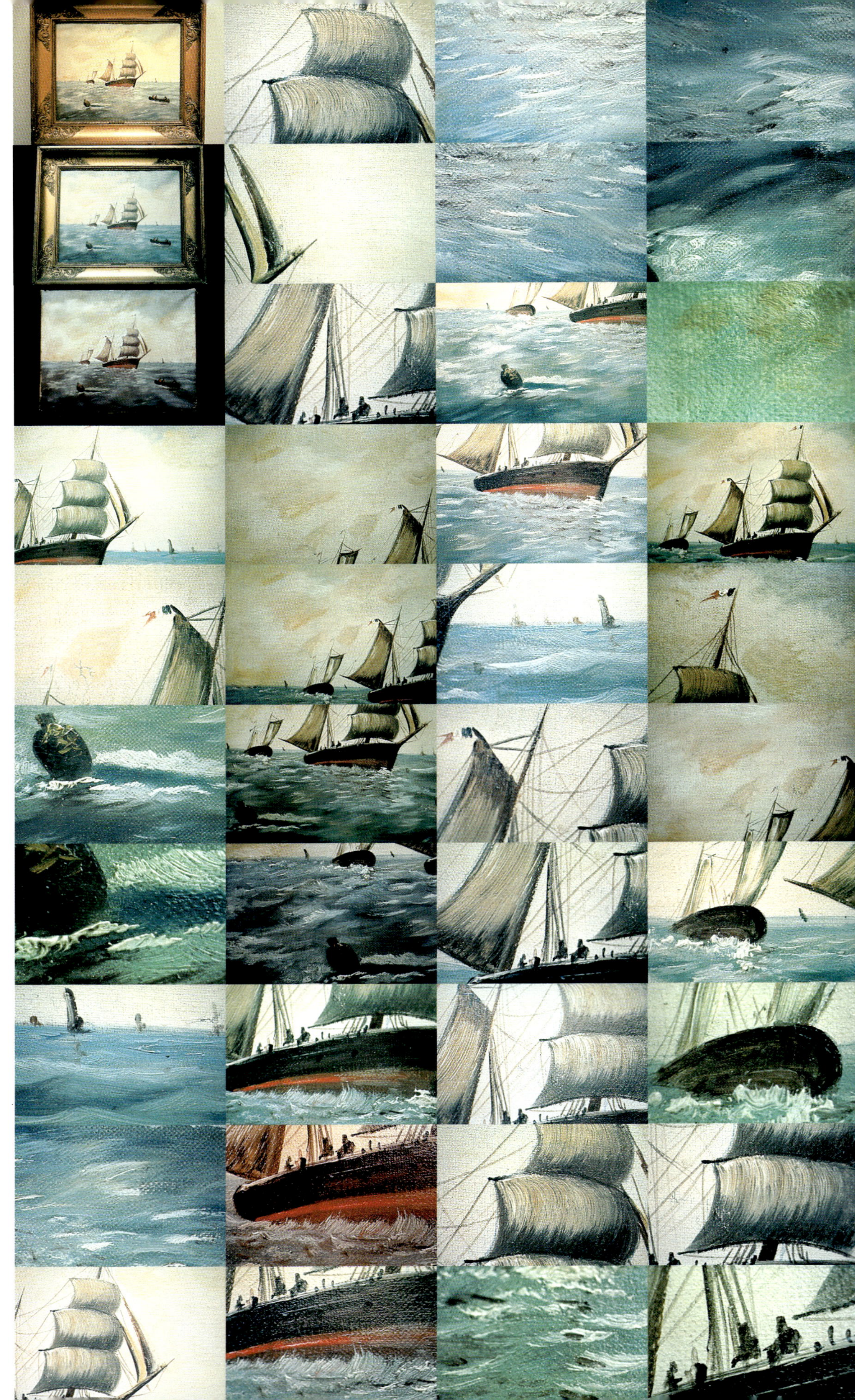

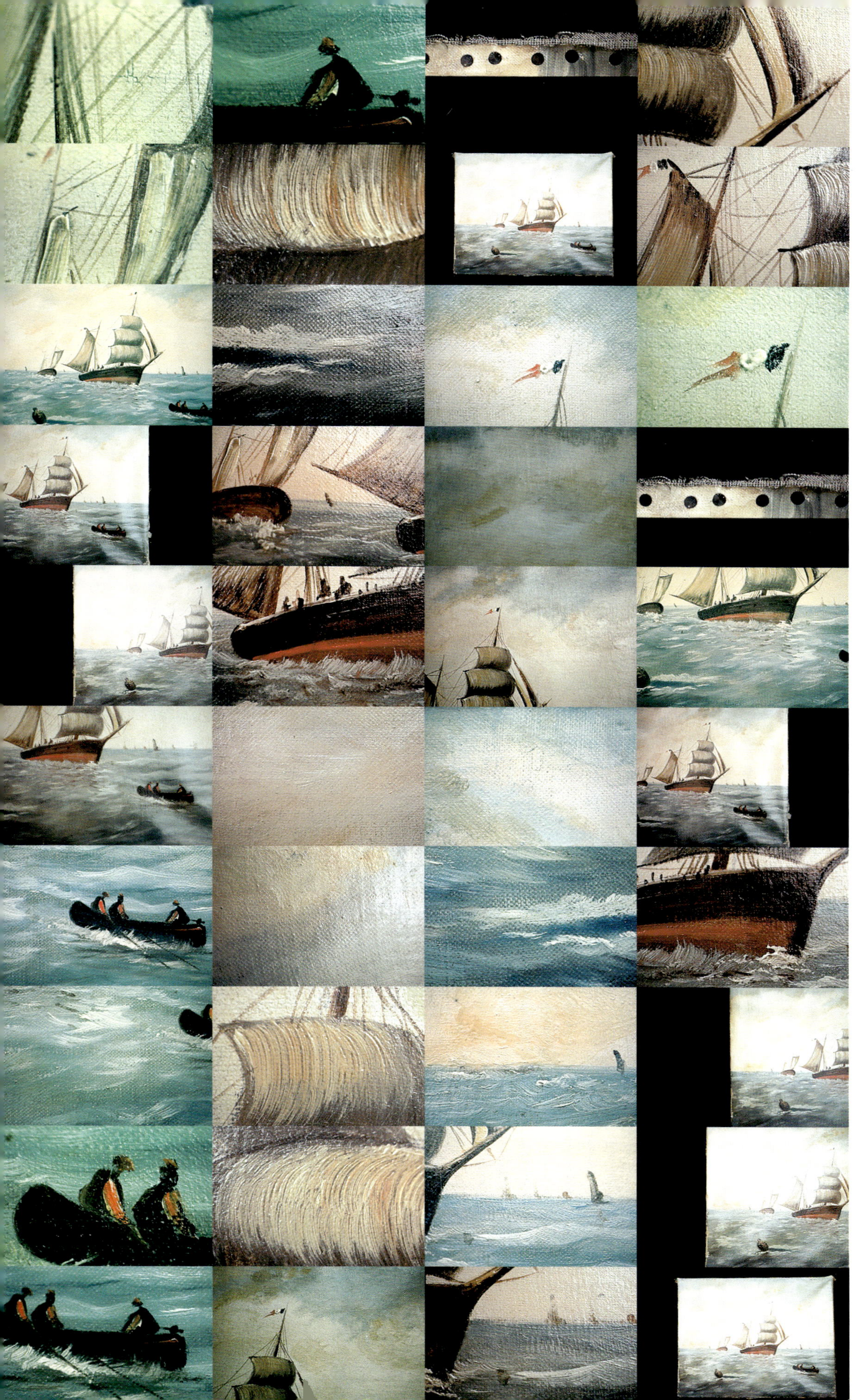

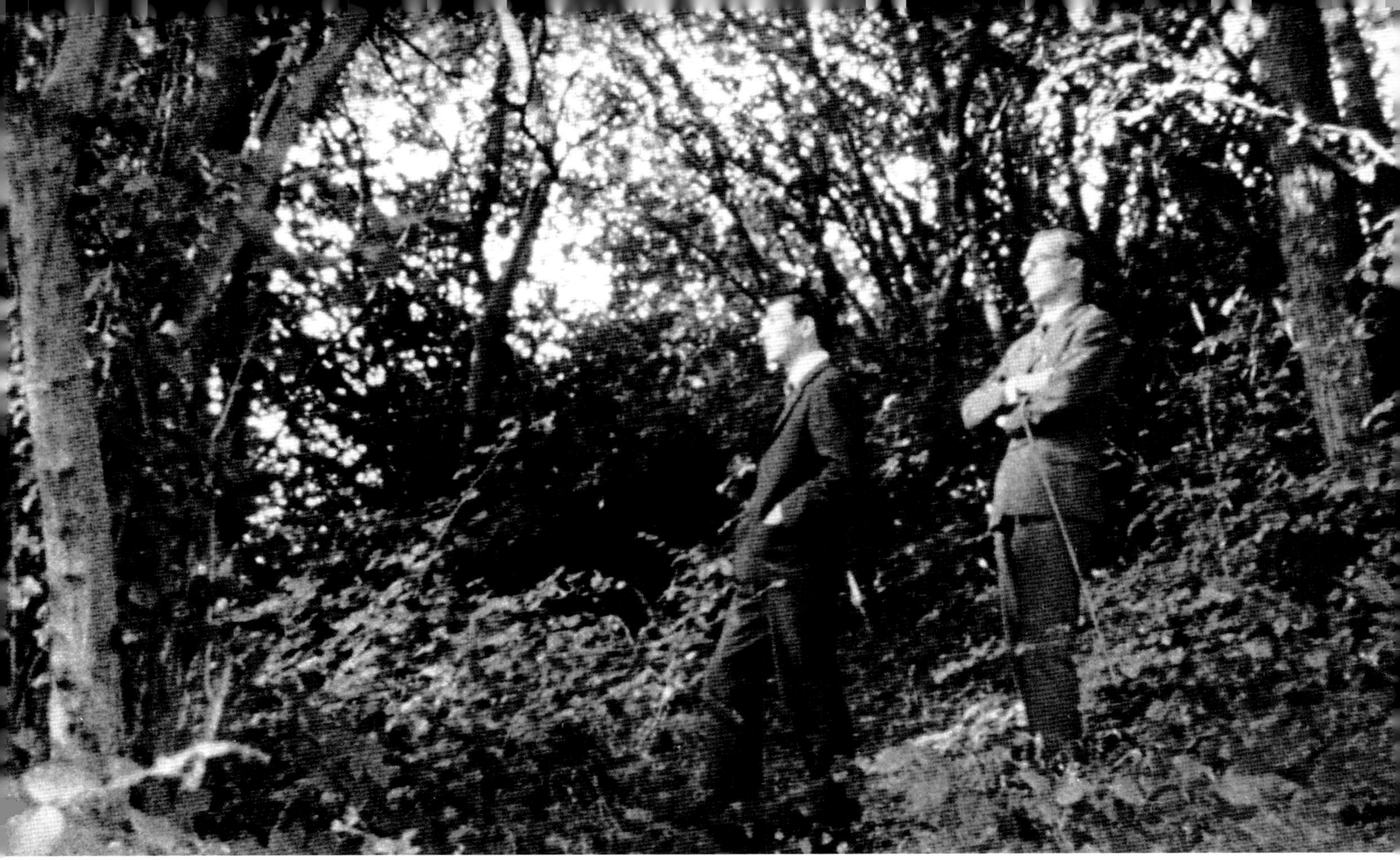

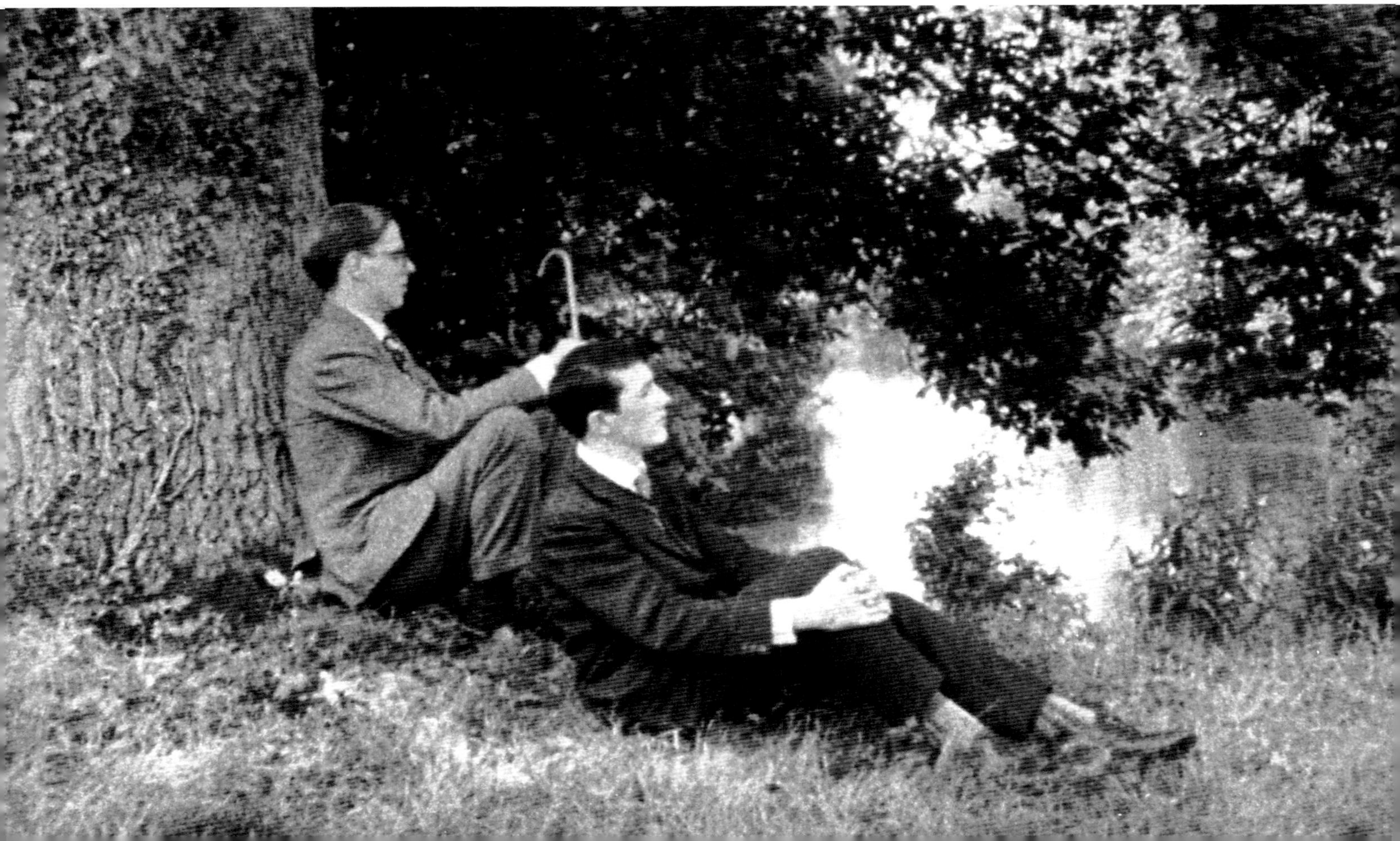

GILBERT & GEORGE

THE NATURE OF OUR LOOKING (1970)

A PORTRAIT OF THE ARTISTS AS YOUNG MEN (1972)

+++++ In the world of Gilbert & George, everything is sculpture. The film and three videotapes made in the early 1970s, at the beginning of their career, are "film" and "video" sculptures, just as their work in other media is variously subtitled "singing sculpture," "story sculpture," "postal sculpture," "living sculpture," and "large charcoal on paper sculpture." Both artists set out to make "all the world an art gallery" and every

action art: "Being living sculptures is our lifeblood, our destiny, our romance, our disaster, our light and life."[1]

Gilbert & George's use of the term *sculpture* to describe their work in video, film, drawing, performance, photography, and mail art emerged out of their training at Saint Martin's School of Art in London, which had become a center of the avant-garde. It also reflected the expanded definitions of sculpture that emerged in both America and Europe during the late 1960s. Gilbert & George's definition illustrates Rosalind Krauss's argument that this widespread "expanded" use of the term concealed a historicism: "The new is made comfortable by being made familiar. . . . We are comforted by

Plates 13–16
GILBERT & GEORGE,
The Nature of Our Looking,
1970, film stills.

Overleaf:

Plates 17–20
GILBERT & GEORGE,
A Portrait of the Artists as Young Men,
1972, video stills.

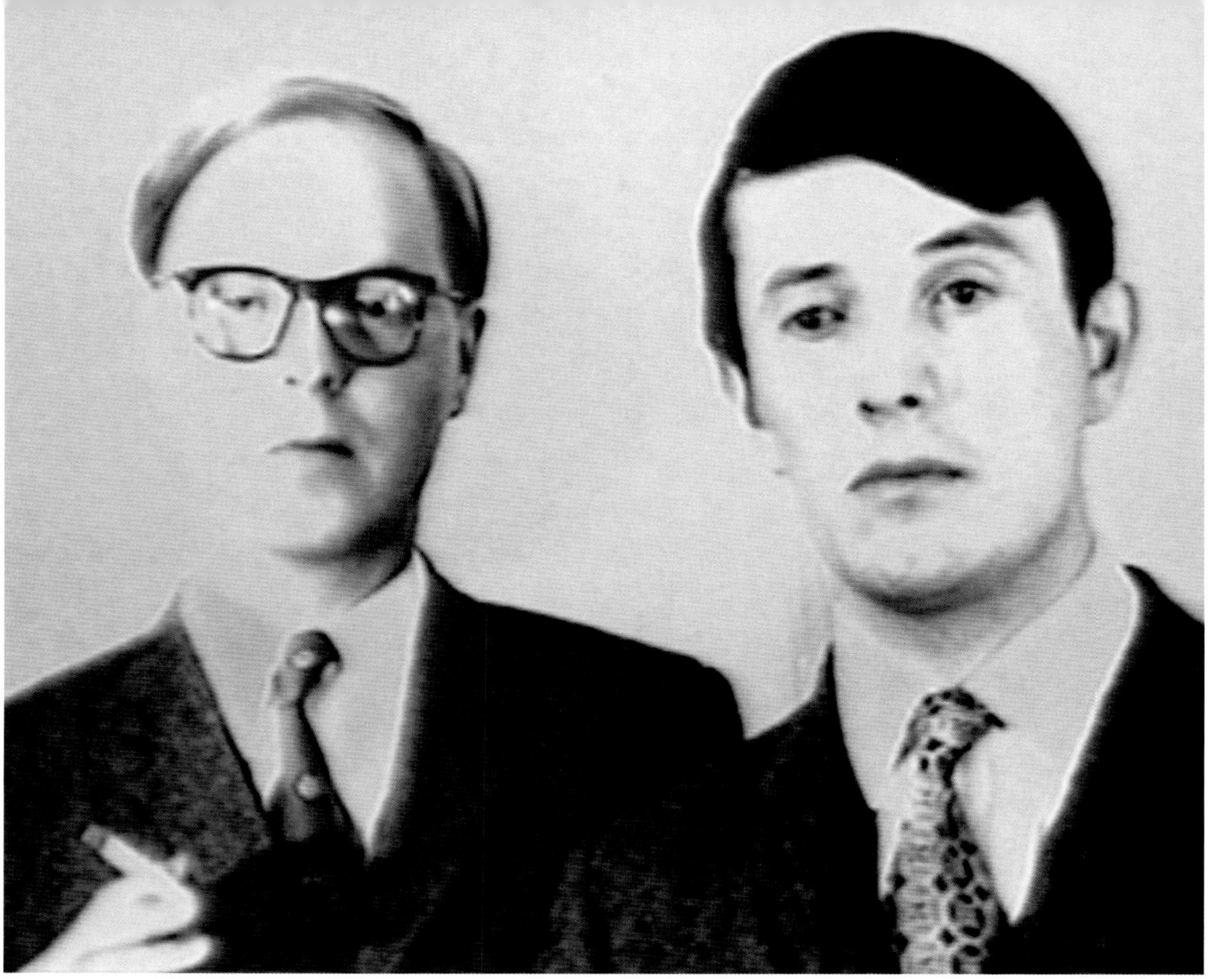

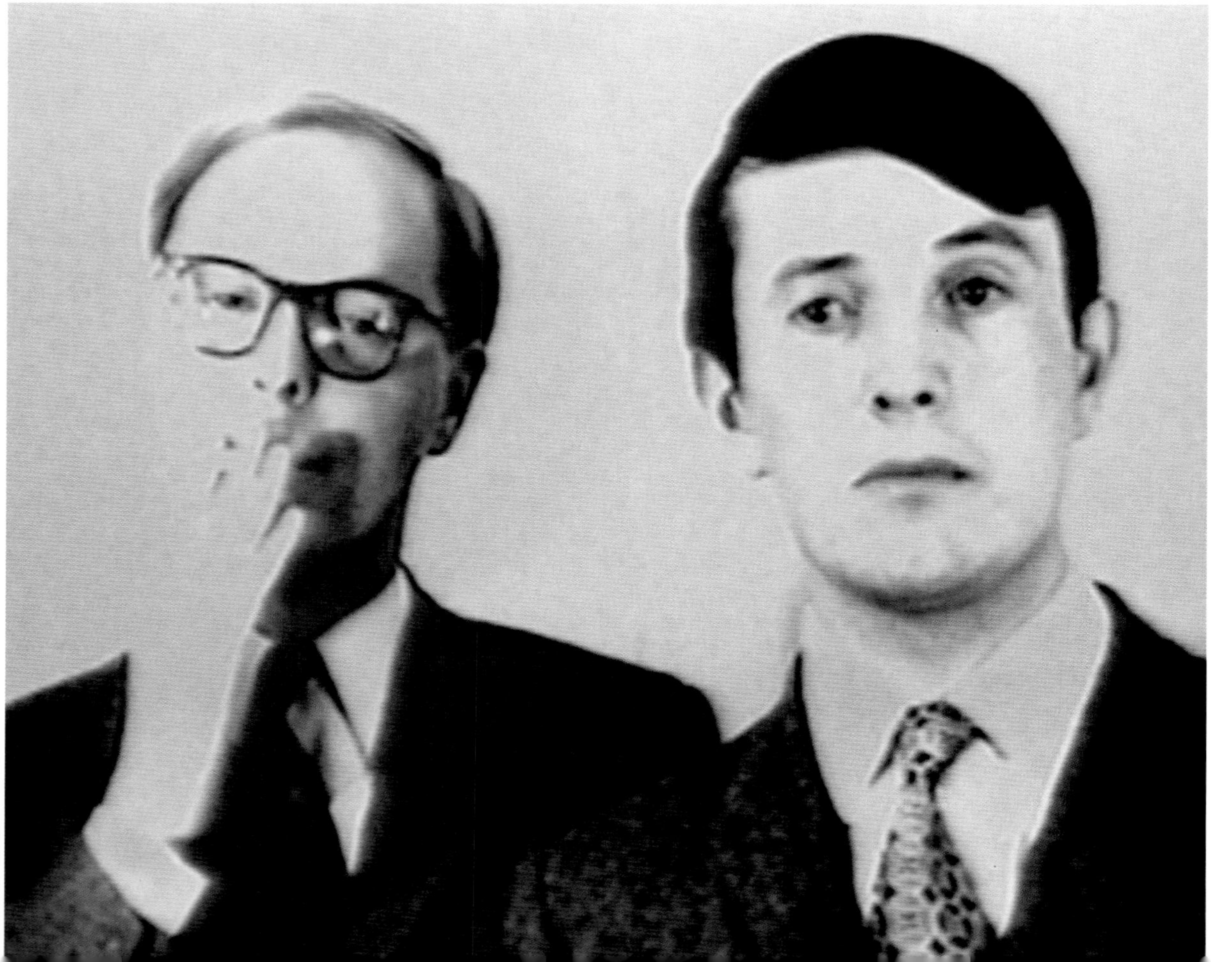

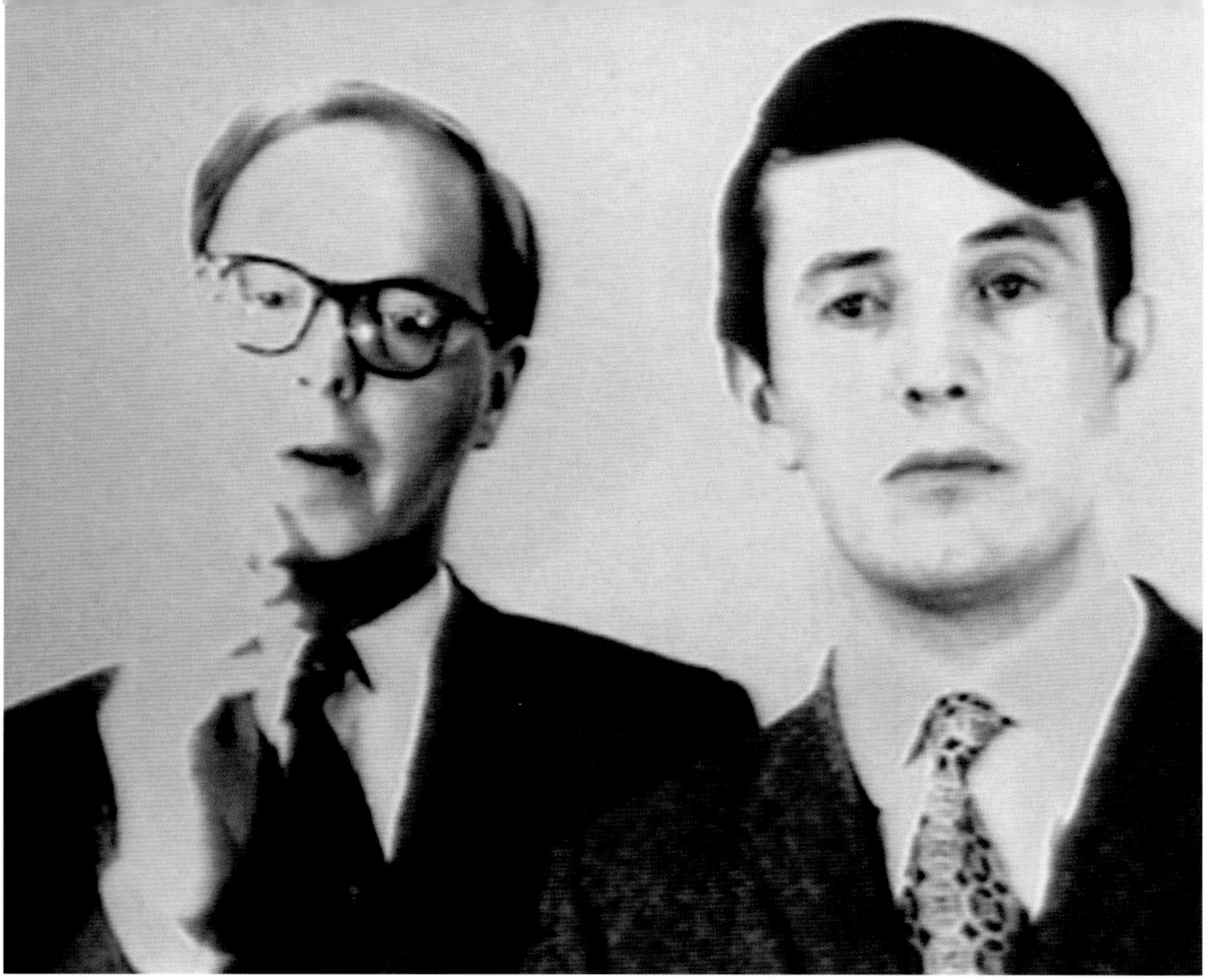

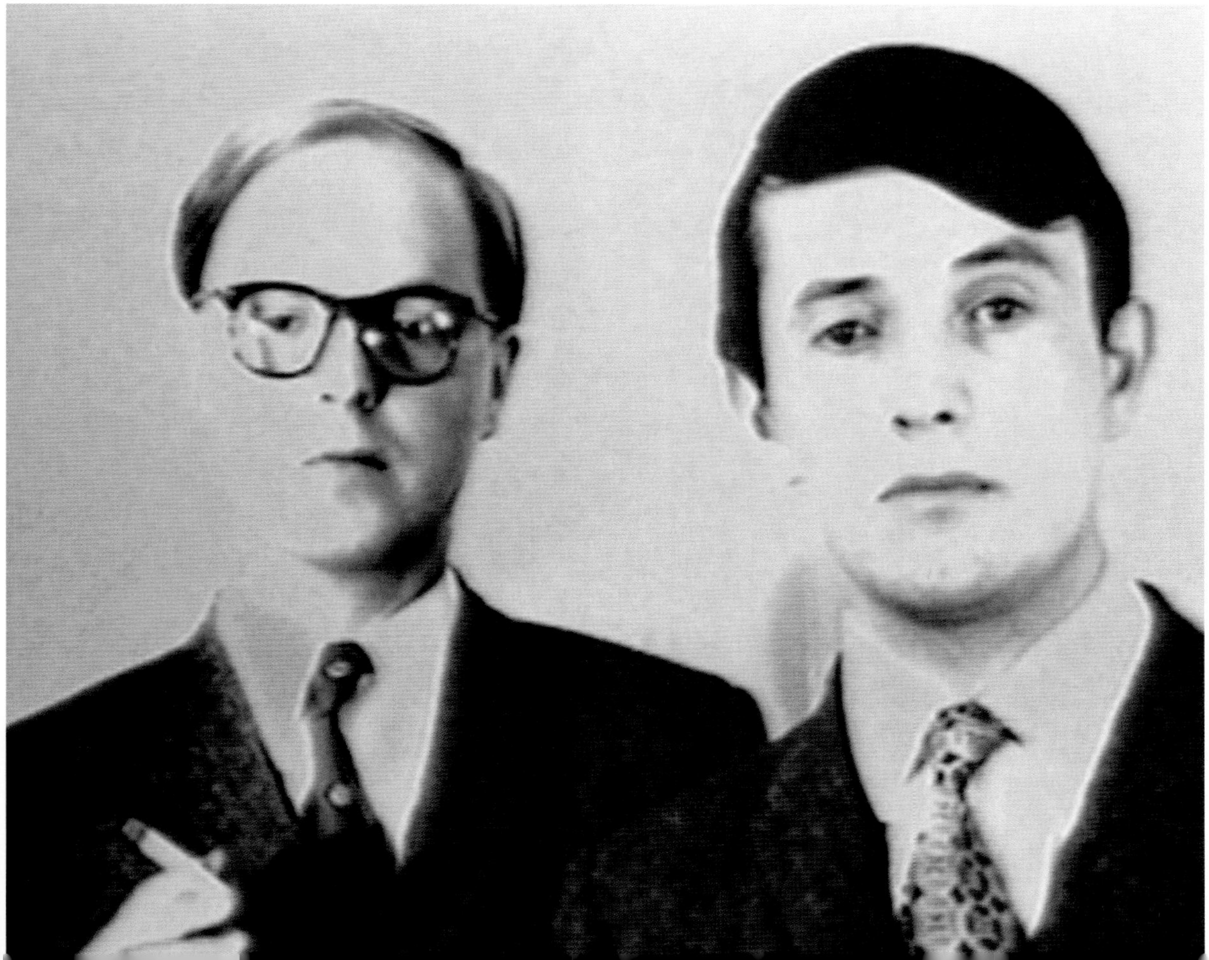

this perception of sameness, this strategy for reducing everything foreign in either time or space, to what we already know and are."[2]

This desire for familiarity, here expressed through a nostalgia for English traditions (gin drinking, pastoral landscape, old-fashioned suits, good manners, Victorian poetry, and music hall songs), forms the core of Gilbert & George's work. Their childlike approach to the world, and the accompanying suppressed aggression, belies an anxiety about the rapid cultural, social, and political shifts ushered in by the 1960s, which threatened to alter permanently the traditional English way of life.

The Nature of Our Looking (1970) begins with a verse by the Victorian poet Norman Gale: "Here in the country's heart/where the grass is green/life is the same sweet life/as it e're hath been." Repunctuated and appropriated as Gilbert & George's own words, the text clearly aligns the artists with Gale's desire for everything to remain exactly as it was in the past. The two artists are shown side by side, immobile and looking into the distance, in two successive fixed-frame black-and-white shots, first standing in wooded countryside, then seated under a large tree. A soundtrack of Victorian music hall piano tunes, an oblique reference to silent cinema, gives the only indication that time is passing. The artists' immobile, "sculptural" presence freezes them into a pictorial composition that recalls not so much photography as the eighteenth-century portrait paintings of Thomas Gainsborough.

As Carter Ratcliff has observed, in the work of Gilbert & George the gaze is of paramount importance.[3] The gaze occupied an important role in the Georgian concept of the picturesque, in tableaux constructed through portraiture. Here the gaze takes on a specific connotation. In works such as *In the Bush*, which shows the artists at a great distance, moving slowly through English woodland, their roaming, and our observation of it, makes ironic reference to the gay male ritual of cruising.

Gilbert & George's studied homoeroticism is echoed in *A Portrait of the Artists as Young Men*. Both artists, shot in close-up head and shoulders, stand in silence, looking intently into the middle distance. Their affected stance in front of the camera is underlined by George's repeated draws on a cigarette, which he lifts slowly to his mouth at regular intervals. The combination of intimacy and formality within the double self-portrait, whose format presents them as a couple, simultaneously reveals and represses the erotic and emotional depth of their relationship. As Ratcliff argues, their rigidity and formality make us aware of our own personae: "We are all a touch sculptural, all enclosed on occasion by public selves."[4]

1. GILBERT & GEORGE, quoted in Carter Ratcliff, "Gilbert & George and Modern Life," in *Gilbert & George, 1968–1980* (Eindhoven: Stedelijk Van Abbemuseum, 1980), 7.
2. ROSALIND KRAUSS, "Sculpture in the Expanded Field," in *The Originality of the Avant-Garde and Other Modernist Myths* (Cambridge: MIT Press, 1985), 277.
3. RATCLIFF, "Gilbert & George and Modern Life," 10.
4. Ibid., 8.

Plate 21
GILBERT & GEORGE, *The Nature of Our Looking*, 1970, film still.

In *Gordons Makes Us Drunk*, the dark underside of Gilbert & George's world becomes evident for the first time. The nihilism of their drinking was to be explored in numerous pieces during 1972 and 1973—including *Falling*, *Staggering*, *Reeling Drunk*, and *The Secret Drinker*—in which its destructive effects became increasingly evident. If, as Ratcliff suggests, Gilbert & George's double persona acts as a kind of armor to shield wounded personalities, the self-control demonstrated in *Gordons Makes Us Drunk* hints at the potential collapse of the artifice, as it gradually gave way, in later work, to

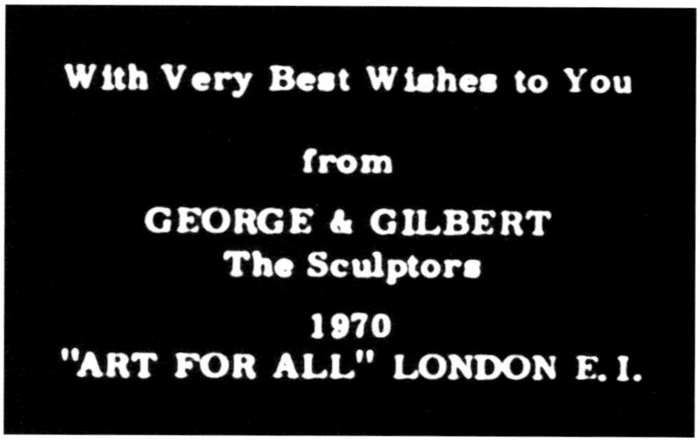

With Very Best Wishes to You
from
GEORGE & GILBERT
The Sculptors
1970
"ART FOR ALL" LONDON E. I.

blurred vision, sexual imagery, anger, blood, and violence. As debauchery created another kind of doubling, the dual persona began to fall apart.

Despite its apparent discipline, the artifice through which Gilbert & George's every action is filtered could not, in the end, regain paradise lost; nor could it heal the pain of social unacceptability. Their work arguably belongs to the political and aesthetic tradition of English gay cultural pioneers such as Oscar Wilde, and their early film and video pieces express a uniquely English kind of existentialism, whose power is achieved through a fusion of the conceptual and the erotic with the picturesque.

JANE AND LOUISE WILSON

STASI CITY (1997)

+++++ In the installations of Jane and Louise Wilson, the dreamlike space of cinema is rendered conceptual. Large double images are projected onto opposite or adjacent walls of the gallery, showing deserted domestic and industrial spaces whose evocative atmospheres act as a trigger for a filmic memory. Yet the projected loops give literal form to the inherent mirroring properties of video, refusing the linearity of cinematic narrative.

Stasi City[1] represents a further shift in this dialectic, from the artifice of cinema toward the realism of the video documentary. Powerful political, historical, and ideological meaning is embedded in buildings and sites throughout the city of Berlin. The double projections expose the city's most potent architectural symbol of postwar East German government repression: the abandoned headquarters of the Staatsicherheit, the notorious secret police known as the Stasi, in an area of East Berlin nicknamed Stasi City. In contrast to previous works, here the location of the film is clearly identified, through both the title and the imagery, and becomes the subject of the piece itself, rather than a metaphor for another, fictional space. This fictional space, or film memory, is replaced by another kind of memory—that of the horrific events that took place during the communist regime—which continues to pervade the empty buildings.

In two double-wall projections, almost identical panning shots move rapidly through abandoned hallways, elevators, and padded interrogation rooms, all left in a state of disarray and decay. The horizontality of the interior corridor shots are contrasted with the verticality of the open elevators, which can be seen, framed by their doorways, moving rapidly up and down between floors. As though silently articulating the need to witness the destruction of the feared Stasi administration's hidden heart, now ripped open and exposed to public scrutiny, the camera adopts a searching, quasi-documentary role. The Wilson's voyeuristic surveillance of the Stasi headquarters mimics the all-pervasive surveillance activities for which the East German secret police became infamous, penetrating the once-secret territory with the camera lens in an almost political statement of liberation. The sense of freedom is echoed in the first shot, in which the lights in the office of the Stasi's ex-director, Erich Mielke, are all switched on simultaneously, in a symbolic reference to his fall from power.

This surreal moment is echoed throughout the piece by the slightly out-of-sync pairs of images, which give the quasi-documentary nature of the footage a sense of unreality. As in all the Wilsons' work, two subtly differing images are brought together to create a third space. Superficially, this space arguably alludes to the artists' joint creative process as twins. On a deeper level, it operates as a metaphor for the space of memory, a hidden place inside which a different reality can be freely imagined, when immediate circumstances have been severely repressed.

1. Produced during a DAAD (Deutscher Akademischer ustauschdienst) artists' residency in Berlin, awarded to Jane and Louise Wilson in 1997. The video nstallation forms part of a larger, three-part piece, whose other ments include photographs and a culptural reconstruction of partial views of the interiors.

2. JANE AND LOUISE WILSON, erviewed by Raimund Kummer, in *asi City* (Hannover: Kunstverein Hannover, 1997), IX.

Plate 22

JANE AND LOUISE WILSON, *Stasi City*, (Floating figure), 1997, Cibachrome print on aluminum produced in conjunction with the video, 108 x 108 in.

Overleaf:

Plate 23

JANE AND LOUISE WILSON, *Stasi City*, 1997, installation view.

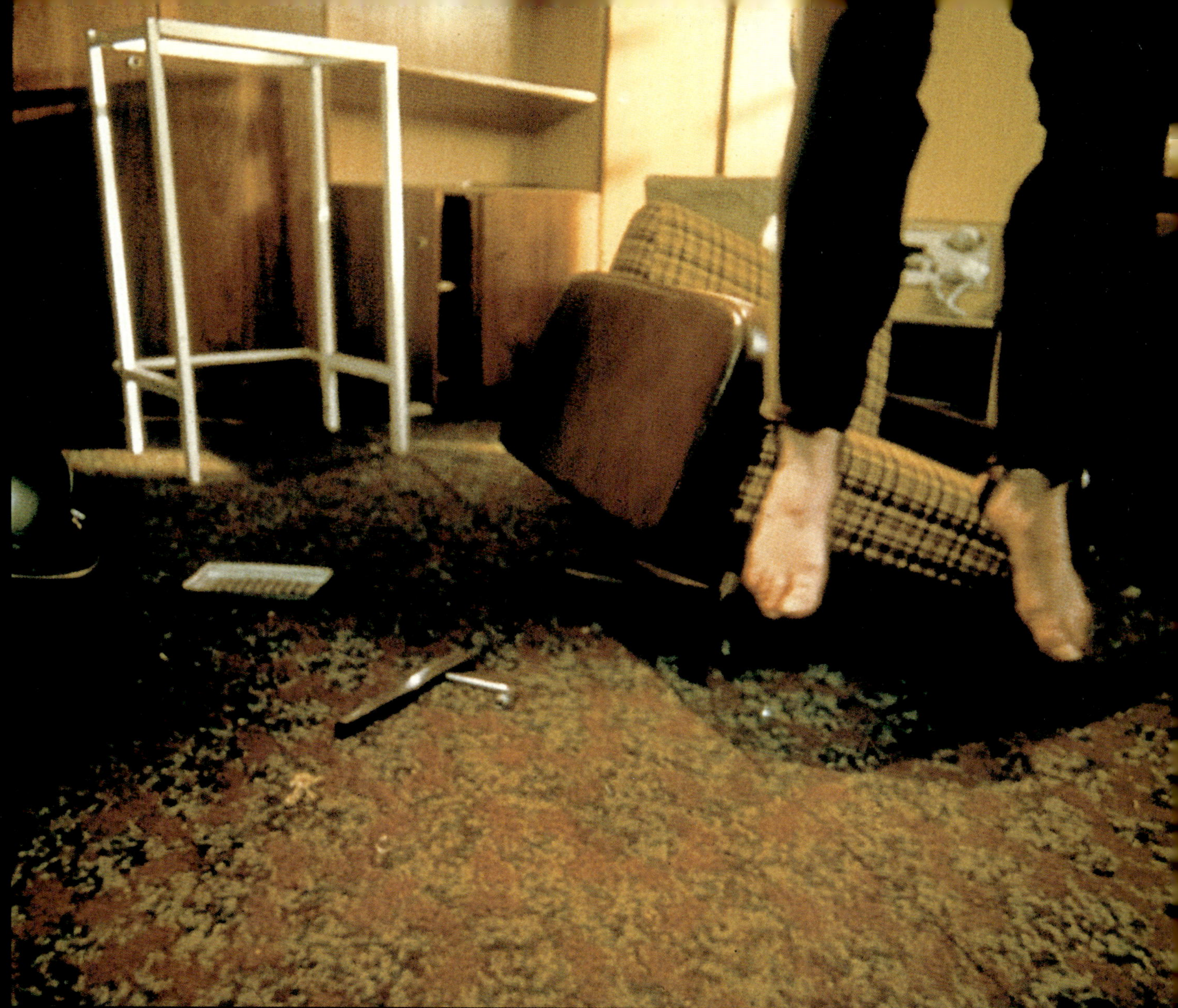

The fantasy potential contained within this space of memory is crystallized in the final shot, in which a figure free-floats in space for several seconds, inside one of the interrogation rooms. People under extreme conditions of mental or physical torture often cope with their ordeal by removing themselves mentally from their physical situation. In an interview the Wilsons made a direct reference to the symbolic freedom of antigravity, citing the importance of space travel to East Germans, for whom it represented unlimited freedom.[2] Like the Wilsons' previous works, *Stasi City* creates an uncertain ambiguity in its tension between fantasy and the real. In the final shot, when a flask falls, the force of gravity is reasserted and, with it, the grim realities of the all-too-recent past.

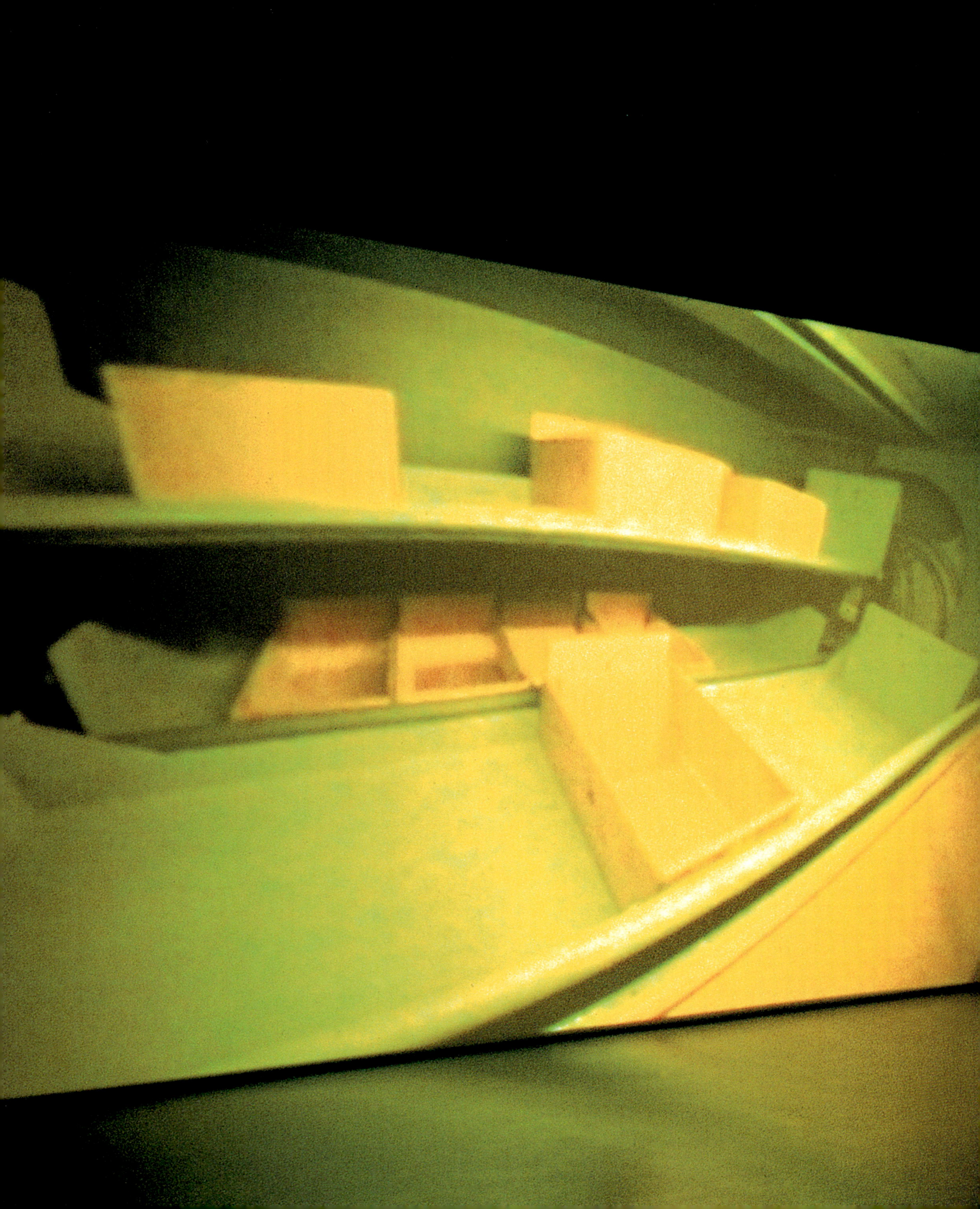

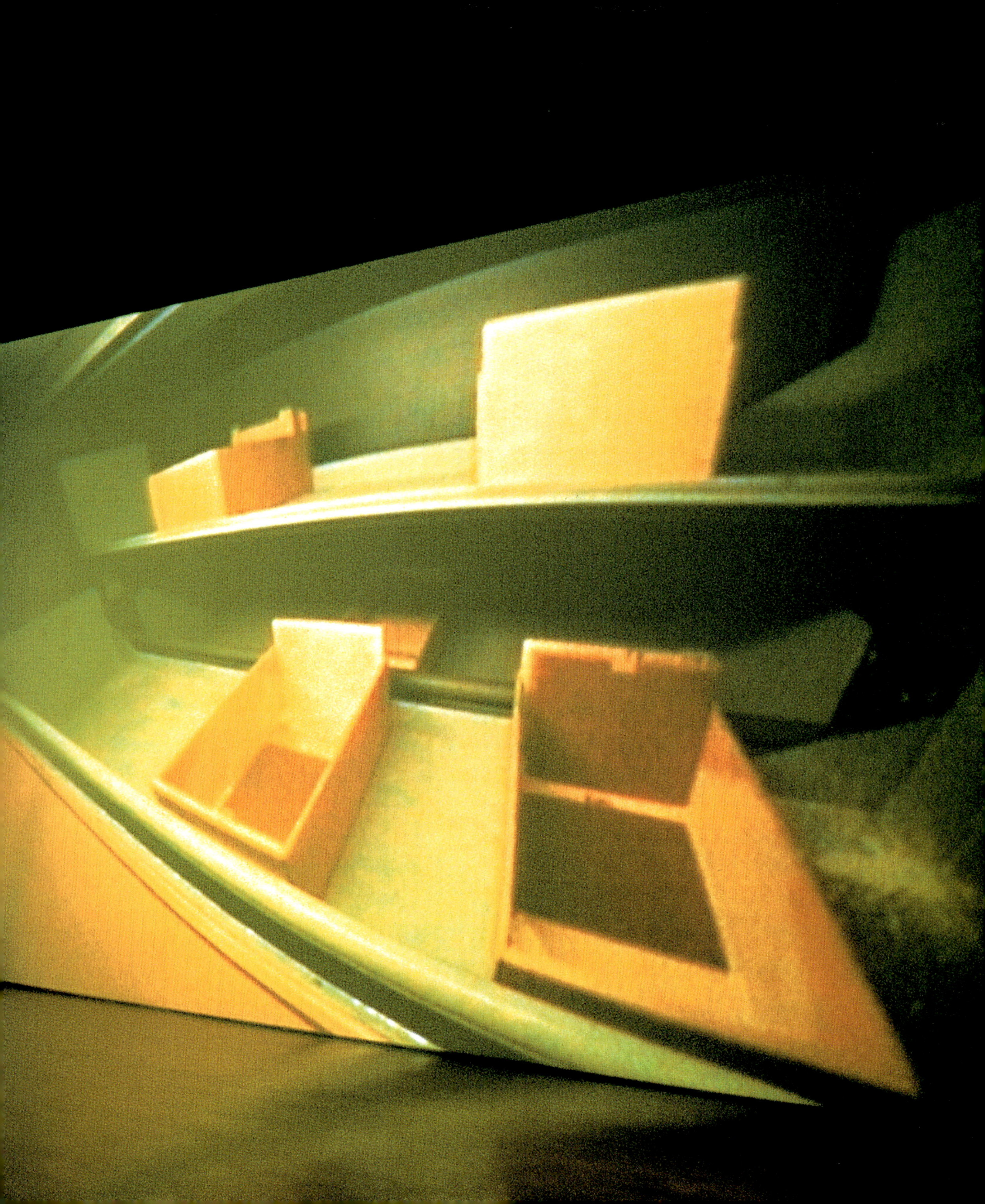

DAN GRAHAM

BODY PRESS (1970–72)

+++++ From 1969 to 1973 Dan Graham made a group of conceptual films that epitomize the key concepts of feedback and splitting, which underpin all his work in performance, videotape, installation, and conceptual photography and his architectural pavilions.[1] The principles explored in these five double-screen films, of which *Body Press* has become the best known, emerged out of Graham's interest in self-perception, the theories of Marshall McLuhan, and the role of the spectator, stimulated by the popularity of the psychological and phenomenological theory that developed during the late 1960s.

Graham used super-8 film for the same reason that he used Kodachrome slide film for his photographs: its simplicity, availability, and cheapness—all features of both media's domestic and educational use.[2] The exploration of the concept of feedback in Graham's early films is highly significant for the history of video, whose instant-feedback properties are generally assumed to have been the sole conduit for the investigations into self-reflexive ideas such as feedback and splitting which took place in the late 1960s and early 1970s. In fact, *Body Press*, like Andy Warhol's first double-screen film, *Outer and Inner Space* (1965), reveals a parallel attempt in film to present multiple viewpoints, parallel time, and the camera as an extension of the body.

In *Body Press*, two naked performers—one male, the other female—stand back-to-back inside a mirrored cylindrical structure. Each performer holds a film camera, which they rotate around their bodies slowly, in a spiraling figure-eight movement, from waist to eye level. The movement is then reversed, until the camera is back at waist level, behind the performer and facing the other performer's body, at which point both performers exchange cameras.

In the two films, the body appears alternately as a clear representation and as a distorted image reflected in the mirrored surface. Both images are projected at large scale onto opposite walls of the gallery, re-presenting both performers' coexistent viewpoints, mirrored three times over: in each other's actions; by the mirrored interior walls; and by the exchange of cameras halfway through, which creates a third "splitting" of the action and image. As Graham points out, the viewer is unsure of whether to identify with the camera or the performer, since the camera becomes part of the performer's body, leading the viewer to identify with both simultaneously. This reverses the normal condition of film viewing, in which "the film . . . detaches the viewer from present reality."[3]

The pressing of the camera against the skin of the performer during the making of *Body Press* lends the process of filming a tactility, which, as Graham observes, can be "felt" by the spectator as surface tension. This tactility is echoed in the curved surface of the structure's inner walls, whose circular format reappears

1. See BRIAN HATTON, "Feedback: An Exchange of Faxes," in *Dan Graham: Architecture* (London: Camden Arts Centre, 1997), 7.

2. For technical reasons, *Body Press* was made in two versions: the first, in Super-8 film, in 1970, and the second, in sixteen-millimeter, in 1972.

3. DAN GRAHAM, *Video, Architecture, Television: Writings on Video and Video Works, 1970–1978*, ed. Benjamin H. D. Buchloh (Halifax: Press of the Nova Scotia College of Art and Design; New York: New York University Press, 1979); quoted in Anne Rorimer, "Dan Graham, an Introduction," in *Dan Graham: Buildings and Signs*, ed. Anne Rorimer (Chicago: Renaissance Society at the University of Chicago; Oxford: Museum of Modern Art, 1981), 10.

Plate 24
DAN GRAHAM, *Body Press*, 1970–72, production still.

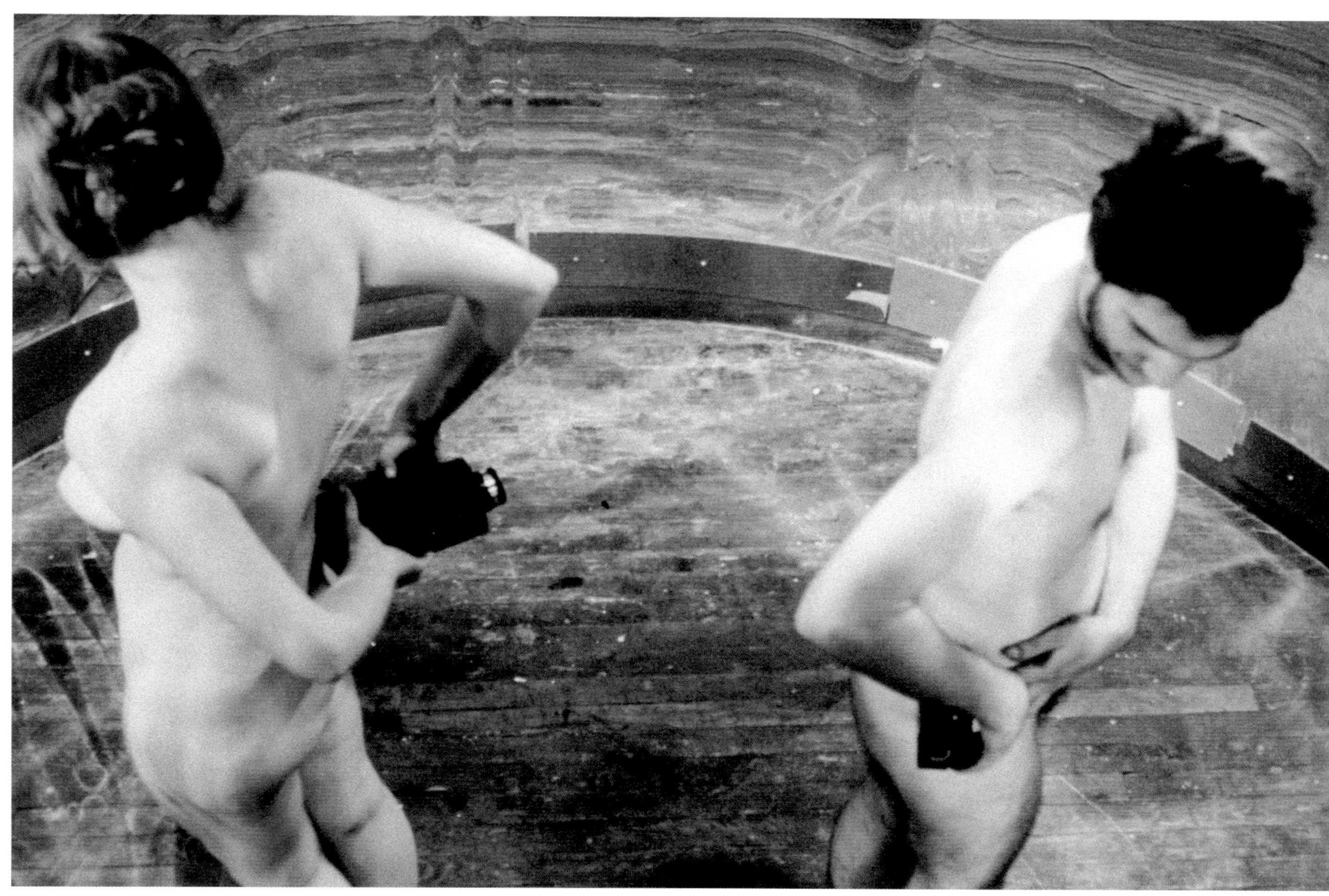

in several subsequent architectural pieces, including *Two-Way Mirror Cylinder inside Cube* (1981/91) on the rooftop of the Dia Center for the Arts in New York. Graham's use of the circular structure connects the cylindrical volume of the human body, and the curve of its contours, to the 360-degree circumference of the skyline beyond. This simple but profound connection marks *Body Press* as perhaps the earliest physical expression of Graham's deep understanding of the social and psychic body and its relationship to urban architectural form.

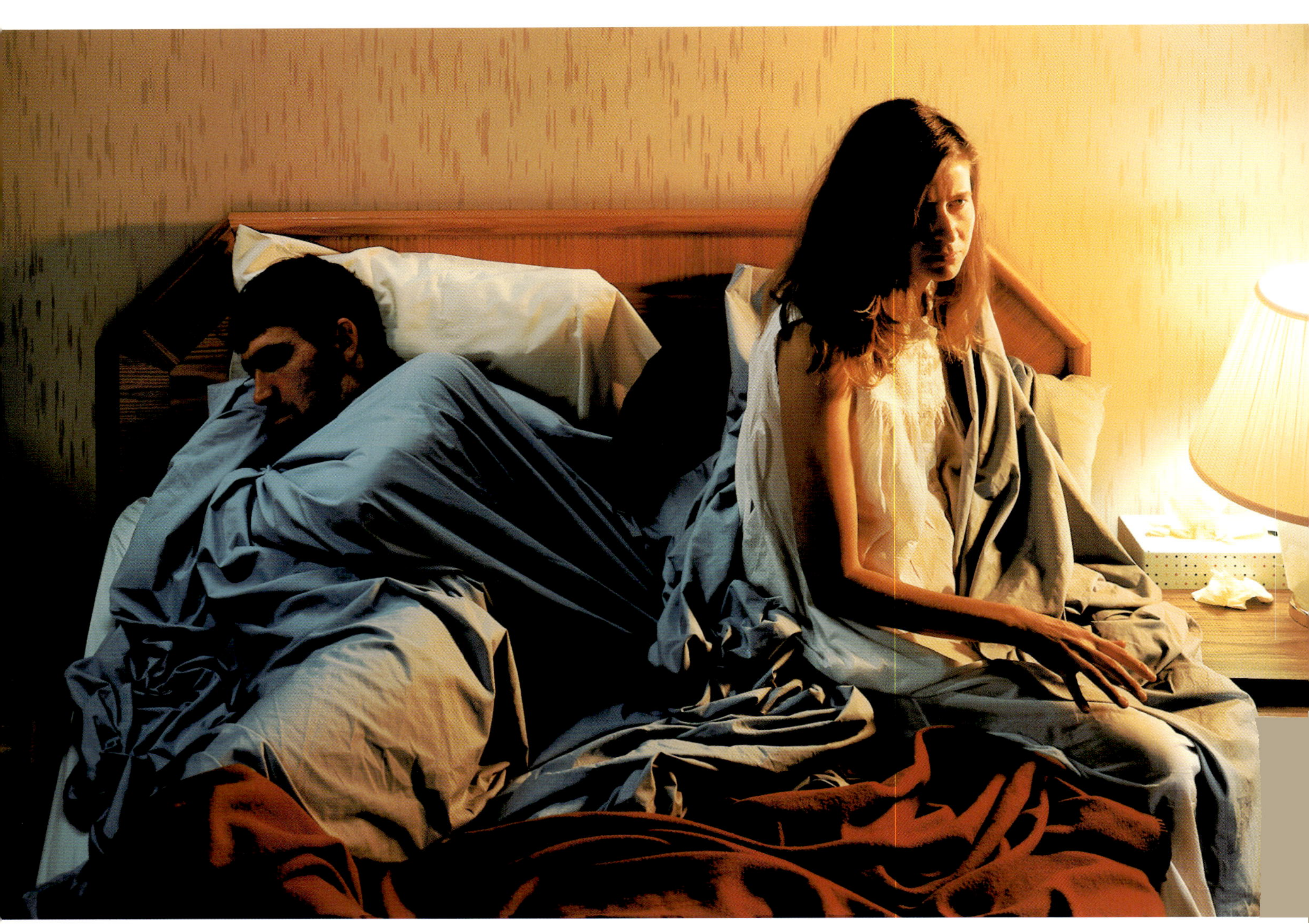

JEFF WALL

THE QUARREL (1988) UNTANGLING (1994)

+++++ The elaborately constructed photographic light boxes that have characterized the work of Jeff Wall from 1977 to the late 1990s are defined by a methodology drawn from photography, history painting, and cinema. Wall's radical strategy, heavily influenced by social theory and art history, emerged out of the conceptual photographic practices developed during the late 1960s in Vancouver, where he showed his work alongside that of Dan Graham, Bruce Nauman, and others. As Gary Dufour has argued, Wall's reworking of the photograph, into the commercial advertising form of the light-box transparency reflects both its conceptual role during the 1970s as a document of a performed action or a critical, social intervention and its subsequent metamorphosis into 1980s photo-conceptualism.[1]

Wall's involvement with social theory and art history, both as student and lecturer, merged his conceptual thinking with a deep interest in nineteenth-century French painting, in particular the work of Gustave Courbet, Eugène Delacroix, and Edouard Manet. His meticulously composed large-scale photographic tableaux treat contemporary social subjects—racism, domestic problems, job exploitation, Native American issues—in the grand nineteenth-century style of history painting. Like paintings, all his pieces is unique. Their luminous surfaces, as Dufour has observed, both emanate light and absorb their environment, like a cinema screen.[2] Combined with a precise and detailed composition, a kind of hyperpictorialism emerges, evocative of the large-scale narrative paintings of Georges Seurat. These intertwined references to painting and cinema appear throughout Wall's work. Each transparency is constructed in the manner of a film shoot. Actors are hired, a suitable location is found, and a composition is carefully built up, using props, costumes, and lighting. The theatricality of each frozen moment is underlined by Wall's method of rehearsing a single gesture with the actors before it is eventually photographed. In many cases, an image represents the moment after an emotional outburst, often triggered by a female's spoken words.[3] Thomas Crowe has observed that Wall uses shock as a central organizing principle in his work, which he defines in Benjaminian terms as "the defining feature of modern experience, the sensory assault that lends to urban life its perpetual aspect of the uncanny."[4]

In *The Quarrel* (1988), this sense of the uncanny is depicted in an emotional urban domestic scene of a couple in bed, in the miserable and exhausting phase after an argument has taken place with no resolution. While the man turns away, gathering the disheveled bedclothes around him as he lies staring silently into the middle distance, his partner sits on the bed, one of the sheets draped around her shoulders, distraught and frozen in thought, perhaps on the point of leaving the scene. Her half-raised right hand, fingers splayed, implies an action or reaction about to take place. The dramatic lighting of her profile by the bedside lamp,

Plate 25
JEFF WAL
The Qu
1988.

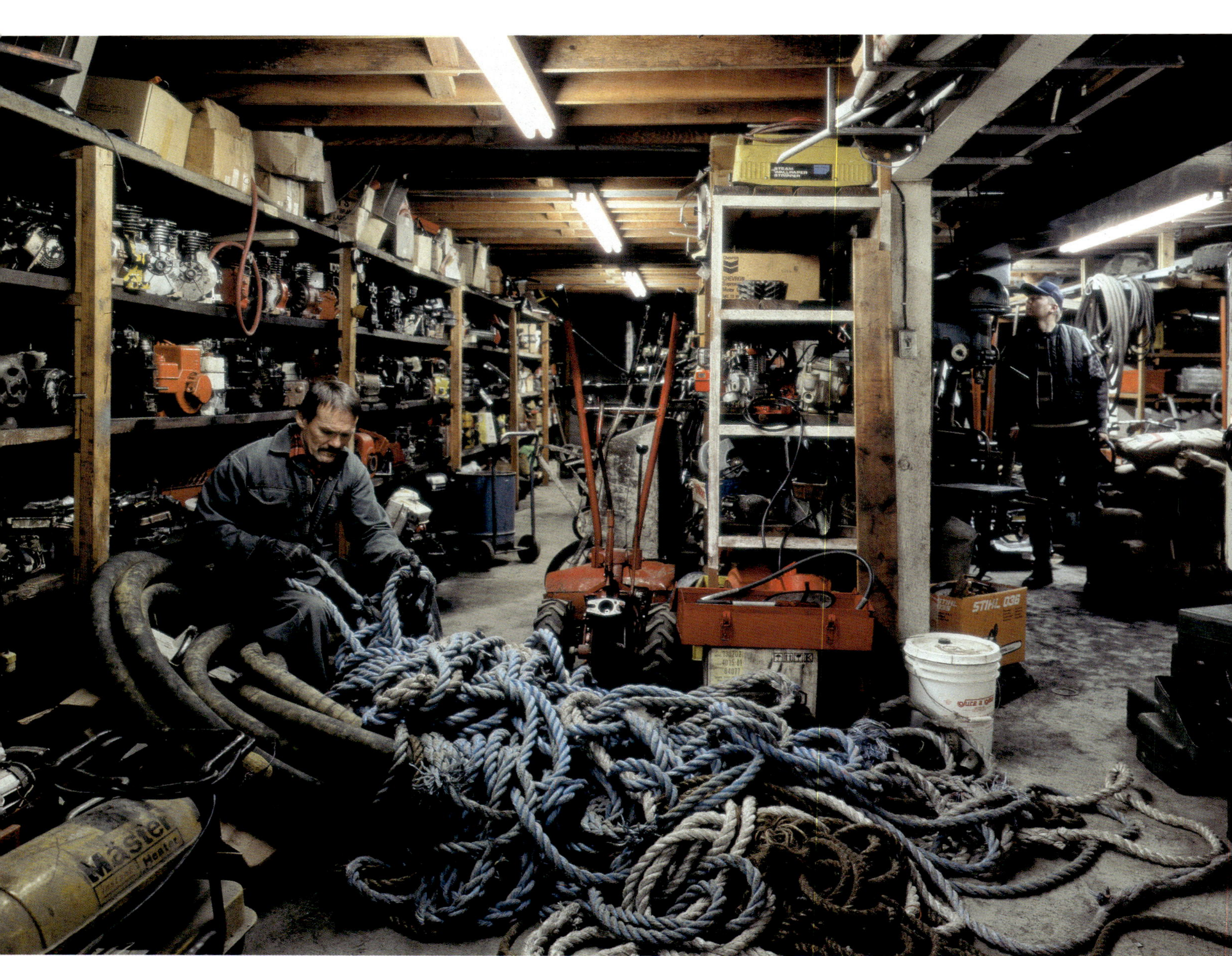
STIHL 036
Master
Heater

placing the focus on her emotional state and anticipating another dramatic moment, suspends the viewer between past and future action. Wall uses both the cinematic and painterly techniques of formal composition to depict the emotional distance between the couple. A large gap is created between the figures, pillows, and sheets, splitting the double image apart. The rumpled bedclothes are carefully arranged, like the drapery in a Netherlandish painting, to depict a very modern kind of sorrow.

If the emotional intensity, shallow perspective, and symmetrical frontal composition of *The Quarrel* evoke both earlier artworks and classic scenes from Hollywood film, *Untangling* (1994) contains a more direct allusion to allegorical painting. In the 1990s Wall began to construct more complex compositions using digitized computer techniques, which he likens to the studio practice of painting. The manipulations allowed by this process intensified his strategy of destabilizing the viewer's habitual reading of the image in order to suggest new possibilities for interpretation.[5]

In *Untangling*, an apparently ordinary scene in a mechanic's garage storeroom obscures a deceptively complex composition. A mechanic sits in a basement room full of mechanical parts, untangling a mass of blue rope, like a fisherman mending his nets. In the background another man stands looking at one of the shelves, as though searching for a piece of machinery. Yet the mass of rope seems too large for the room. It occupies the central position within the composition, its knotted mass contrasting with the relative order of the shelves behind. As Jean-Paul Criqui has suggested, it is as though the rope were a mythological monster with which the mechanic is quietly grappling, a metaphor for "the individual's struggle to escape the tangled threads of fate that control his destiny."[6] Wall's disconcerting image folds the everyday reality of the working mechanic, in a highly functional interior usually invisible to the outside world, inside an art historical metaphor. The possibility of new readings implied by this bringing together of two opposing representational codes permeates all of Wall's tableaux, forming the core of his overall aesthetic and theoretical strategy of redefinition and renewal.

1. GARY DUFOUR, "Against the Reality/Fiction of History," in *Jeff Wall*, 1990 (Vancouver: Vancouver Art Gallery, 1990), 59.

2. Ibid., 60.

3. Ibid., 62.

4. THOMAS CROWE, "Profane Illuminations: Social History and th[e] Art of Jeff Wall," *Artforum* 31 (February 1993): 68.

5. DUFOUR, "Against the Reality/Fiction," 62.

6. JEAN-PIERRE CRIQUI, "Jeff Wall[,"] *Artforum* 34 (March 1996): 119.

Plate 26
JEFF WALL,
Untangling,
1994.

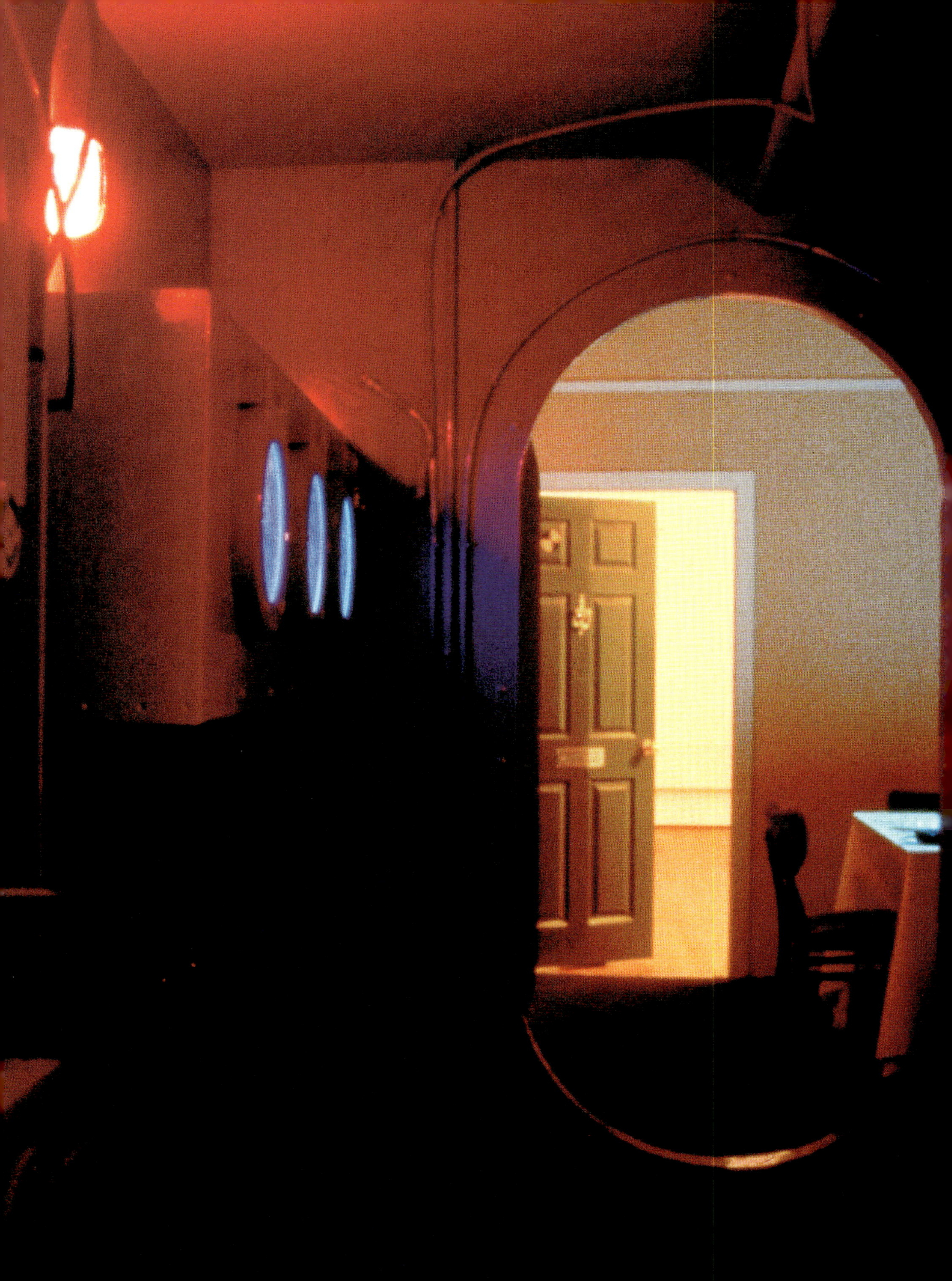

KEITH TYSON

ARTMACHINE ITERATION AMCHII-XLII: ANGELMAKER PART II QUADRUPED (1995)

+++++ For artists from Leonardo da Vinci onward, art and technology have always been inextricably linked. Keith Tyson's method of art making invokes the role of the artist as inventor—an intermediary between technology and the human imagination. All Tyson's work is produced by the "Artmachine," a computer program that instructs the artist to make artworks from templates constructed using disparate elements trawled randomly from virtual information sites, including libraries and the Internet.

The Artmachine's choices are made without any aesthetic intervention by the artist. For Tyson, their significance lies in their irrational unpredictability and the absence of any trace of illustration. Sometimes Tyson does not like what the Artmachine

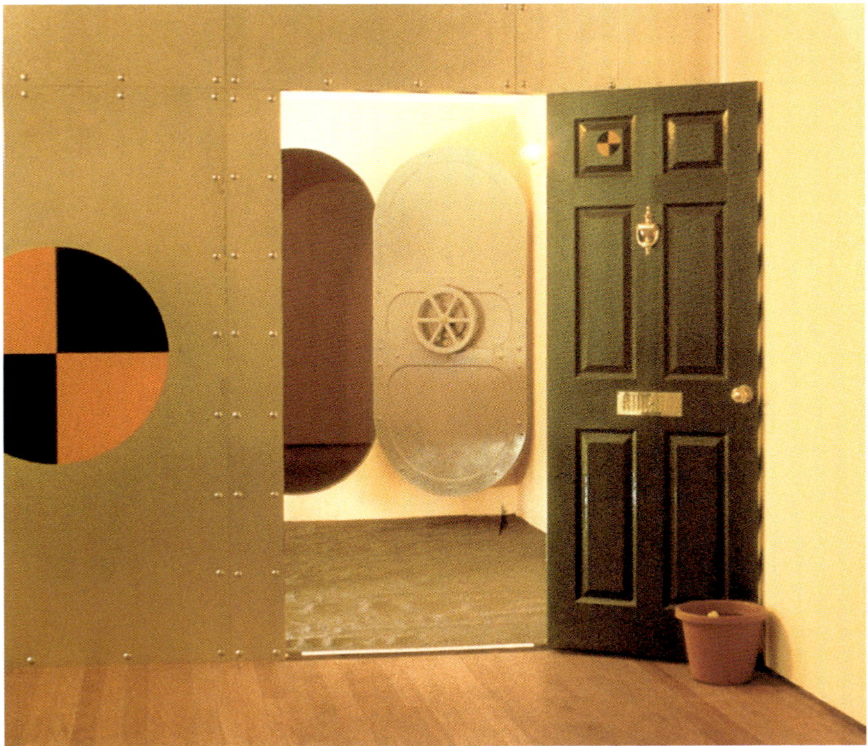

suggests but is obliged to make it nevertheless, in order to preserve the integrity of the concept. Each piece is realized because of a decision made by a curator, collector, or dealer. Tyson's insistence on rejecting any contribution from the artist to each idea suggests an extension of the tenets of Minimalism set out by Sol LeWitt in his *Sentences on Conceptual Art* (1967), in which the idea takes precedence over its physical manifestation. Yet Tyson sees his method as essentially traditional and allies his ambivalence toward the computer's proposals to struggling with a painting that refuses to conform to the artist's intention.

Plates 27–28
KEITH TYSON,
Artmachine Iteration AMCHII-XLII: Angelmaker Part II Quadruped,
1995, installation views.

Tyson's method was strongly influenced by the writings of the Argentine writer Jorge Luis Borges, in particular his story "The Library of Babel." Tyson's machine can be likened to Borges's labyrinthine library: "The Universe (which others call the library) is composed of an indefinite and perhaps infinite number of hexagonal galleries with vast air shafts between, surrounded by very low railings. Over many hundreds of years . . . it becomes clear that all the books are made from the same elements . . . and that there are no two identical books."[1]

Artmachine Iteration AMCHII-XLII: Angelmaker Part II Quadruped is one of a group of works realized from an Artmachine template. Its complex structure was created by an unfathomable logic. The piece consists of four rooms, which together form a quasi–stage set that the viewer is allowed to enter. Each room is titled: "Submarine Mock-up," "Dining Room," "Chinese Cabinet," and "Kitchen." There is no rationale behind the structures, yet each contains a complex set of references, which combine to form a bizarre spatial narrative. The "Submarine Mock-up" room is entered via a heavy submarine capsule door, which reveals three deep blue, porthole-shaped light boxes on one wall, a glass projection screen showing a radar image on another, a map on a third, and a periscope area. In "Kitchen," three vacuum cleaners, placed on a checkered floor and attached to a monitor opposite by lengths of red plastic hosing, are activated by the soundtrack of a videotape. Titled "Automatic Oxygen Debt," the tape sequence shows a man choking each time the vacuum cleaner's suction is triggered.

"Dining Room" continues the obscure logic. A video loop showing multiplying bacteria is projected onto the floor, while an accompanying sound track of a heartbeat and the sounds of everyday family life, played backward, triggers family photographs on an adjacent wall to light up. In "Chinese Cabinet," a case fashioned like a bamboo hut and placed on a table presents a miniature Chinese city with tiny pagodas. Chinese music and a rumbling noise from an otherwise blank-screened video monitor cause the table to vibrate, as though in an earthquake. In each room, the electronic activity is triggered by a particular sound pulse, which, as thunder in an open area beyond, triggers strobe lights to flash. If the sound changes to birdsong, a shaft of light appears on the outer walls, reflecting an image of angels, and smoke appears. Red safety lights are positioned in each room and on the external walls.

This bizarre operatic drama has been realized through a completely random set of instructions, gathered by the Artmachine from an infinite number of possibilities. As Jeremy Miller has observed, this system evokes John Cage's use of an IC computer program to simulate the I Ching. Tyson uses chance similarly as a means to counteract habit and predictability.[2] If his refusal to become involved in the decision-making process hands over aesthetic power to a machine, the vulnerability and the potential failure of technology, expressed in the strange vulgarity and ultimate irrelevance of the Artmachine's aesthetic choices, is also contained within it.

1. JEREMY MILLER, "The Sony Kit," in book *Keith Tyson* (London: Delfina, 1999), 2.

2. Ibid., 6.

Plate 29
KEITH TYSON,
Artmachine Iteration AMCHII-XLII: Angelmaker Part II Quadruped,
1995, installation view.

LOTHAR BAUMGARTEN

"DA GEFÄLLT'S MIR BESSER ALS IN WESTFALEN" ELDORADO 1968–1976

1. Lothar Baumgarten, conversation with the author, March 1999.

+++++ In the work of Lothar Baumgarten, nothing is what it appears to be. Each image, meticulously constructed, contains a double layer of meaning, creating a tension between artifice and reality that becomes evident only through careful observation. In addition to its representational ambiguity, each photograph also conveys a sense of time beyond its identity as an individual image, suggesting that it is part of a larger, perhaps filmic, whole. Yet although Baumgarten's images could be said to operate somewhere between film and photography, their substance as individual frozen "frames" of time also locates them within the more concrete definition of "sculpture," in its most conceptual form.

"Da gefällt's mir besser als in Westfalen" Eldorado 1968–1976 began in 1968 as a democratic, dematerialized artwork. Baumgarten's desire for ephemerality, born out of the radically charged political and cultural milieu of the late 1960s, led to the appearance of the images first as a series of unframed photographs of sculptures, glued directly onto the wall and destroyed at the end of the exhibition. Baumgarten's photographs manipulated the reality of the sculptural objects, subtly shifting their visual context to give them new form. By the early 1970s the images appeared in the finalized format of a single slide sequence, accompanied by a soundtrack.

The 187 thirty-five-millimeter color slides that form *"Da gefällt's mir besser als in Westfalen" Eldorado 1968–1976* trace the gradual transition from a thundery night to day, and back to night, in what appears to be a tropical forest. This notion is reinforced by the title's reference to El Dorado, in a sentence taken from Voltaire's novel *Candide* ("I like it better there than in Westphalia"). In the novel, which Voltaire criticizes the rigid mentality of Prussia, where he lived for a short period, and yearns for what he perceives as the liberated, civilized life of native South America.

On close scrutiny, the sumptuously photographed "sculptures," apparently from within this arcadian continent—including close-up shots of trees, leaves, pools of water, birds, toads, a nest of eggs, ants, turtles, and plants—are revealed to be a subtly manipulated artifice. What appears to be the skin of a snake is actually a section of a hose. An armadillo shell is the surface of an old tire. A stick inserted into a pool has been deliberately placed. The serrated edge of a leaf, which at first glance appears to be the natural form of an exotic plant, has been cut by Baumgarten with pinking shears. The subject of the work is revealed to be not nature, but culture. The area so seductively photographed is not El Dorado, but a triangle of no-man's-land on the Rhine River between Cologne and Düsseldorf, polluted by toxic waste. A map, a paddle, a gun cartridge, a small boat, a knife and pot, all found abandoned in the woods and covered by leaves, are carefully re-presented to

Plate 30
LOTHAR BAUMGARTEN,
"Da gefällt's mir besser als in Westfalen" Eldorado 1968–1976,
1968–76,
detail of image no. 68a (1970).

suggest the presence of an explorer. But the objects transformed into fragments of an exotic narrative are all urban detritus, abandoned in the woodland by casual visitors and reclaimed by Baumgarten.

This subtle shifting of our perception of the world reveals both an ethnographic and an ecological meaning. Yet *"Da gefällt's mir besser als in Westfalen" Eldorado 1968–1976* is defined more broadly by a kind of animistic conceptualism. Halfway through the slide sequence, a single shot of the interior of the room Baumgarten worked in while shooting the piece appears, filled with books and film reels. The source of the piece's making is suddenly revealed, and its existence is shown to be primarily in the mind. Baumgarten's desire for ephemerality is thus expressed in both physical and conceptual terms.

If the mercurial nature of his sculptural-photographic constructions defies a fixed reality, this shifting meaning serves, to quote Baumgarten, as "a draft for a grammar of the interaction between language and form."[1] Language is transformed into the three-dimensional, which is, in turn, dematerialized. The subtle shift in perception created by this manipulated re-presentation of the forgotten and the over-looked is used to imply an oblique social critique, diffused through the lens of a poetic conceptualism.

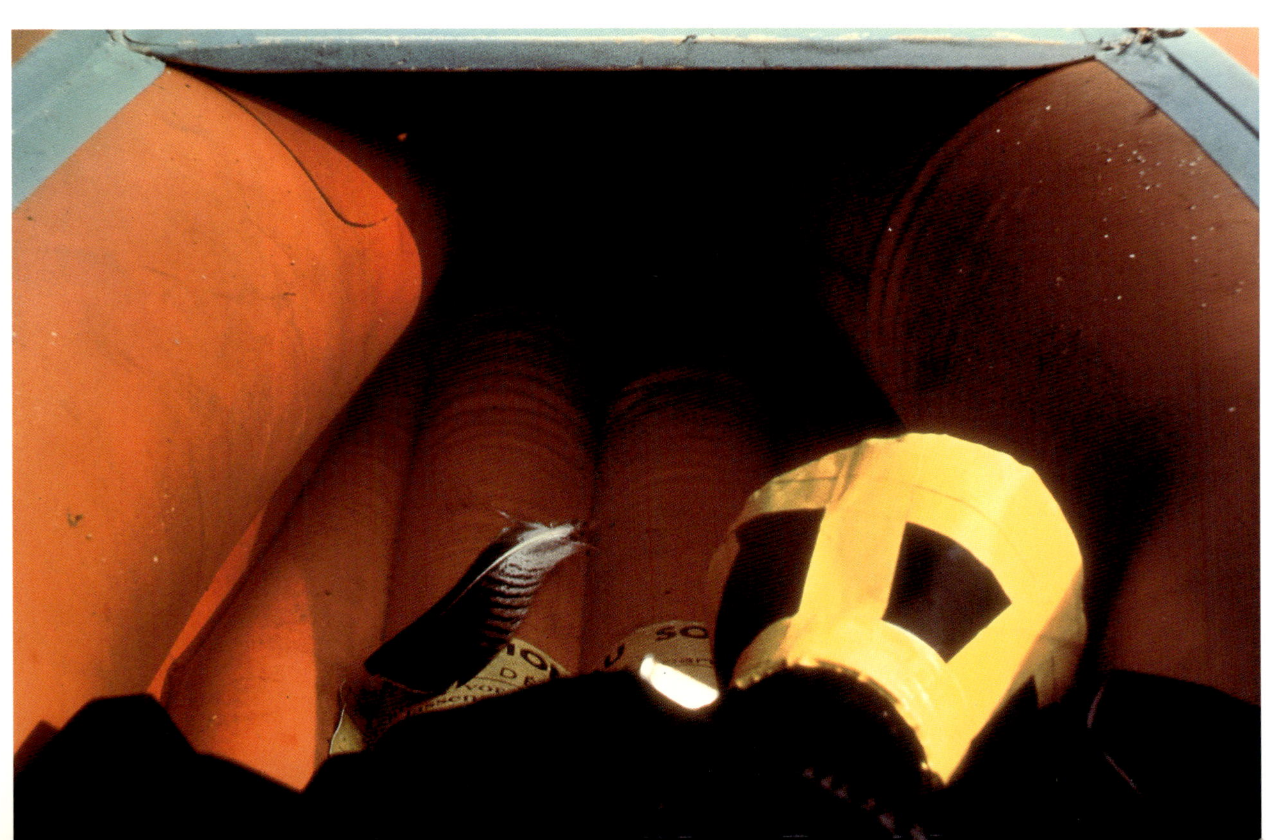

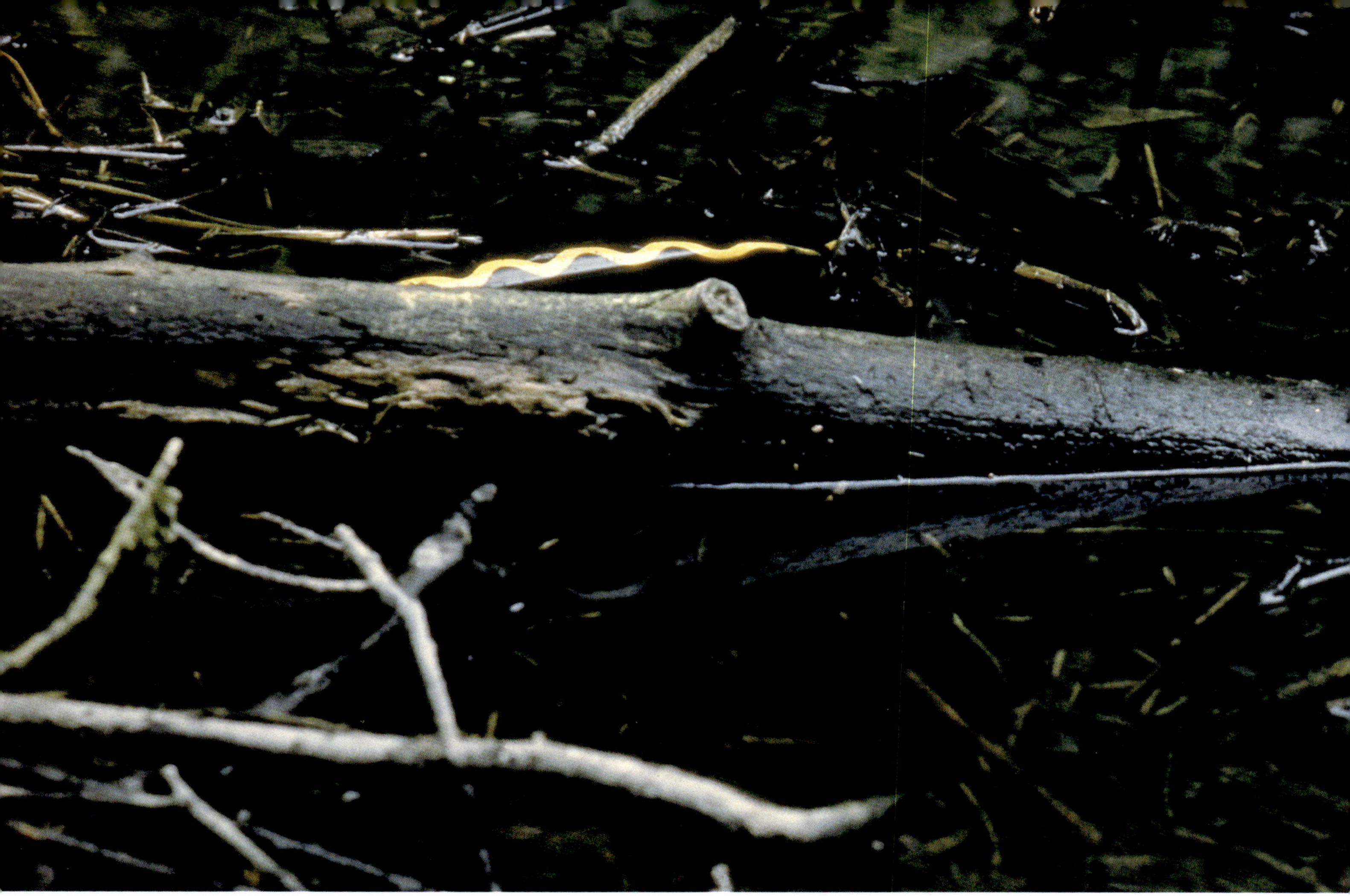

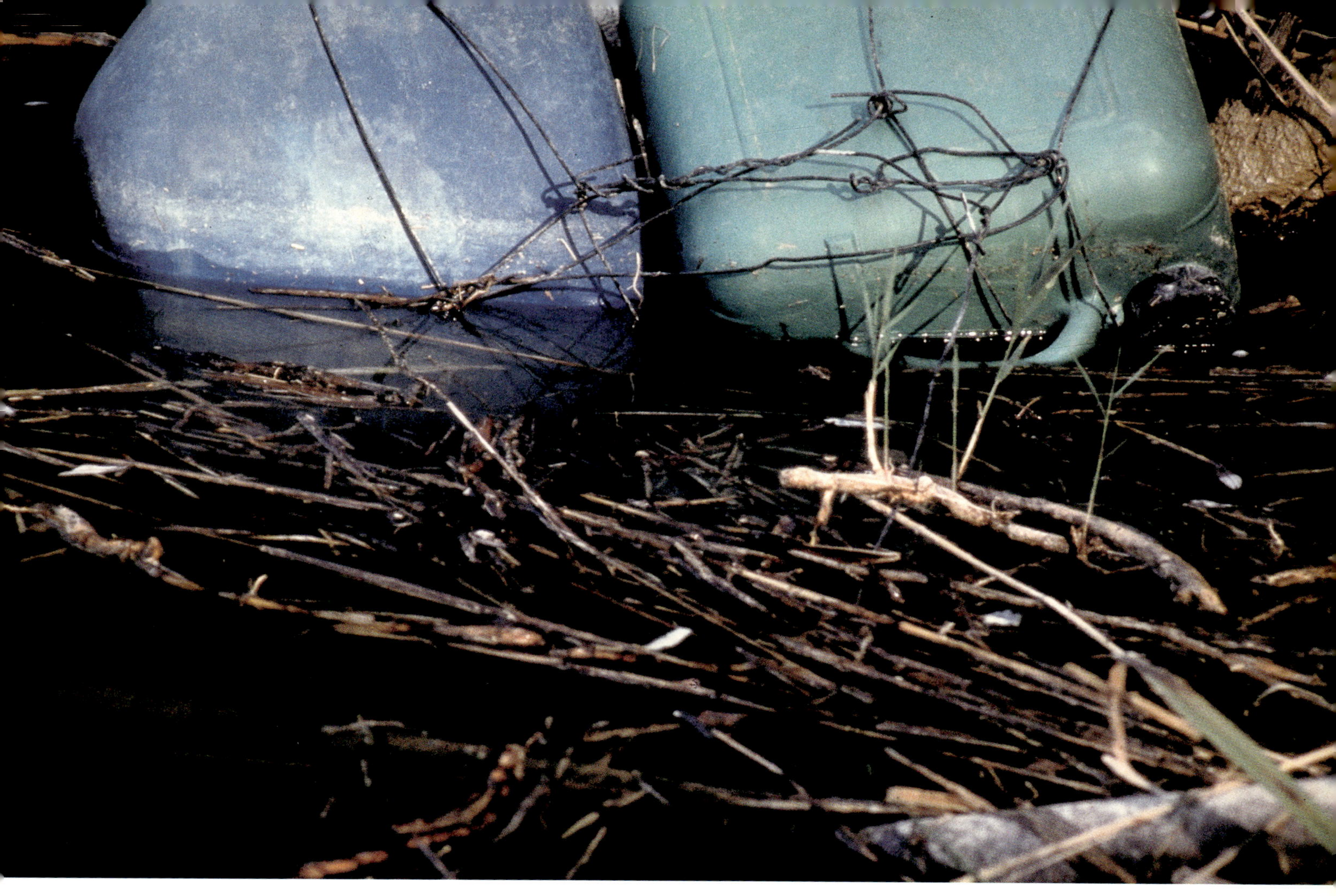

Plate 31 (left)

LOTHAR BAUMGARTEN,

"Da gefällt's mir besser als in Westfalen" Eldorado 1968–1976,

1968–76,

detail of image no. 24b (1971).

Plate 32 (right)

LOTHAR BAUMGARTEN,

"Da gefällt's mir besser als in Westfalen" Eldorado 1968–1976,

1968–76, image no. 67a (1968).

THOMAS STRUTH

LOUVRE 1 (1989)

The photographic work of Thomas Struth is inherently taxonomic. Its classificatory nature bears a complex relationship to the late nineteenth century's deterministic approach to photography. Not long after photography's invention, photographers in Germany, France, and England carried out a methodical documentation of architecture, the museum, the body, disease, and culture, creating an archive that was assumed to be based on "scientific" truth. Like his teachers Bernd and Hilla Becher, Struth both reinforces and undermines this argument.

Unlike the Bechers, Struth does not limit his archival project to a single subject or location. His museum series, of which *Louvre 1* is a part, belongs to a larger group of works that include people, architectural interiors, and urban spaces, photographed both in Europe and across the world. As Russell Roberts has pointed out,[1] the invention of photography in the late 1830s paralleled the rise of the museum, whose ordering principles were both hierarchical and deterministic. In each of Struth's self-reflexive images of museum interiors, viewers find themselves observing other works of art—or viewers observing other works of art, on other walls. Both the act of viewing and the museum environment appear to be captured as an objective and "real" record. *Louvre 1* could be argued to belong to an archive created by Struth, which mimics the process of museum collecting. Yet there is no suggestion of drama; the viewers in Struth's photograph are caught in the mundane act of cultural consumption, standing, sitting, or walking through the galleries of the Louvre, one of the most visited museums in the world.

This depiction of the museum as public, touristic site, rather than a space for aesthetic contemplation, conforms to what Benjamin Buchloh has described as Struth's tendency to universalize his subjects. The museum space in *Louvre 1* becomes equal not only to other spaces in his museum series but also to other, indoor and outdoor, public urban spaces. This is only possible, Buchloh has suggested, because of the ubiquitousness of commercial photography, which has expanded the spatial possibilities for the flaneur. The most important element in *Louvre 1* is not the paintings, but the group of viewers gathered in the grand space of the gallery. In an increasingly virtual world, this kind of social gathering in a single physical space takes on a new significance, which has, for Struth, become increasingly important. Like the photographers of the nineteenth century, "Struth . . . is building an archive of . . . a globally disappearing world of the 'real'—in this case, the reality of inhabited and experienced social space. . . . [His] images of urban architecture already appear as part of an archive of the past that was still animated by utopian aspirations toward public experience, social interaction, and a sense of spatial and temporal reality."[2]

1. RUSSELL ROBERTS, "Taxonomy: Some Notes towards the Histories of Photography and Classification," in *In Visible Light: Photography and Classification in Art, Science, and the Everyday*, ed. Chrissie Iles and Russell Roberts (Oxford: Museum of Modern Art, 1997), 12.

2. BENJAMIN H. D. BUCHLOH, "Thomas Struth's Archive," in *Thomas Struth: Photographs* (Chicago: Renaissance Society at the University of Chicago, 1990), 11.

Plate 33
THOMAS STRUTH, *Louvre 1*, 1989.

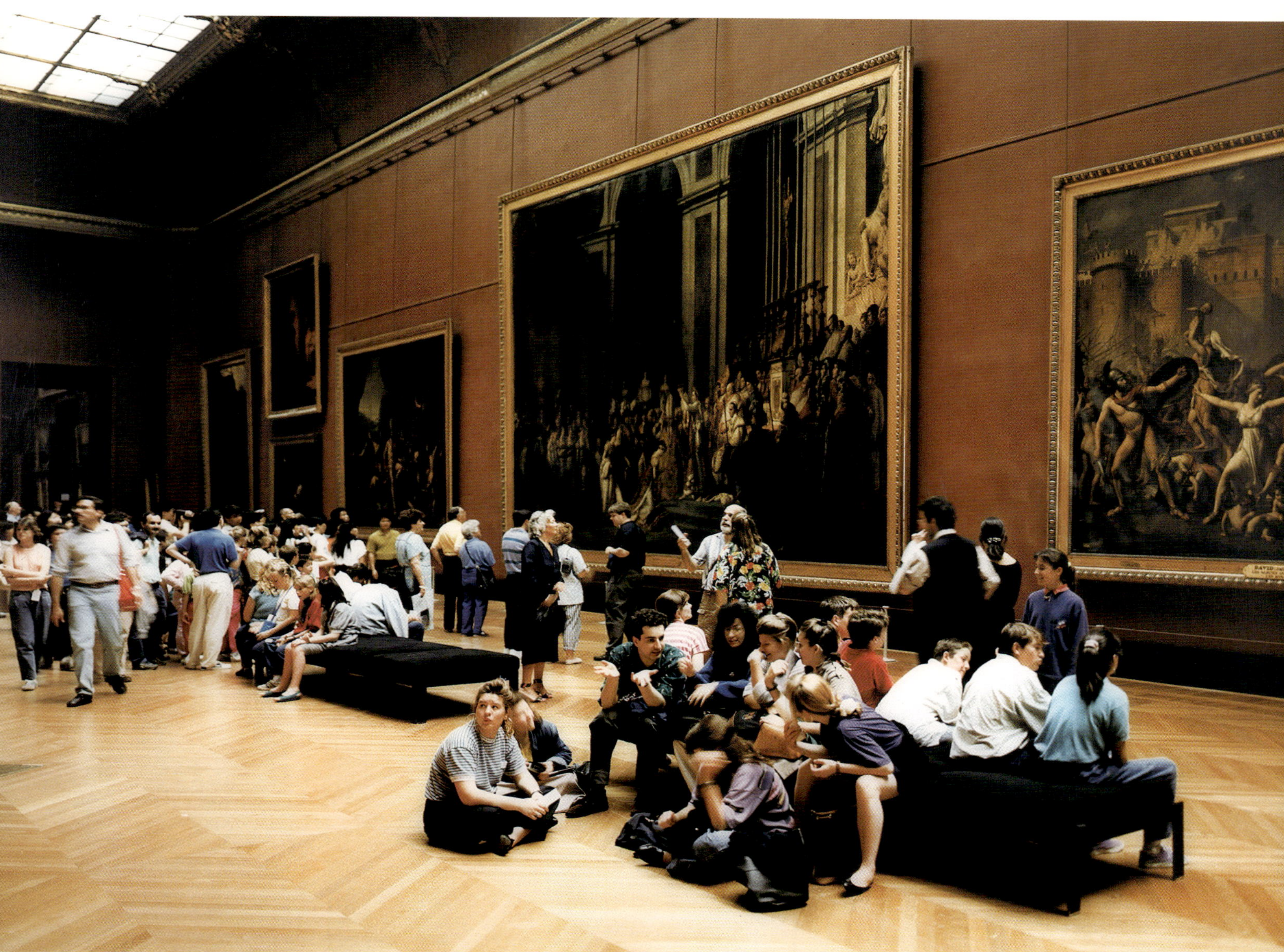
DAVID

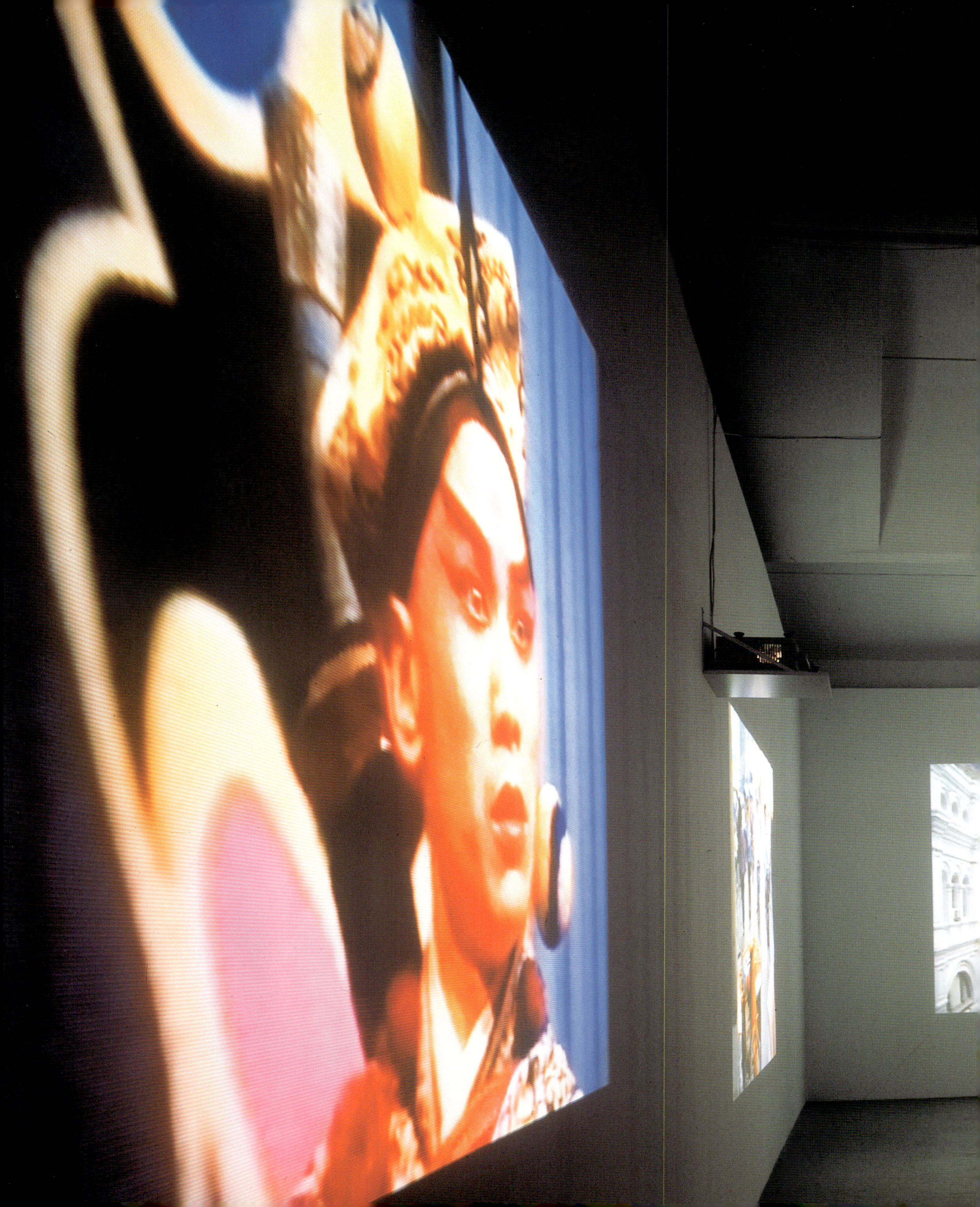

THOMAS STRUTH AND KLAUS VOM BRUCH

BERLIN-PROJECT (1997)

++++

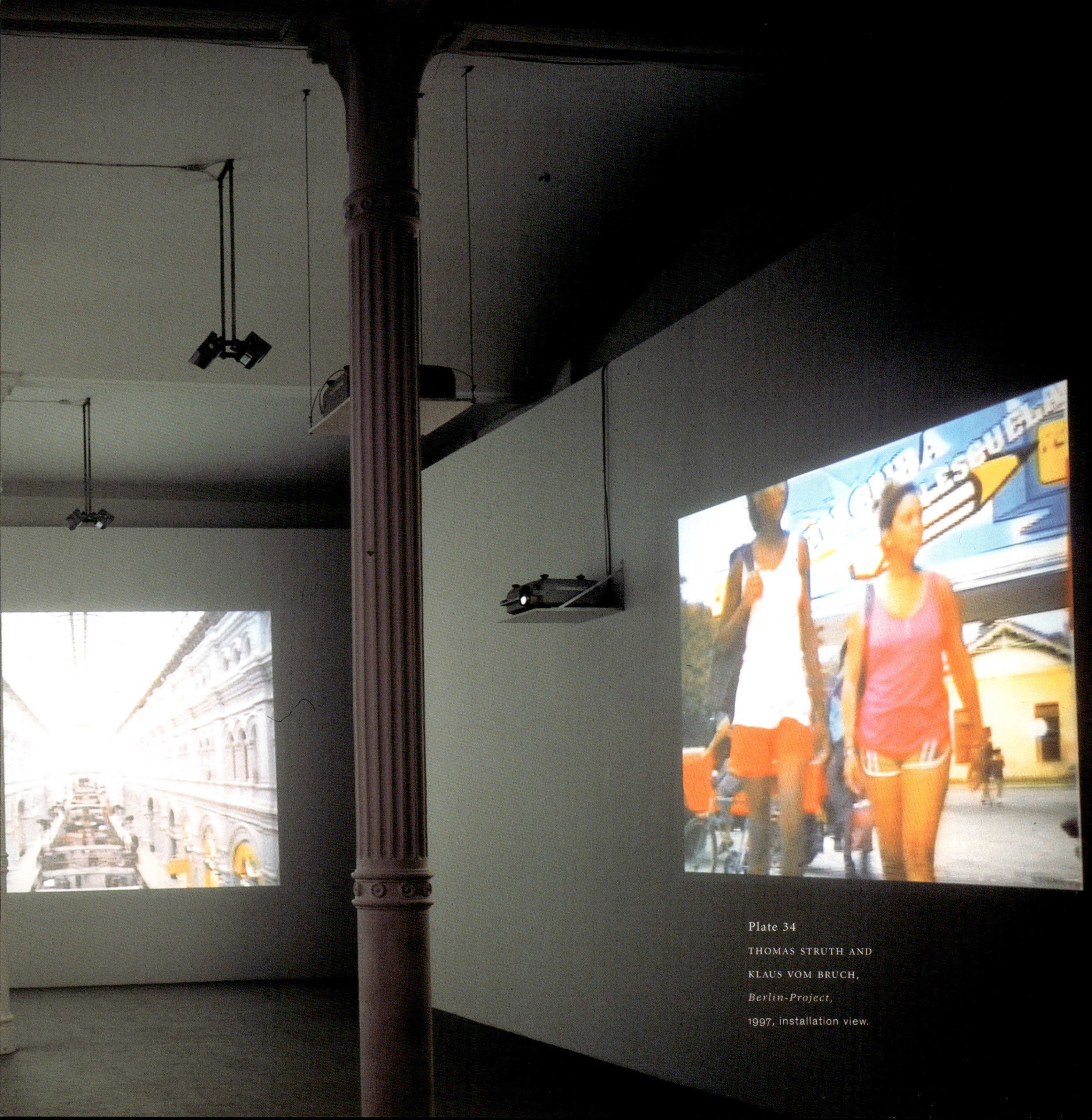

Plate 34
THOMAS STRUTH AND KLAUS VOM BRUCH, *Berlin-Project*, 1997, installation view.

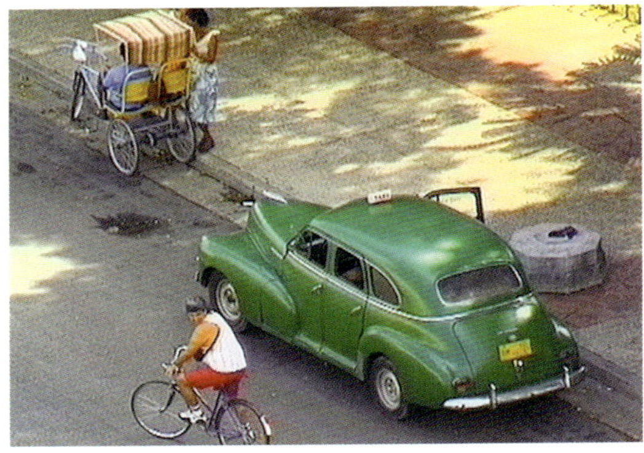

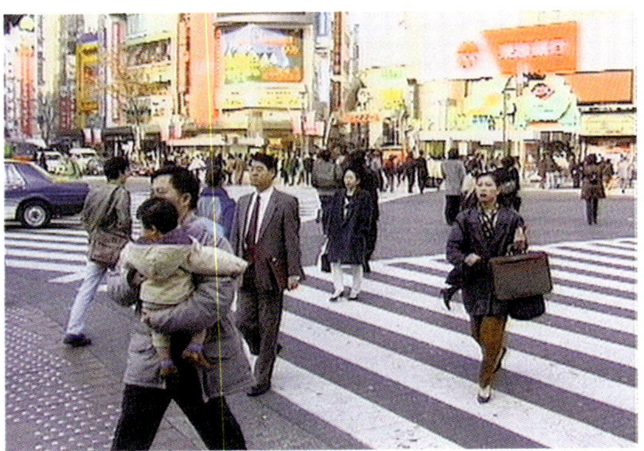

+++++ A profound shift has occurred in the role of the visual image at the end of the twentieth century. As Jonathan Crary has observed, the image no longer describes the viewer's position within "a 'real,' optically perceived world. . . . Increasingly visuality will be situated on a cybernetic and electromagnetic terrain, where abstract visual and linguistic elements coincide and are consumed, circulated and exchanged globally."[1] The global territory suggested in *Berlin-Project*, a collaborative video installation by Thomas Struth and Klaus vom Bruch, evokes a collective public experience of social space within Crary's cybernetic terrain, or what Jean Baudrillard calls "hyperspace."

Such a "virtual" space exists in sharp contrast to the inescapable German historical context of a self-conscious past, shared by both Struth and vom Bruch, and made visible in the changing architectural postwar landscape of urban centers such as Berlin. *Berlin-Project* began as an open-air projection piece for a square in the city whose role as the capital of Germany was shortly to be reinstated. The projection in an open-air Berlin location of large-scale images of street scenes from around the world—including other German cities, such as Düsseldorf and Cologne; other European cities, such as Lucerne and Rome; other world capitals, such as New York, Havana, Shanghai, and Hong Kong; and remote non-urban areas, such as the Gobi Desert and towns in Tunisia—underlined the transformation of the city from an isolated "island" within the communist eastern bloc to a free space, openly connected to the outside world.

One of the ways in which Berlin maintained a connection with the outside during its postwar isolation was through the international network of the art world. The inspiration for *Berlin-Project* came to Struth in Japan, where he observed the vast advertising video walls attached to the sides of buildings, mimicking the classic American billboard format (which in turn echoed the monumentalism of the Hollywood cinema "big screen"). Struth and the Berlin-based video artist Klaus vom Bruch transformed the language of corporate capitalism into an oppositional statement, which both reflects Berlin's new entrepreneurial status and critiques it. This paradox is echoed in Struth's solo photographic work, which, as Benjamin

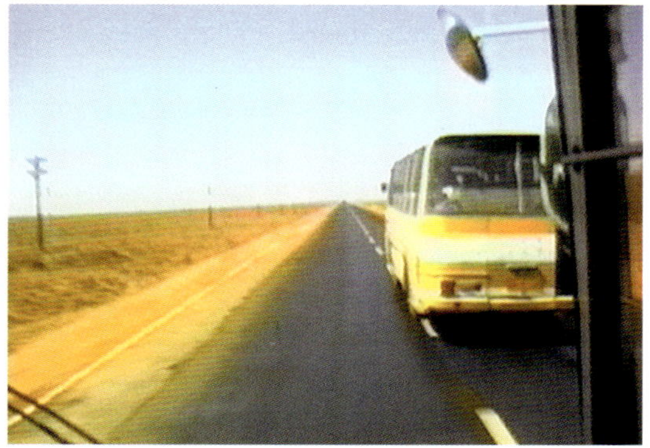

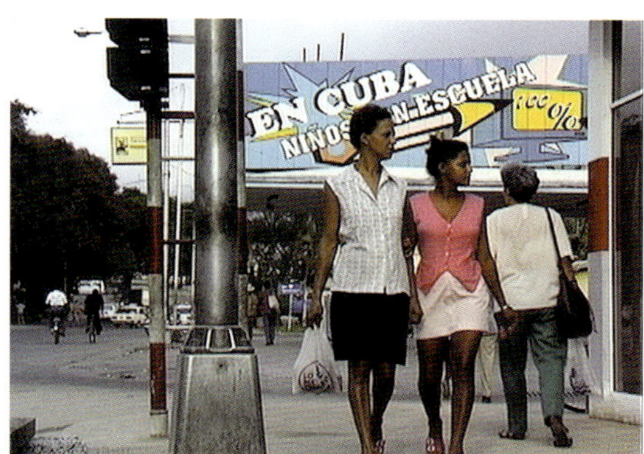

Buchloh has observed, creates "an archive of a globally disappearing world of the real," which "could [not] have been conceived before the age of global tourism and advertising, both of which have qualitatively transformed the historical and spatial limits of the scope of the flaneur."[2] In this new cybernetic social space, Buchloh has suggested, the observer of life in the street is not so much an urban flaneur as a global itinerant.

In the four large-scale projections of *Berlin-Project*, the artists gather their experiences as both flaneurs and global itinerants into a single space and time. Street scenes from around the world, filmed by the artists during a year of intensive travel, are projected onto the four walls of the gallery, uniting Berlin and Tokyo, Helsinki and the Gobi Desert. This flattening of space and time also unites the artists' respective disciplines. The video footage evokes the ubiquitous imagery of television, to whose monolithic power vom Bruch's video work has always worked in opposition, while the juxtaposing and universalizing of radically different geographical locations is a hallmark of Struth's solo photographic work, in which, as Buchloh has pointed out,[3] ancient architecture is made to sit comfortably next to high-rise apartment blocks, in a refusal to adhere to fixed specific historical and geographical boundaries.

This transitional approach can also be seen in the paradoxes contained within single cities such as Berlin, where the ideology of prewar buildings contrasts sharply with the progressive vision of contemporary architectural projects. If Struth's photographs work from the premise that all social space is collectively constructed, the collaborative structure of *Berlin-Project* takes this paradox a stage further, erasing difference and substituting the sense of a global, ubiquitous present, in which, as Buchloh has suggested, "the spaces of electronic communication and media technology . . . have . . . become the only sites where the experience of the 'real' is managed and determined."[4]

1. JONATHAN CRARY, *Techniques of the Observer: On Vision and Modernity in the Nineteenth Century* (Cambridge: MIT Press, 1990), 2.

2. BENJAMIN H. D. BUCHLOH, "Thomas Struth's Archive," in *Thomas Struth: Photographs* (Chicago: Renaissance Society at the University of Chicago, 1990), 11.

3. Ibid., 9.

4. Ibid., 11.

Plates 35–38
THOMAS STRUTH AND KLAUS VOM BRUCH, *Berlin-Project*, 1997, video stills.

STAN DOUGLAS

TELEVISION SPOTS (1987–88)

+++++ From the earliest moving images of cinema to the contemporary medium of television, technology has transformed the landscape of human perception. Samuel Beckett acknowledged this when, toward the end of his career, he embraced both film and television as media ideally suited to his ideas regarding the antiauthoritarian, antiheroic self. Stan Douglas, who became deeply involved with Beckett's work in the mid-1980s, was also interested in television's power to shape consciousness and representation, particularly through the structure of commercial advertising. In 1987, inspired by Beckett's *Teleplays*, an exhibition of which he had recently organized, he created *Television Spots*, twelve short pieces to be broadcast on television, inserted between advertisements during commercial breaks.

As Jean-Christophe Royoux has observed, each of these brief narrative fragments uses the same ironic mimicry as the readymade, in this case parodying "not . . . the manufactured object, but . . . the form of communication these objects have inspired."[1] This parody is achieved by disrupting the viewer's narrative expectations. In stark contrast to the fast-edit mini-dramas of commercial advertisements, the *Television Spots* present slow, single shots of urban locations, in which very little happens. A woman walks away from the camera in an underground parking lot, pausing briefly to sneeze. A parking lot attendant reads the newspaper in his booth, looking up briefly when an overhead lamp suddenly stops working. A couple walk down a deserted street. She asks, "What's the matter?" He replies, "Nothing." An ice cream van drives along a deserted urban street. The often humorous, deadpan fragments, without dramatic dénouement, suggest a world beyond television, in which, as in Beckett's work, ordinary habits and banal moments of everyday life are brought from the margins into the center and invested with meaning. Douglas's choice of drab urban locations—industrial zones, parking lots, street junctions—further reflects, as Scott Watson argues, "the Vancouver aesthetic of the 1980s, in which the urban fabric became a semiotic landscape."[2]

This mechanism returns the viewer, as Miriam Nichols has observed, to that moment when reality began to disappear, "conquered [in advertising] by impossible fantasies . . . [and] the exchangeability not just of things, but of feelings, ideas, and meaning itself. . . . Stan Douglas undoes the [invisible] seams between times, spaces, programs and ads, and the seams between cinema and television."[3] In doing so, Douglas suggests the possibility of alternative forms of representation, inspired by Jenny Holzer, whose *Truisms*, presented anonymously on street posters, were a model for *Television Spots*.

Although the banality of *Television Spots* subverts the drama of television advertising, the work contains another kind of dramatic narrative, which owes much to cinematic language. In "Box Office," the sound track is a narrative clip from the Alfred Hitchcock film *Marnie*, evoking a connection between the power relationship between the black female ticket seller and her white male customer and the vulnerability of Hitchcock's female victims.

In "Answering Machine," a distinctly cinematic scene is evoked by a long tracking shot of a domestic interior and the sound of a telephone ringing repeatedly. The camera comes to rest by a table, at which a woman sits, calmly listening to the telephone, but refuses to answer it. Eventually the answering machine takes the call, as she continues to smoke impassively, demonstrating what Watson has described as "an everyday, private assertion of freedom and autonomy . . . a kind of disobedience."[4]

Many of the gestures in the *Television Spots* express refusal, negation, or miscommunication, in a direct challenge to the dramatic conventions of advertising. This challenge is reinforced by the issues of race and class that Douglas inserts into the dialogue. Drawing the viewer's attention to a world beyond the constructed space of television, he interrupts the idealized fantasies of advertising with the political and social realities of contemporary urban life, presented in a new, hybrid cinematic form.

1. JEAN-CHRISTOPHE ROYOUX, "The Conflict of Communications," in *Stan Douglas* (Paris: Centre Georges Pompidou, Musée National d'Art Moderne, 1994), 66.

2. SCOTT WATSON, "Against the Habitual," in *Stan Douglas* (London: Phaidon, 1999), 52.

3. MIRIAM NICHOLS, *Stan Douglas: Television Spots* (Vancouver: Contemporary Art Gallery, 1988) 5.

4. WATSON, "Against the Habitual," 53.

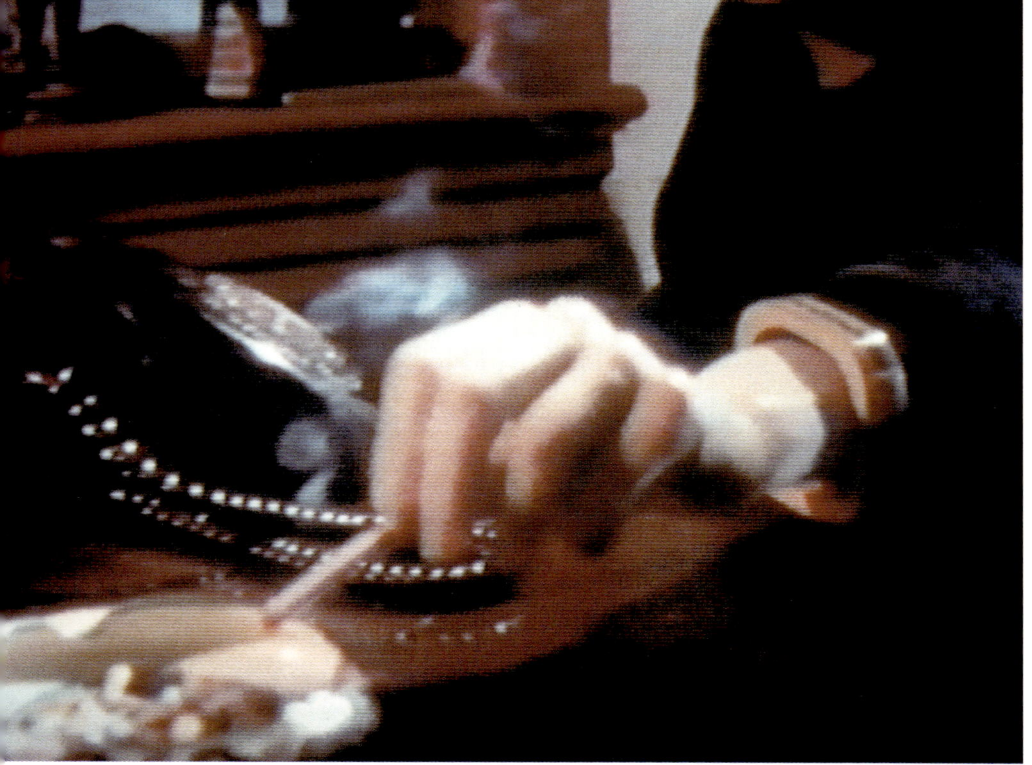

Plate 39
STAN DOUGLAS,
Television Spots,
1987–88, video still from "Answering Machine."

Overleaf:

Plate 40 (left)
STAN DOUGLAS,
Television Spots,
1987–88, video still from "Sneeze."

Plate 41 (right)
STAN DOUGLAS,
Television Spots,
1987–88, black-and-white gelatin silver print framed with text, from "Sneeze" (detail).

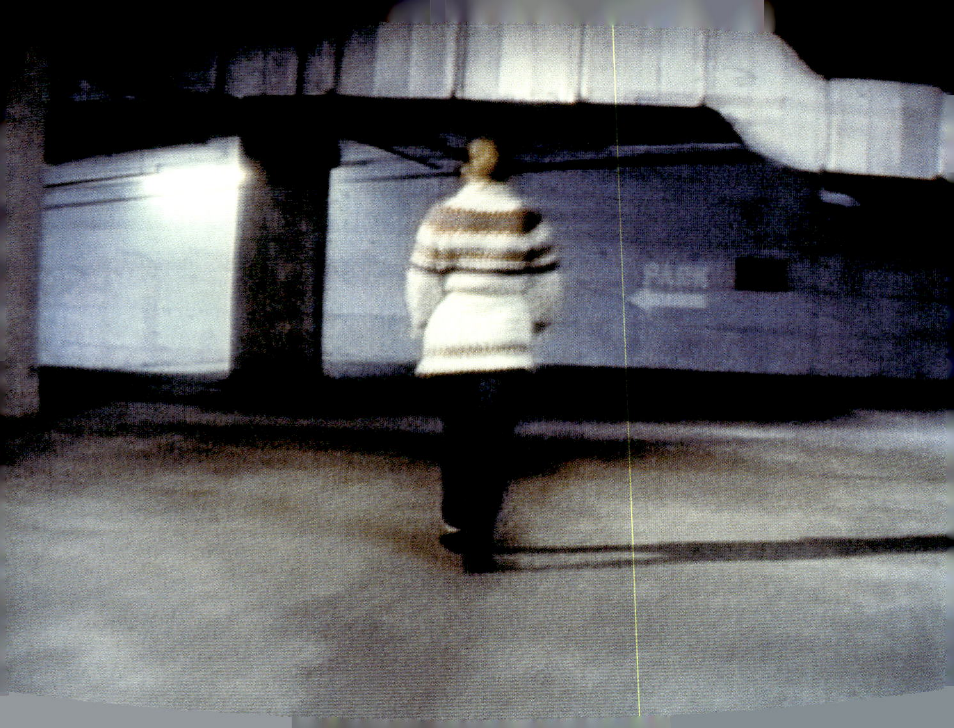

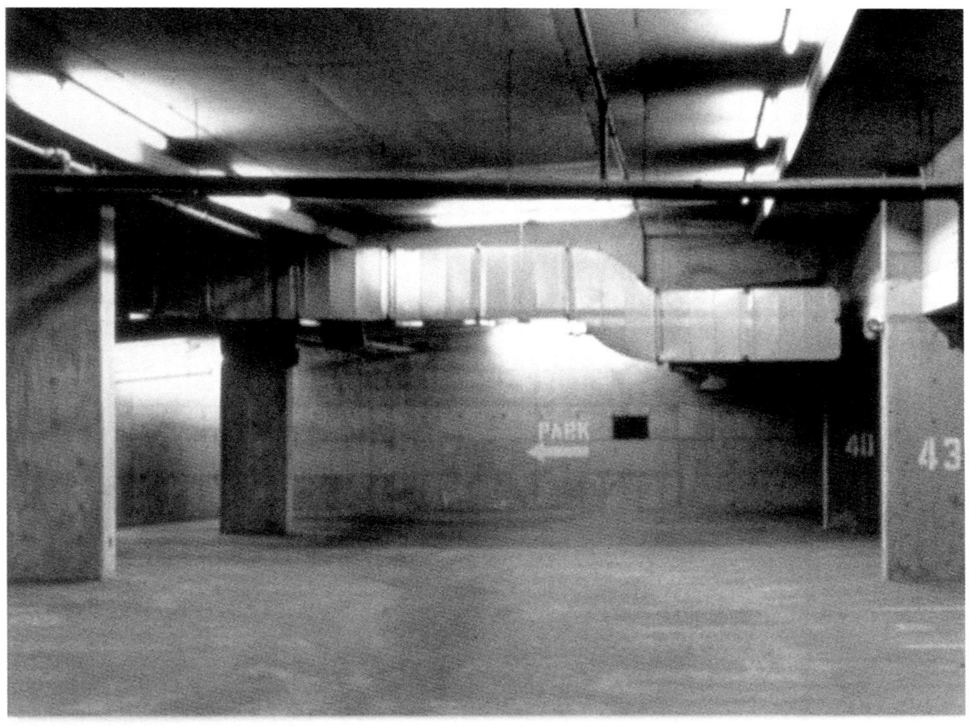

SNEEZE

A woman walks alone in an underground parking lot, passing rows of vacant stalls. Suddenly she stops and sneezes. After this pause she resumes her stride and soon turns, following the path of an exit ramp which spirals downward. Apart from the sneeze, the only sound is that of footsteps in a cavernous space.

1. Iris open to a tracking shot of the woman walking. The camera follows her from behind, slightly to her right.
2. The woman pauses and the camera stops abruptly as she sneezes.
3. She turns her head, as if to better hear the echo she has caused, and then walks on.
4. Iris in to black as she approaches the exit ramp.

STAN DOUGLAS

MONODRAMAS (1991)

1. SCOTT WATSON, "Against the Habitual," in *Stan Douglas* (London: Phaidon, 1999), 53–54.

+++++ In 1991, several years after he made his *Television Spots*, Stan Douglas made a second group of short works for television. Titled *Monodramas*, these ten "mini-fictions" contained a clear narrative structure that parodied the television melodrama. Influenced by the work of Cindy Sherman, in particular her *Film Stills*, these pieces also evoke the early photographic and conceptual work of Dan Graham.

Each monodrama, as Scott Watson has observed, is "a parable of dysfunction and inner disorientation, miscommunication and distraction, or, inversely, freedom from the codes of communication and recognition."[1] In "Encampment," a man walks purposefully through a darkened industrial unit, agitatedly rehearsing an argument out loud, until he is silenced by encountering two young women in a trailer around the corner. In "Disagree," a school bus and a car nearly crash into each other at a street corner. Miscommunication takes on racial implications in "I'm Not Gary," in which a white man greets a black man on a shopping street, mistaking him for someone else, implying his symbolic social invisibility.

In the three-part "Guilty," mental dysfunction is suggested by the description of an almost schizophrenic state, which, by implication, is also latent in the television viewer. In a format that merges the television interview, the psychoanalytic monologue, and the literary text, three ordinary people in the street, their faces deliberately blurred by computer as though confessing something socially unacceptable, are "interviewed." All recite the same Beckettian speech: "My punishment was to feel guilty.... Even when I'm listening to music, the words still come to me involuntarily . . . each voice is different, and beautiful.... Only when I'm talking out loud or to other people do the sounds disappear." By implication, the insidious social effects of technology and the media on the human psyche are all-pervasive. The deadpan delivery of the oblique text both heightens the mood of alienation and, by revealing the tableau's artifice, underlines the theoretical point being made.

Plate 42
STAN DOUGLAS, *Monodramas*, 1991, black-and-white gelatin silver print framed with text, from "I'm not Gary."

Overleaf:

Plate 43 (left)
STAN DOUGLAS, *Monodramas*, 1991, video still from "I'm not Gary."

Plate 44 (right)
STAN DOUGLAS, *Monodramas*, 1991, video still from "Guilty II."

Each monodrama, while mimicking the conditions of television, undermines melodramatic reality. "As Is" superficially resembles a television car advertisement. Against the disco soundtrack of Chic's "I Want Your Love," three large 1970s cars appear in three successive sequences, being fixed in the driveway, being driven fast along the highway, and being smoothly parked in a parking lot. The teenage social ambition implied by this sequence is underlined by the disco music. Yet the sequence is impersonal; no characters are presented, no "product" is being sold, and the conclusion leaves the viewer in a state of suspended anticipation, waiting for the "human" story behind the cars.

"Eye on You" employs a more direct cinematic reference, within a circular structure. A man walks through his apartment and onto his

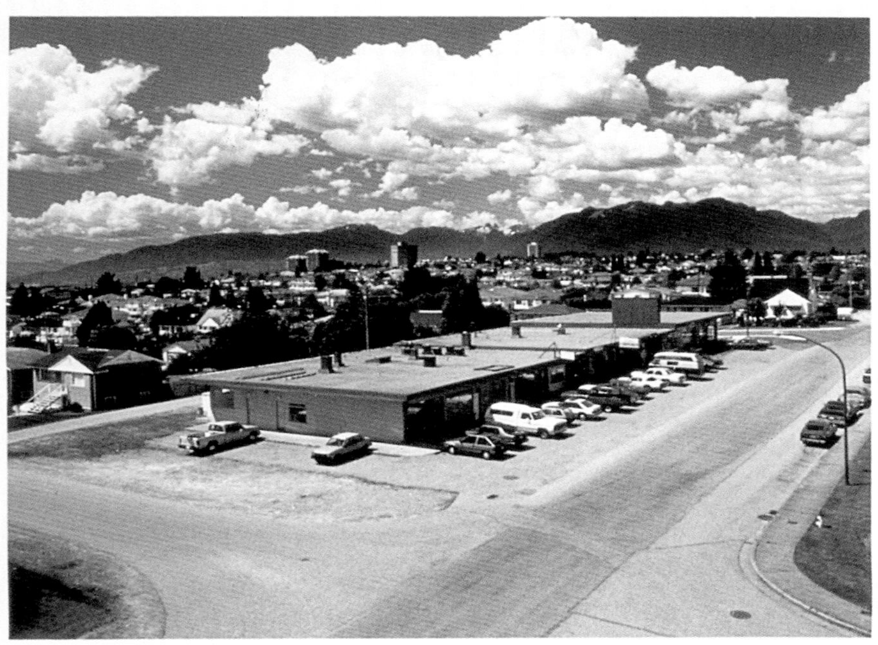

"I'm not Gary"

A one-block market street. It might rain. Both characters no doubt have reasonably well-paying day jobs, but the second most likely has the day off.

1. An establishing shot presents the surrounding landscape and only a few people on the street shopping, going to and from work.

2. A tracking shot follows our protagonist, as he walks under the covered sidewalk: another man walks toward him, grinning, and otherwise doing his best to make eye contact.

3. Reverse tracking shot: the protagonist approaches, and then issues one of those involuntary twitches that often derive from conceit, but more generally occur when one is attempting to ignore the fact that a stranger is looking at oneself. The second man is now very close as he hurries to remark, "Hi, Gary."

4. Return to shot 2. The two men, now about three metres apart, as the protagonist man looks long at the face of the second.

5. A close-up of the interlocutor, smiling and saying, as one does to an old friend, "How you doing?"

6. The protagonist is seen in a close-up; he is not entirely sure of himself but replies anyway, "I'm not Gary."

balcony, where he observes a stranger standing below him among the foliage, in the darkness. Alarmed by his presence, he dashes outside. Both the balcony and the space below it are shown to be empty. The man then appears below his own balcony and looks up at the camera, which has taken the place of his gaze downward. Popular cinema's staple ingredient of fear is invoked, as an anticipated sinister conclusion is suggested by the enticing of the man from the comfort of his apartment to the darkness outside. In *Monodramas*, as in *Television Spots*, the languages of cinema, television, and literary theory are interlocked. In the resulting critique of television's social impact, Douglas opens up a space for the spectator to reenter the work, within a broader, multicultural dialogue.

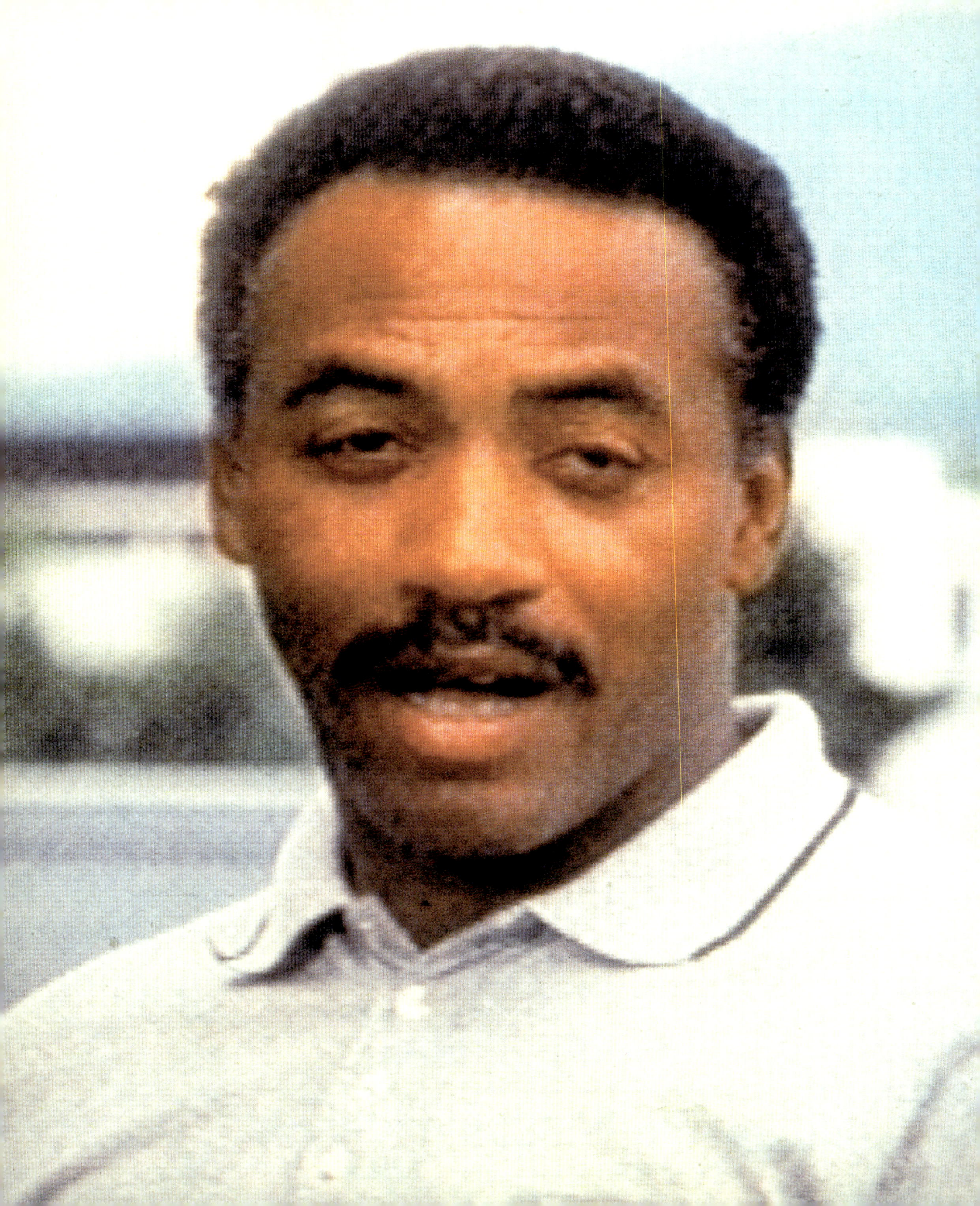

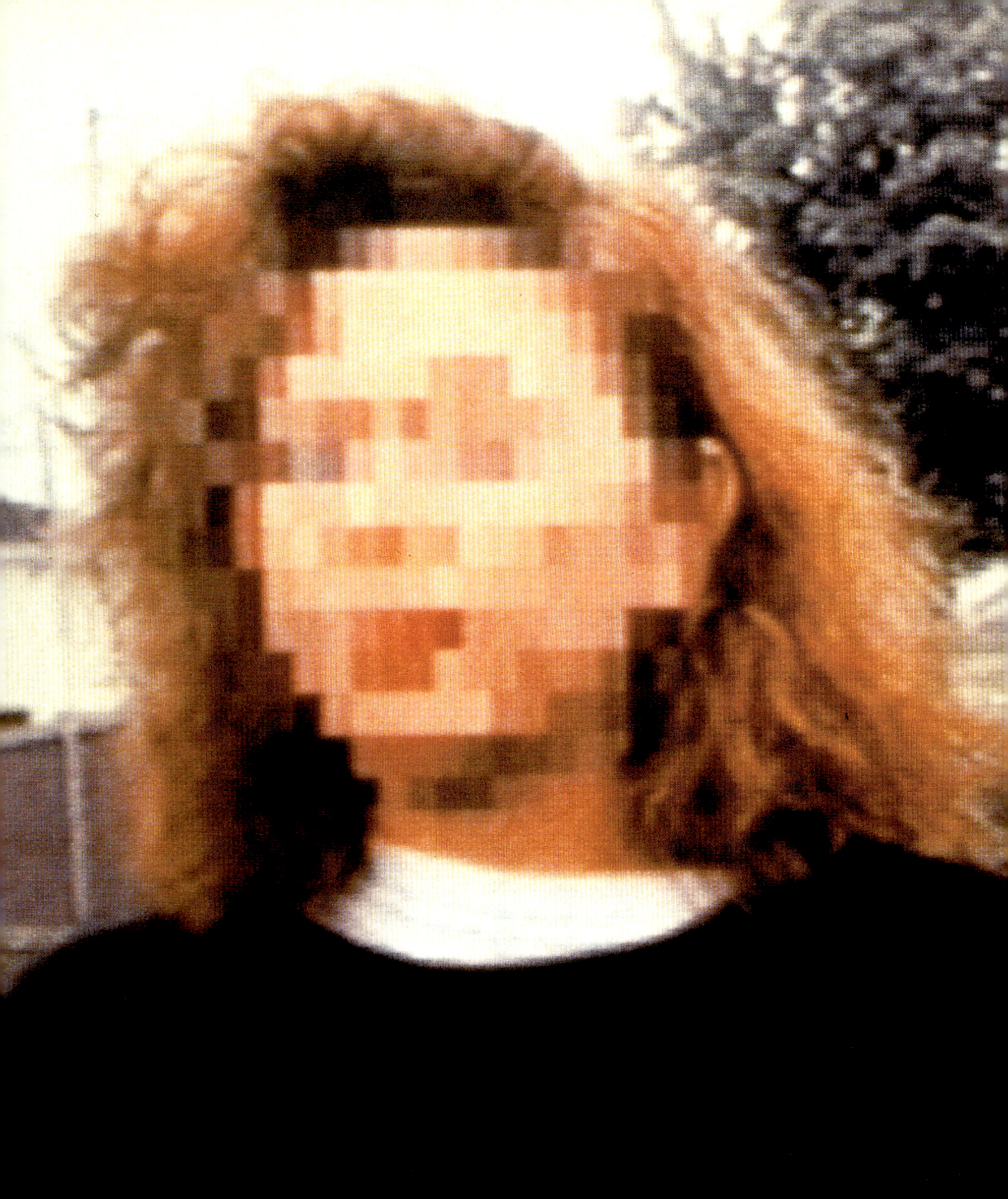

DARA BIRNBAUM

TIANANMEN SQUARE: BREAK-IN TRANSMISSION (1988–90)

+++++ Since the late 1970s Dara Birnbaum has used the video medium to question and subvert the power of mainstream television in shaping social consciousness. In early videotapes such as *Wonder Woman* (1978), she appropriated images directly from prime-time television, prefiguring a practice that was to become ubiquitous in video during the next decade. From 1987 onward, she began to take street protest as a major subject, using footage of youth demonstrations, filmed by others but never used, to create an alternative televisual experience.

Birnbaum's interest in political subject matter and television emerged out of her experiences during the 1960s at the University of California, Berkeley, where she witnessed the powerful energy of mass youth demonstrations for civil rights and against the Vietnam War. She also observed the power of television in relation to direct action. At one event, she noted, "They had a TV on the podium.... The new left was already fragmented ... fighting each other, and ... someone with a mallet said 'Are we listening to this?' because the news was on, showing the expansion of the war in Cambodia, and with the mallet they broke the TV and it exploded." From that moment on, Birnbaum recognized television's role as a medium of mass communication and felt that it was important to speak its language.[1]

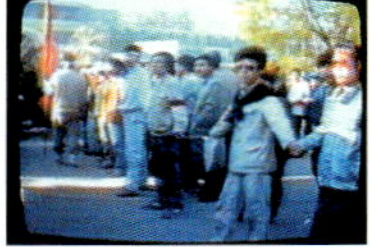

Throughout the 1980s video appeared in Birnbaum's installations as an individual element within a larger architectural whole, framed by painted sections of wall and large-scale photographic panels. *Tiananmen Square: Break-in Transmission* marks a shift, both in formal terms and in subject matter. Previous installations had interwoven social and political issues within a fictional narrative. Dramatic political street action, as mediated through television, now became the primary subject. Four small LCD video screens, a larger monitor, and five video players hang suspended in the gallery space, supported by a sculptural network of tubular metal rods hanging from the ceiling. It could be argued that the presentation reflects, in physical terms, Birnbaum's observation that, in countries undergoing radical political change, television is often used by demonstrators as a tool, functioning like "a central control nervous system; a networking communication device."[2]

As the title of the piece suggests, this networking attempts to penetrate commercial television broadcasting. In contrast to the large-scale drama of Birnbaum's earlier installations, the video images in *Tiananmen Square: Break-in Transmission* can be watched only close-up, underlining Birnbaum's focus on the communication and reception recorded by colleagues. In one case, the demonstrators sing a song composed by students; in the other, students attempt to communicate with the outside world through fax machines. The repression of free speech in communist China renders these interventions particularly radical.

1. Unpublished interview between Dara Birnbaum and Judy Cantor, quoted in *Dara Birnbaum* (Valencia, Spain: IVAM Centre del Carme, 1990), 40.

2. Ibid., 36.

Plates 45–47
DARA BIRNBAUM, *Tiananmen Square: Break-in Transmission*, 1988–90, video stills.

Overleaf:

Plate 48
DARA BIRNBAUM, *Tiananmen Square: Break-in Transmission*, 1988–90, installation view.

On a fifth monitor the four channels of recorded material are randomly interwoven into a nonlinear, single-channel narrative, dissolving the boundaries between commercial and noncommercial reportage. In the space created by this hybrid, the accepted "truth" of broadcast television, in both Western and communist terms, is replaced by multiple viewpoints, from which the viewer is invited to judge events. *Tiananmen Square: Break-in Transmission* both distills, and moves beyond, the issues raised by the demonstrations taking place in Beijing, to become a metaphor for a broad utopian vision of universal freedom.

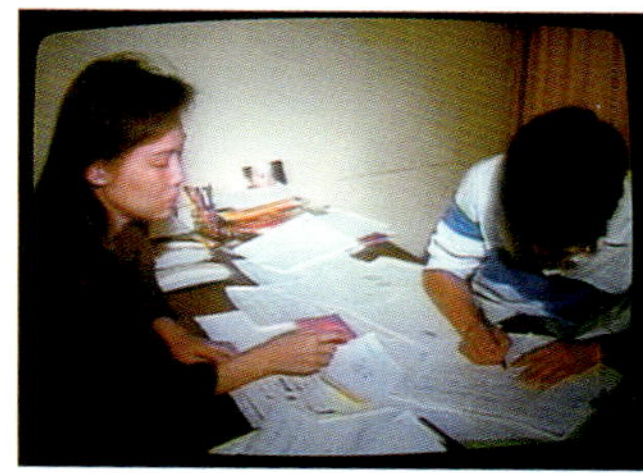

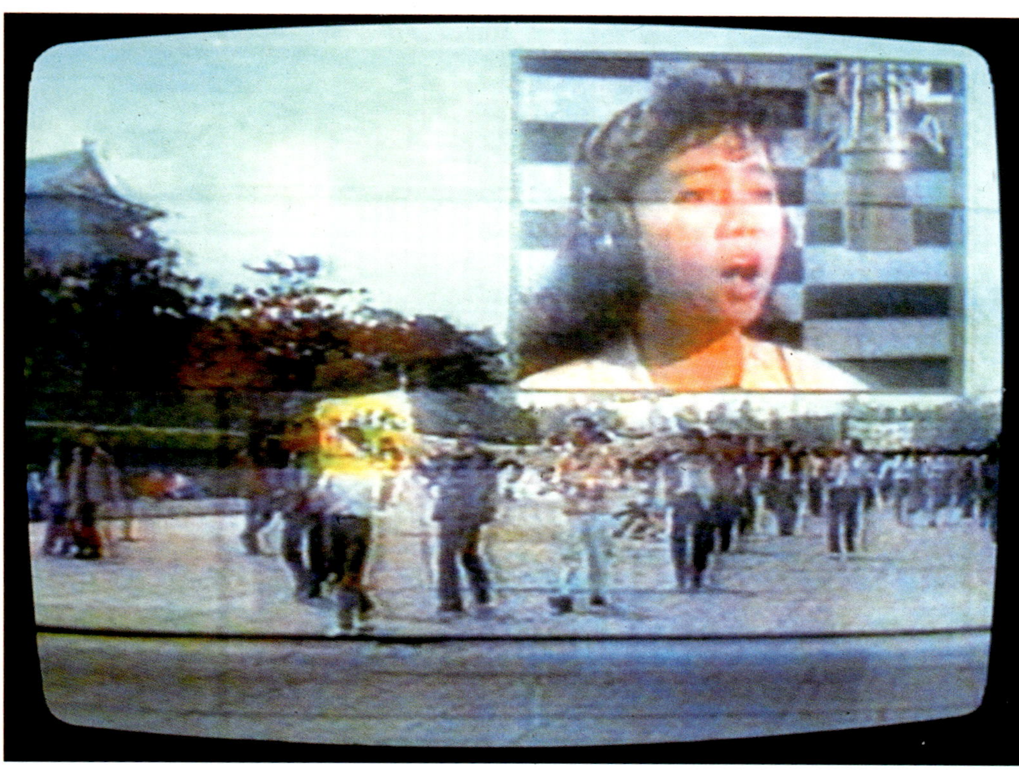

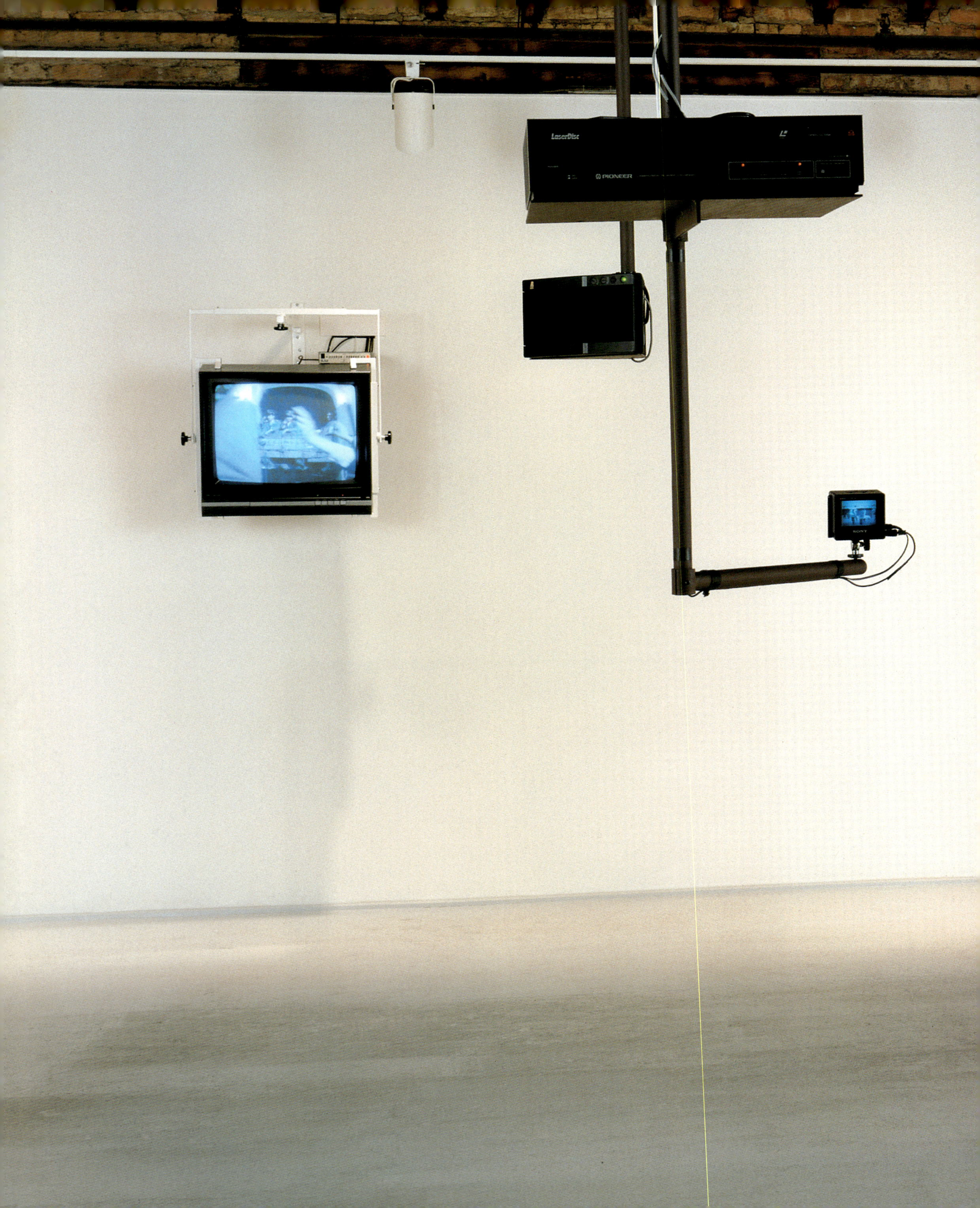
LaserDisc
PIONEER

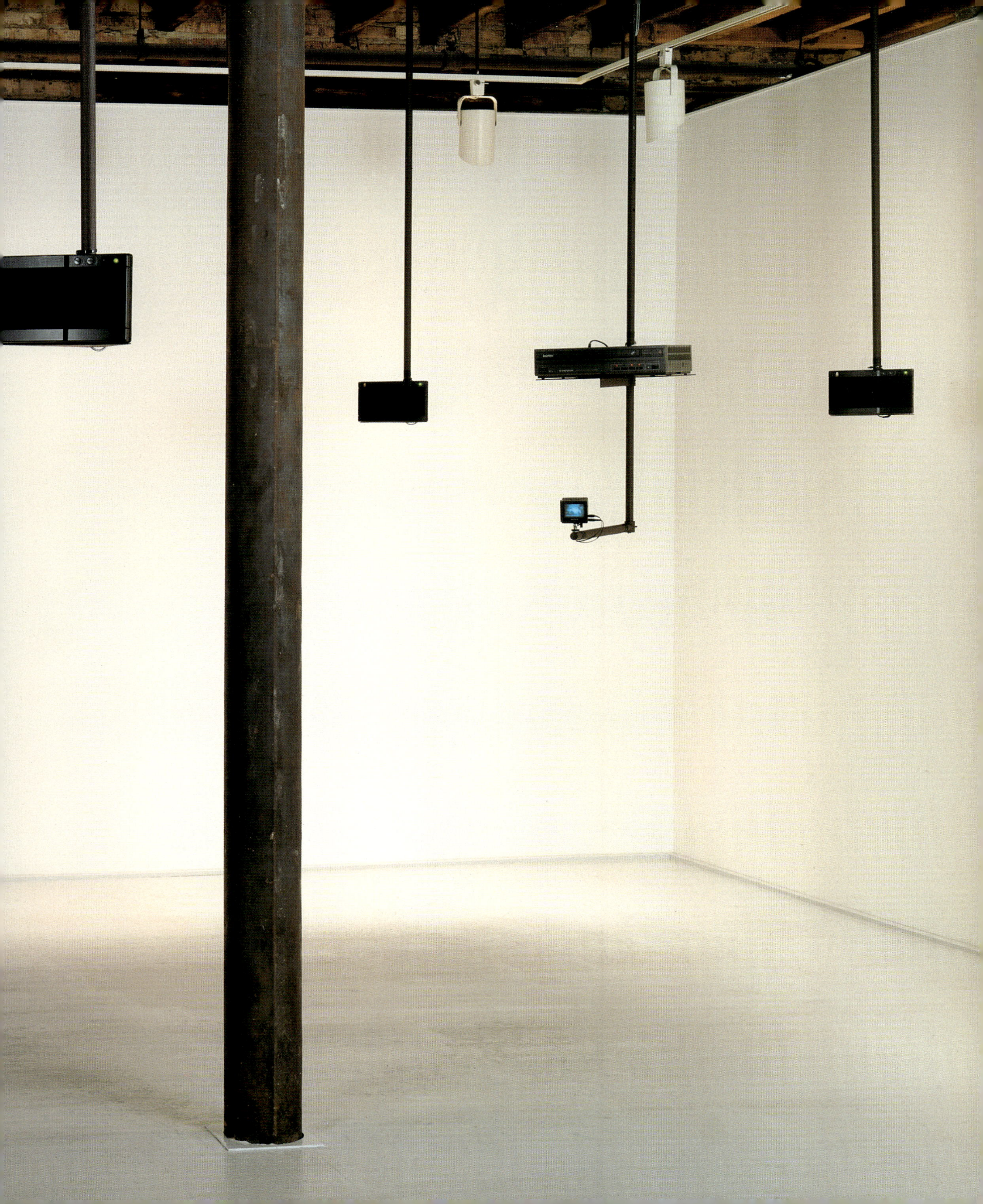

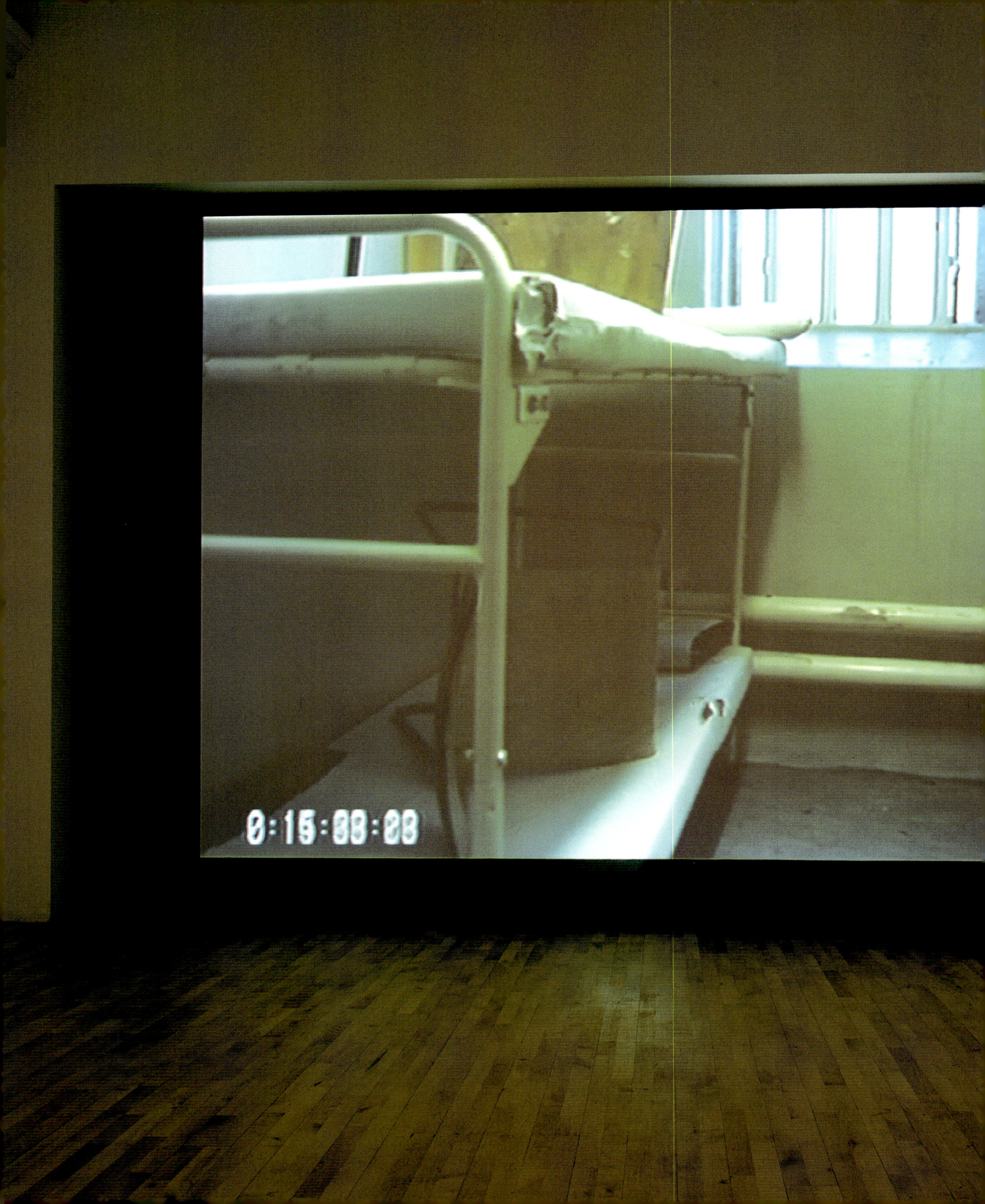

DARREN ALMOND

H.M.P. PENTONVILLE
(1997)

+++++

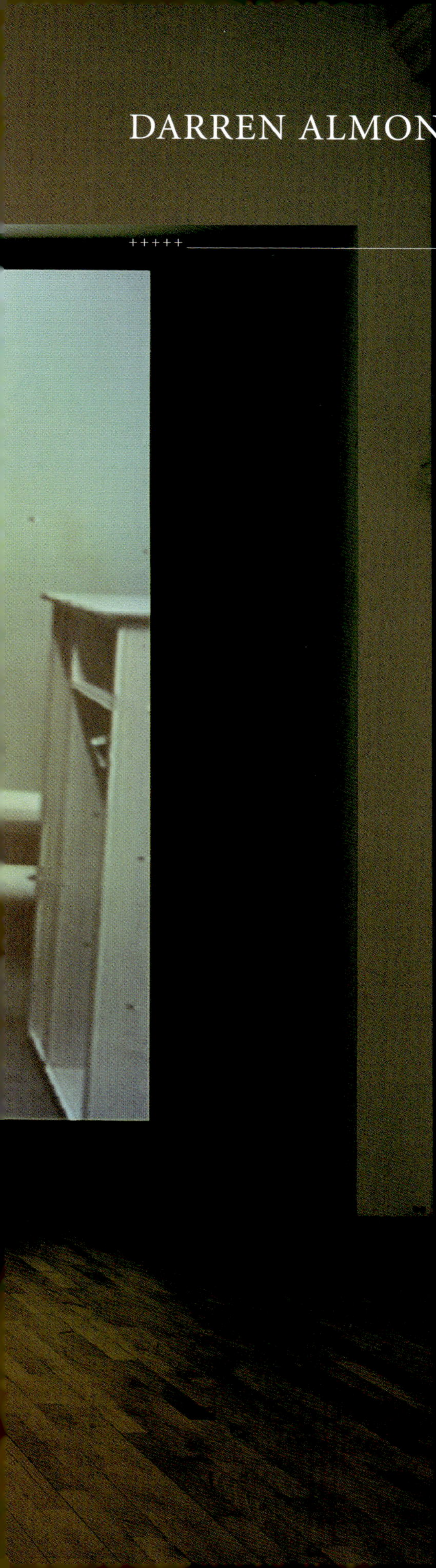

Plate 49
DARREN ALMOND,
H.M.P. Pentonville,
1997, installation view.

+++++ ________________ On May 7, 1997, Darren Almond connected an empty prison cell in Pentonville Prison with one of the galleries in the Institute of Contemporary Art, London, by a live satellite video link. For one hour the viewer was able to scrutinize an otherwise inaccessible space, via a video projection onto a wall of the gallery, in real time. This installation re-presents the hour-long live video link as an hour-long prerecorded image. Almond's connection of two institutional spaces—one in which public movement is highly restricted, the other in which the public has freedom of movement—temporarily hands one of the basic tenets of power and control—observation—from the prison guard to the viewer, momentarily breaking the closed circuit between guard and prisoner. ________________

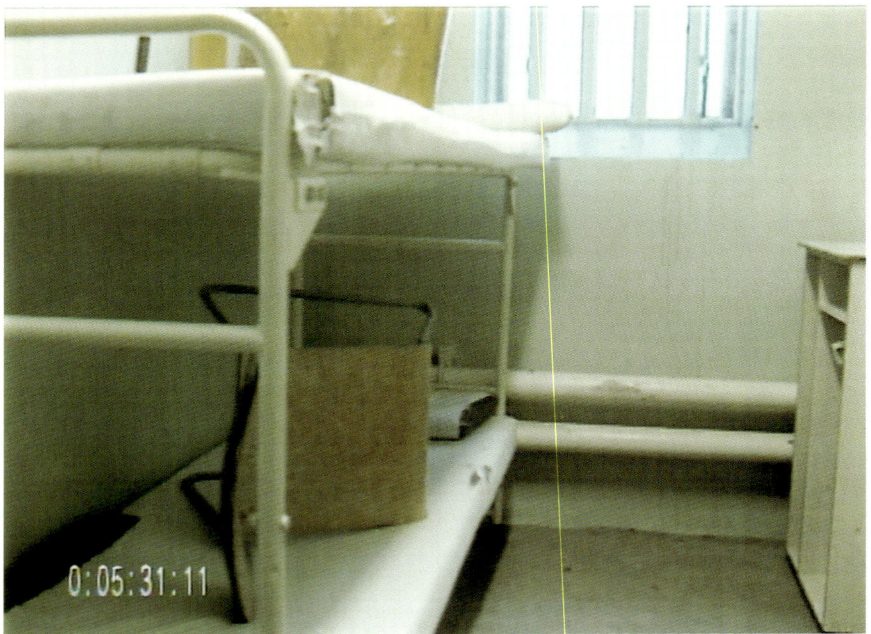

________________ The guard's watchful eye is replaced by the gaze of the camera, which appears similarly to possess the space. The prison cell is rearranged to align it with the formalism of the gallery; no personal belongings are present, and a chair is placed on the bottom empty bunk, shifting the space from living area to formal subject. The viewer encounters the cell as the new prisoner might see it upon first entering, at the moment before occupancy begins. The absence of personal effects or human activity allows our gaze to explore the room over a period of time, taking in details and absorbing the alienating atmosphere of the institutional space. ________________

________________ A separate sound track records the ambient sounds of the prison, including conversational fragments, doors being slammed shut, and the voices of prison guards, as staff and prisoners move through the corridor past the empty prison cell. In a reversal of the usual cinematic predominance of the image, sound propels the narrative, animating the stillness of the cell's interior. The sound marks the passing of time, which is otherwise detectable within the image only from the subtle changes in the light emanating from the barred window as the hour passes.

The stillness of the space and the slowness of time passing allow pause for reflection on all the thoughts and feelings experienced within the locked room in the past, made stronger by the absence of the previous occupants. In the original live presentation, the awareness of the passing of time was heightened by the visual experience of the remote space in real time. The anticipation of possible action about to take place in the otherwise inert space, echoed by the aural presence of unseen prisoners and guards outside, increased the charged atmosphere of the gallery space, rendering the piece performative.

Both the live and recorded versions of the piece suggest the presence of a closed-circuit television camera, emphasizing the voyeuristic role of both viewer and prison guard. In his book *Surveiller et punir: Naissance de la prison* (published in English as *Discipline and Punish: The Birth of the Prison*), Michel Foucault discusses the shift, in eighteenth-century Europe, from public, physical punishment to private punishment "that acts in depth on the heart, the mind, the will."[1] Foucault likens the subdivided unit of the prison cell to its monastic precursor and to its use in other institutional spaces—such as barracks, schools, asylums, hospitals, and factories—as an instrument of authoritarian control.

The primary mechanism within this system of control, as Alan Sheridan argues,[2] is the timetable, by which all the prisoner's physical activities are regulated. The imprisoned body is observed and controlled through a series of highly structured daily actions, executed under strict supervision. Power is maintained by near-permanent observation over time, which turns the body into an objectified unit, for which physical punishment has been replaced by a punishment of the soul. The empty prison cell in Almond's installation could, on one level, be read as a metaphor for the state of the incarcerated soul. It also represents a temporary rupture of the panopticon-like[3] observation system, since, for one hour, the prison cell is removed from the rigor of the prison timetable, and the rigid structure of the day is experienced only aurally, in the distance, through the sound of the guards and prisoners carrying out their set tasks. The chair placed on the bunk bed, creating a real and symbolic space in the middle of the empty cell, implies that the room has been recently vacated, suggesting the gesture of a body no longer under observation, and connecting the prison cell with the outside world through the liberty of the unseen, freed prisoner and the freedom of the gallery space.

1. MICHEL FOUCAULT, *Discipline and Punish: The Birth of the Prison*, trans. Alan Sheridan (New York: Vintage Books, 1979); cited in ALAN SHERIDAN, *Michel Foucault: The Will to Truth* (London: Tavistock Publications, 1980), 137.

2. SHERIDAN, *Michel Foucault*, 151.

3. The panopticon is a circular architectural structure for disciplined institutional observation invented by Jeremy Bentham (1748–1832).

Plate 50
DARREN ALMOND,
H.M.P. Pentonville,
1997, video still.

REINHARD MUCHA

AUTO REVERSE (1994–95)

1. Mucha has made frequent use of fragments of his childhood within his work, including childhood photographs (in one case, one for every year of his life), photocopied pages from his school notebooks, shoes, and his scooter.

+++++ In the work of Reinhard Mucha, history and autobiography are inextricably intertwined. The past is filtered through a conceptual structure of the present, which, in *Auto Reverse*, interrogates the role of the father in relation to that of the fatherland. In Germany's postwar period of reconstruction, economic success and material prosperity became the building blocks of a new national identity. The car once again became a symbol of economic power, collective achievement, and modernity, just as it had been during the 1930s.

As a result of this strong desire for rehabilitation and reconstruction after 1945, important aspects of collective memory and history were repressed. During the 1960s, when Reinhard Mucha was a child, his parents' generation experienced the emotional vacuum created by postwar German society's collective lack of a credible father figure. Economic prosperity and the apparent recovery from a shameful past masked a deep sense of loss and alienation, from both parent and country.

In *Auto Reverse*, Mucha searches for the father figure, both personally and metaphorically, by identifying with his young son. On one wall of the gallery, a black-and-white photographic transparency, blown up to a large scale, shows Mucha as a child, standing with his scooter.[1] Next to this monumentalized family snapshot, a black-and-white film projects a loop of the artist's son Roman sitting in a child's seat next to his father's bicycle, which leans against a railway bridge. The child repeats the single word *Auto*, echoing the continuous loop of the film. This circularity suggests both an arresting of time and the mechanical action of the heavy machinery that has come to characterize Germany's industrial past.

Whereas Mucha's static childhood image suggests an ordered world in which the scale of the scooter matches that of the child, in the film, impotence and vulnerability are suggested by the difference in scale and power between the child and the adult bicycle. The word *Auto*, repeated insistently by the little boy, implies a desire for the movement, speed, and power of a car, which are beyond his grasp and which the absent father cannot provide. The adult bicycle and railway tracks further underline the difference in power, symbolizing the gap between old-fashioned forms of transport and the powerful modern car for which Germany has become so well known.

Plate 51
REINHARD MUCHA, *Auto Reverse*, 1994–95, installation view.

Overleaf:

Plate 52
REINHARD MUCHA, *Auto Reverse*, 1994–95, installation view.

On the other side of the gallery, two child's scooters, similar to the one in the large photograph, lean side by side against the projector stand. A red pennant showing Düsseldorf's coat of arms is attached to one, identifying it as that of Mucha, who was born in Düsseldorf and studied with Joseph Beuys at the Kunstakademie there. Behind the stand, on the wall, hang two roundels of glass. One contains a mirror, the other a page of a book showing a picture of industrial piping from the factory where Mucha's studio is now located. Once again, a duality is expressed by a juxtaposition of the national and the personal. While the mirror performs the same function for the viewer that the photograph does for the artist, setting up a self-consciousness of looking that pervades all Mucha's work, the illustration of the pipe reinforces the redundancy of the factory's old industrial purpose, just as the film emasculates the bicycle and the railway.

The factory, bicycle, and railway all belong to a past that Germany's economic miracle has left far behind. Yet the two scooters leaning against the projector stand place Mucha on the same level of horsepower as his son, in a rejection of his own paternal authority and power, just as his son calls for it ("Auto! Auto!"). In embracing his own sense of helplessness, Mucha creates a triangle of male authority, linking himself, his son, and the symbolic absent father. In this revisitation of his own childhood vulnerability, he makes a powerful double statement, which fuses the personal with a more general, existential questioning of the deep historical and psychological implications of Germany's postwar "economic miracle."

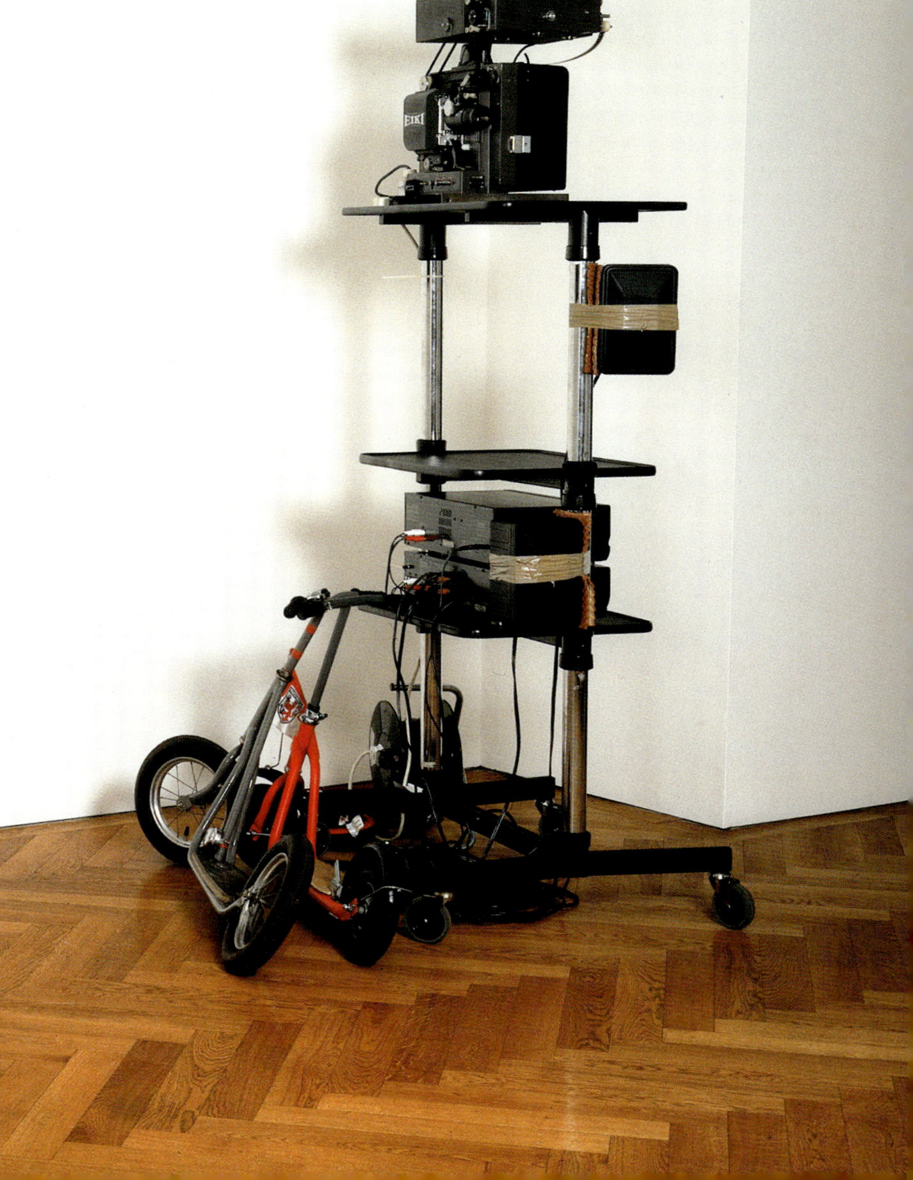

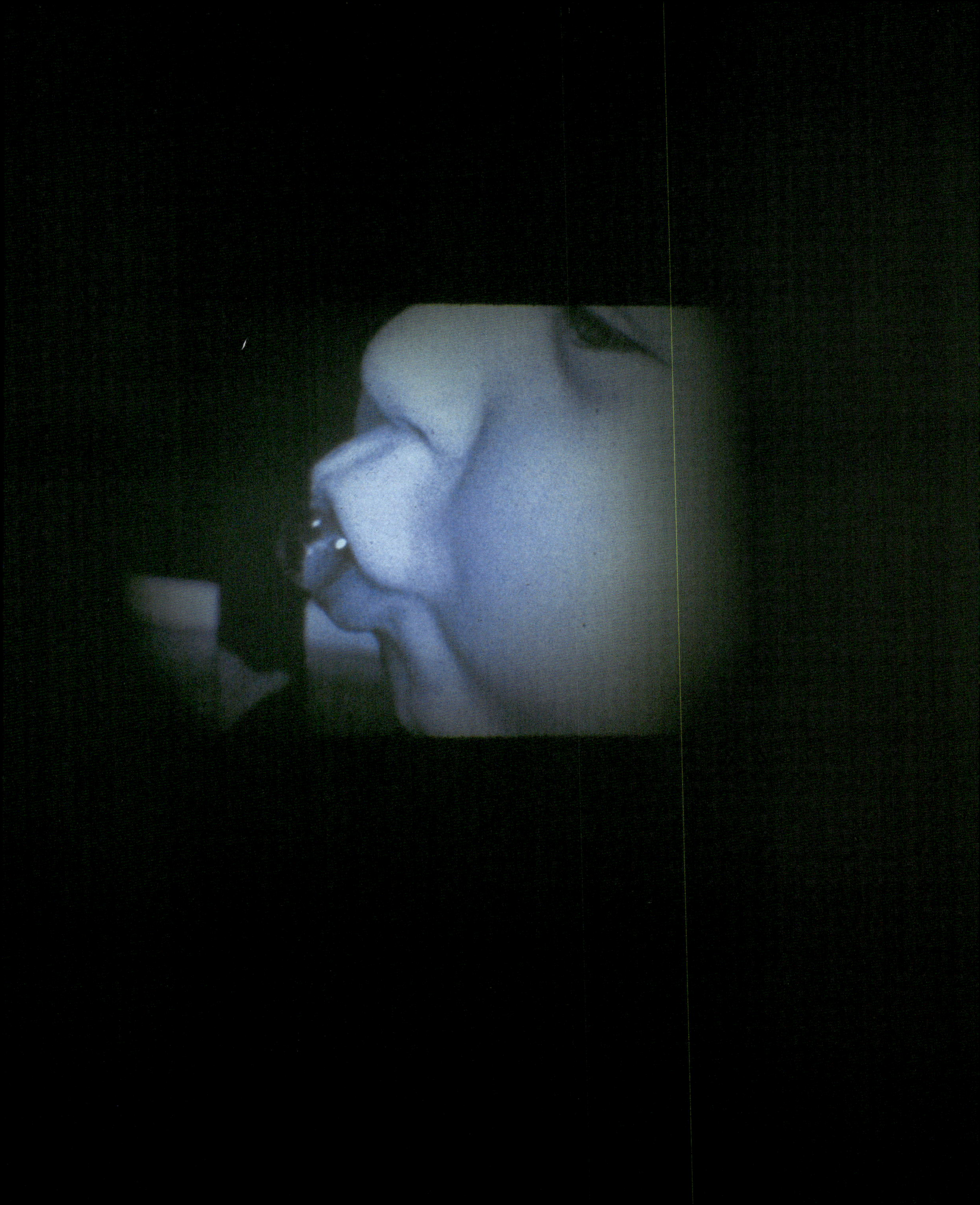

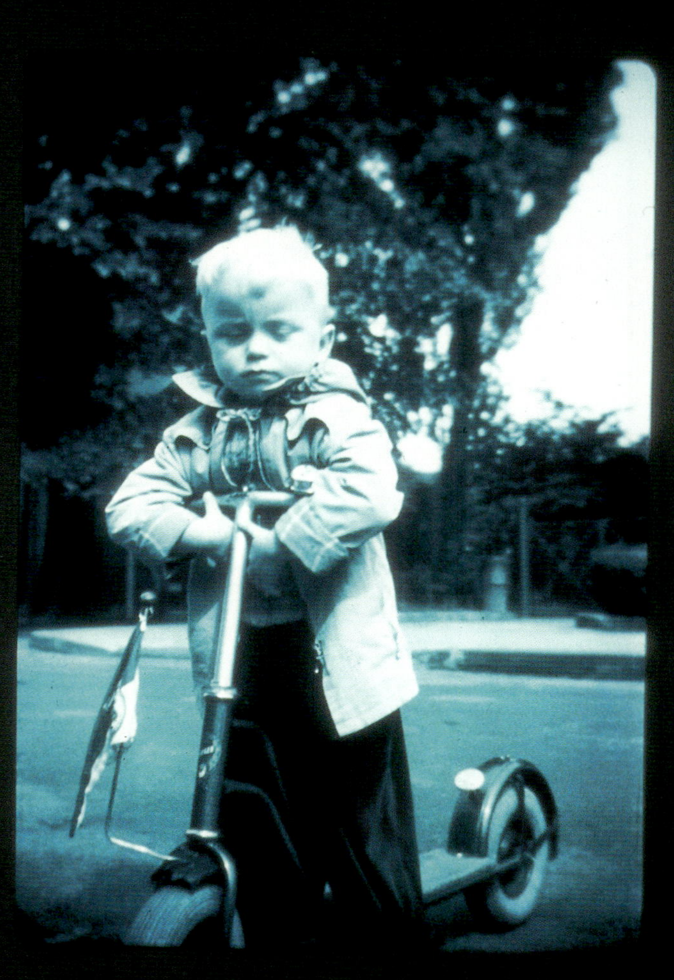

BILL VIOLA

THE GREETING (1995)

+++++ Since the early 1990s the widespread use of video projection has triggered a new cinematic aesthetic in video installation. Television-sized video images on groups of monitors have largely been replaced by large-scale moving images, projected onto walls or freestanding screens, whose content is increasingly merging the aesthetic, cultural, and technical languages of video and film.

Bill Viola was one of the first artists to shift video installation from its multiple-monitor format to that of projection, deeply influenced by the earlier perceptual video projections of Peter Campus as well as by the large-scale commercial moving-image environments of the 1964 New York World's Fair. Unlike most recent projection work, however, Viola's images are not cinematic, either in scale or content. Their impact is, rather, architectural, using the power of scale in a manner highly influenced by his early experience of Italian religious painting and architecture, which he absorbed during a year and a half spent working in Florence in the early 1970s.

The Greeting, perhaps more than any other of Viola's works, shows the profound influence of his Italian experience. It was created as one of five new pieces to be shown in the American Pavilion at the Venice Biennale in 1995, when Viola was chosen to represent the United States. Viola returned to the source that had inspired him at an early point in his career. *The Greeting*, although smaller than most of his other projection pieces, echoes the large, architectural scale of Italian Renaissance church paintings. The video projection, contained within a black frame, adopts a vertical format, whose proportions echo that of painting, rather than film or the standard ratio of the projected video image.

The Greeting was inspired by *The Visitation* (1528–29), a painting by the Italian Mannerist Jacopo da Pontormo,[1] in which two female figures greet each other affectionately, catching each other's arms in an extended embrace, while two other women stand motionless in the background, looking melancholically away from the scene. This composition is repeated almost identically in *The Greeting*, where a friendly conversation takes place between an older and a younger woman—both dressed in long, flowing clothes that evoke the drapery in *The Visitation*—in an artificially constructed Italian architectural setting. The elongated geometry of *The Greeting*'s set design distorts the rules of perspective, obeying the principal tenets of Mannerism, in which exaggeration, elongation, abstraction from nature, and artificiality are emphasized.

After a few minutes, a third woman, striking looking and wearing a red dress, enters from the left and interrupts the conversation, greeting the older woman warmly. The older woman returns her affection, cutting the first younger woman out of the exchange, before awkwardly attempting to bring her back into the conversation.

Plate 53
BILL VIOLA,
e Greeting,
duction still.

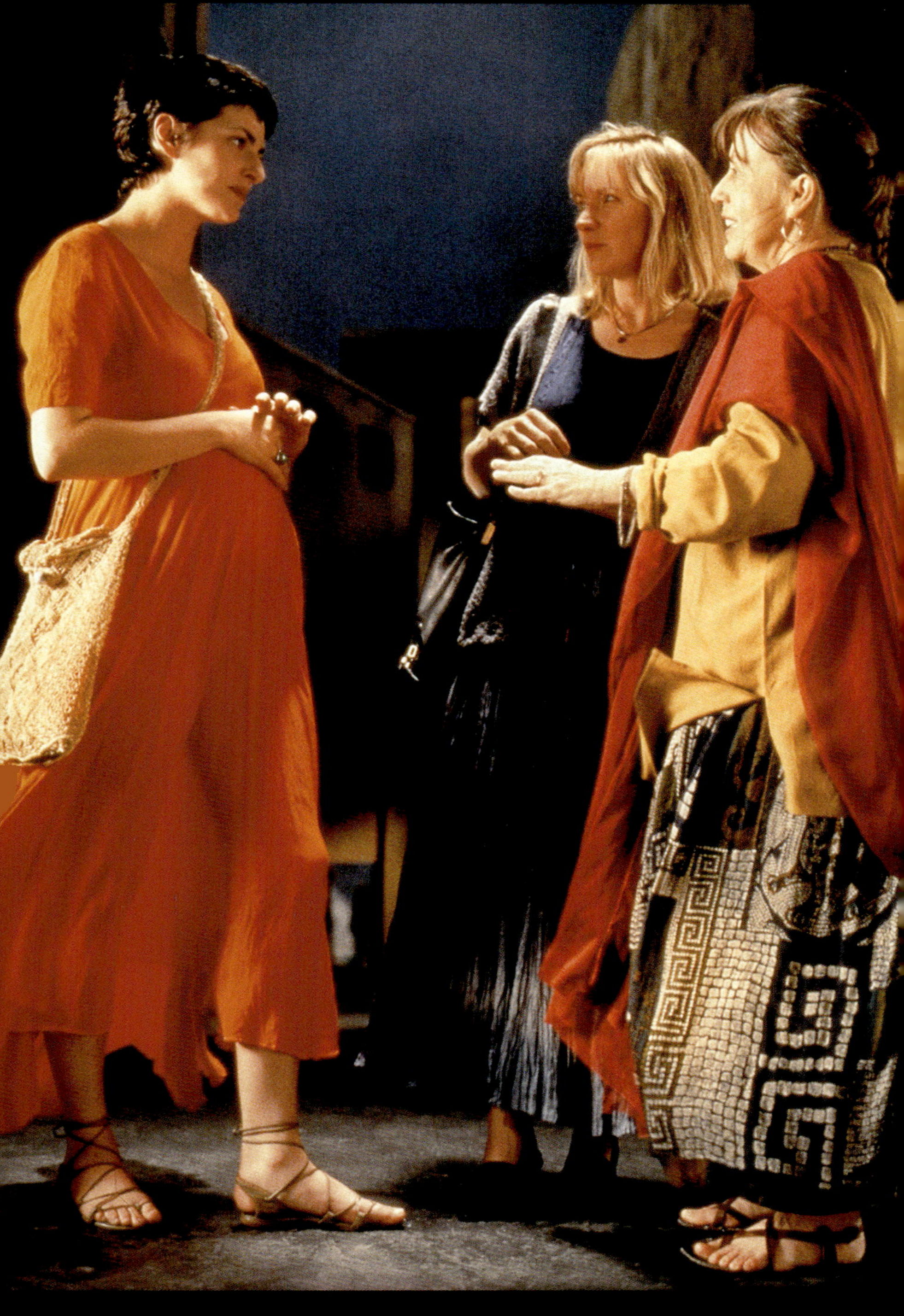

1. In the parish church of San Michele at Carmignano, Italy.

2. BILL VIOLA, *Reasons for Knocking at an Empty House: Writings, 1973–1994*, ed. Robert Violette (London: Thames and Hudson, in association with the Anthony d'Offay Gallery, 1995), 265.

The first younger woman, dressed in blue, recedes into the background, looking crestfallen. The entire encounter, which originally took forty-five seconds, is slowed down, using a slow-motion thirty-five-millimeter film camera, to span ten minutes. Within this extremely extended time frame, tiny details of the women's body language and unconscious reactions, normally invisible to the viewer, are revealed, taking on great significance.

The sequence of *The Greeting* appears to construct the action that immediately preceded the frozen moment of Pontormo's painting, when the Virgin Mary comes to her older cousin Elizabeth and exchanges the news that they have both become pregnant by the grace of God. The mirror image of the two women in Pontormo's composition is repeated in *The Greeting*, where the woman in red, her swollen stomach implying pregnancy, holds her older friend by the arms and whispers something inaudible into her ear, which she receives with delight. Yet, whereas in Pontormo's painting two women look on mournfully in the background, ghostly doubles of the women's former barren selves, in Viola's video sequence the quadruple symmetry has been transformed into a triangle, in which the single, isolated woman in the background exists in the same time as the two main protagonists, and seems jealous, not only of the stronger friendship but of the condition of the woman in red. The suggestion of pregnancy is present but left unstated, as is the overall meaning of the narrative.

Viola's sequence echoes the drama and mystery of Pontormo's mystical paintings, transforming one of the central themes of Christian iconography and Italian painting into an enigmatic contemporary narrative, in which, by implication, birth, one of the major themes in his work, is anticipated. As in all Viola's work, his theme is expressed through a strong physical engagement with the image by the viewer, through its large scale and dramatic accompanying sound track. A rumbling sound evoking an internal emotional state, which becomes increasingly loud as the two women move toward each other, engages the viewer in a fusion of visual and aural intensity. Viola cites the architectural painting of the Italian Renaissance as the source of his first conscious experience of art as related to the body. The physical, sensory inclusiveness of his video projections is echoed in his own description of the importance of a holistic corporeal engagement: "Art has always been a whole-body, physical experience. This sensuality is the basis of its true conceptual and intellectual nature, and is inseparable from it.... In my work, the visual is always subservient to the field, the total system of perception/cognition at work. The five senses are not individual things, but, integrated with the mind, they form a total system and create this *field*, an experiential field which is the basis of conscious awareness."[2]

Plate 54
BILL VIOLA,
The Greeting,
1995, production still (detail).

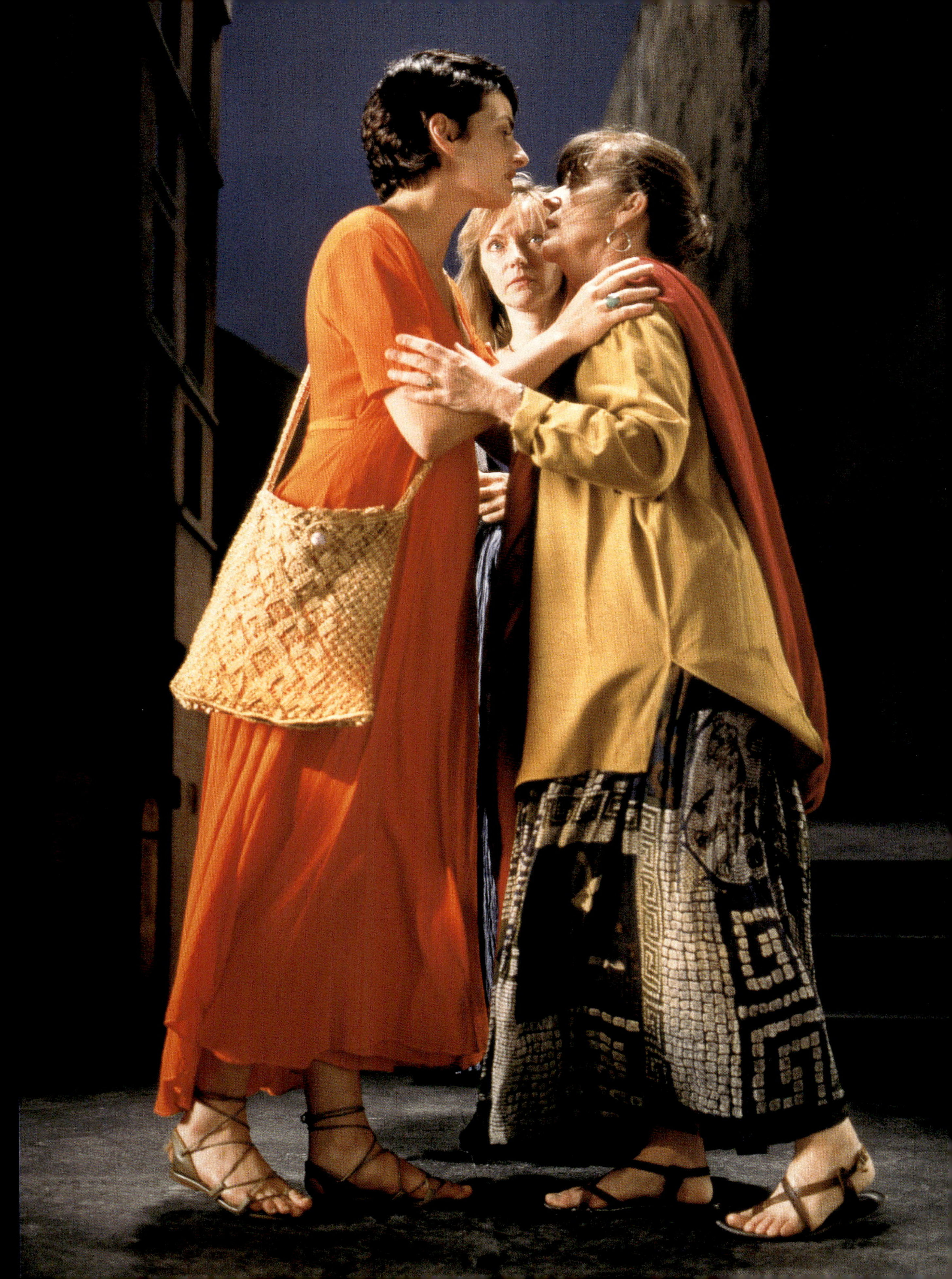

JAMES COLEMAN

INITIALS (1993–94)

+++++ The central concern of James Coleman's work is, as Dot Tuer has observed,[1] to cast the act of seeing into question. For Coleman, the visual image operates not as part of a narrative logic, but as a means to destabilize the viewer's visual cognition. In this sense, his work can be termed structuralist. Since the early 1970s, while based in Milan, he has used the low-key, low-technology medium of slide-tape to construct his inquiry, exploiting its didactic qualities. Unlike film or video, slide-tape, devised for commercial office presentations and educational lectures, has no previous aesthetic history. Coleman uses the physical and perceptual gap between the still slide image and its accompanying sound track, and between one slide and the next, to underline his refusal of a unified narrative or a holistic meaning.

This disjuncture is echoed in the title of *I N I T I A L S*, whose divisions between letters echo the space between the slides within the sequence. *I N I T I A L S* is part of a trilogy that also includes *Background* (1992–93) and *Lapsus Exposure* (1993). As Lynne Cooke has observed,[2] all three pieces involve a group of figures, apparently preparing for a photo shoot, in taxonomic environments: a paleontology laboratory, a recording studio and, in *I N I T I A L S*, a room next to an operating theater in an abandoned tuberculosis hospital outside Dublin, where Coleman lives. Within this local setting, which situates Coleman's inquiry within the context of Irish history and culture, a bare room, piled up with empty hospital beds, begins a fragmented sequence of slowly dissolving, still slide images in which male and female actors dressed in formal eighteenth-century costume and informal twentieth-century clothing adopt a series of theatrical poses.

A disjointed group of narrative texts are read out carefully, and sometimes haltingly, by a young girl. The fragments—extracted from Mills and Boon cheap romance novels, television soap operas such as *St. Elsewhere*, and Irish literature—suggest a realism that disrupts the heavily staged theatricality of the static images. The contrast between the normal speed of the spoken word and the noncinematic speed of the slowly changing images suspends the piece somewhere between film, photography, and theater. The texts include references to Irish history; at one point, the young girl speaks of famine, textile workers, and the depopulation of County Clare as an image of one of the women of the group holding a bolt of fabric appears, spread across a hospital table. The stark hospital room becomes a symbol of absence and loss and, on a more general level, implies a dissection and analysis of the human and, on a more abstract level, the social body.

The repetition of phrases within the sound track echoes Coleman's frequent use in *I N I T I A L S* of what Rosalind Krauss has identified as "the double face-out ... [mined] from the photo-novel, and a major grammatical component of his new 'medium.'"[3] In photo-novels, dramatic moments are often presented by showing two

1. DOT TUER, "Blindness and Insight: The Act of Interrogating Vision in the Work of James Coleman," in *Robert Lehman Lectures on Contemporary Art*, no. 1, ed. Lynne Cooke and Karen Kelly (New York: Dia Center for the Arts, 1996), 175–97.
2. LYNNE COOKE, introduction to *James Coleman: Projected Images, 1972–1994* (New York: Dia Center for the Arts, 1995), 10.
3. ROSALIND KRAUSS, ". . . And Then Turn Away?" in *James Coleman* (Vienna: Wiener Secession; Brussels: Yves Gavaert, 1997), 21.
4. TUER, "Blindness and Insight," 177.

Plate 55
JAMES COLEMAN, *I N I T I A L S*, 1993–94, projected image.

protagonists together in a single close-up shot, refusing the identification with a single character set up by conventional film narrative. Just as the viewer's gaze is suspended in the gap between the two images of this doubling, the darkened space of Coleman's installations suggests another double meaning, as Tuer explains—that of the fixed, individuated space of the camera obscura, and the collective space of cinema, which creates another split for the viewer, between two spatial models. In positioning the viewer in the gap between two different kinds of visual representation, Coleman, as Tuer describes, "unravels the threads that seamlessly bind perception and consciousness. His work becomes a reflection upon blindness and insight: destabilizing visual cognition to link what and how we see to what we can and cannot know."[4]

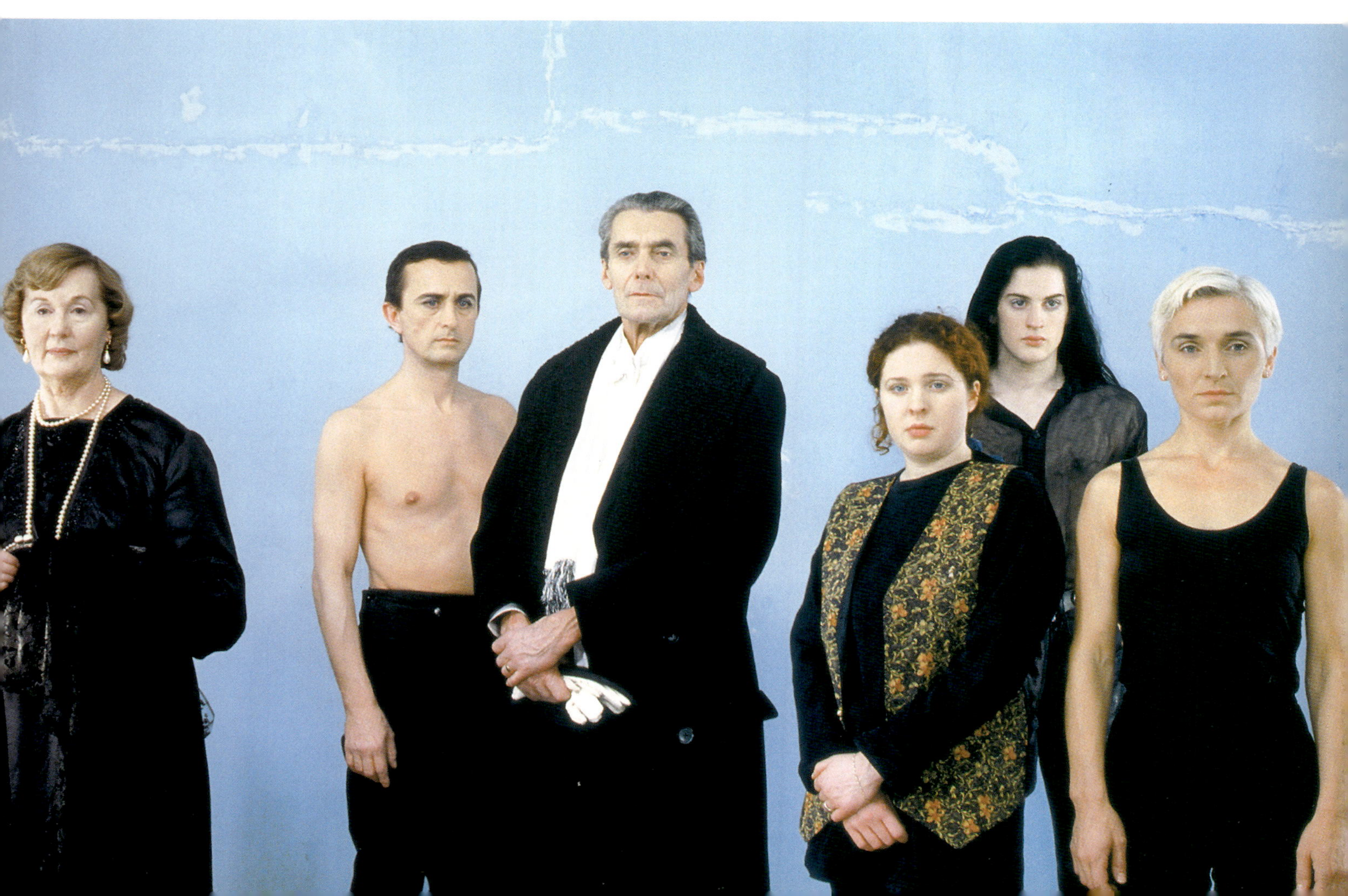

BRUCE NAUMAN

RAW MATERIAL—OK, OK, OK (1990)

+++++ Since his earliest video, audio, and performance works of the 1960s, Bruce Nauman has used sound, movement, and language, all basic functions of behavior and communication, as materials with which to explore the human condition. Nauman's inquiry unites the rigor of conceptual thinking—repetition, extended time, seriality, and boredom—with a subjective emotional content, which always involves anxiety, anger, violence, and alienation. Pieces from the 1990s such as *Raw Material—OK, OK, OK* marked Nauman's reappearance as performer after an absence of more than twenty years, reversing the pattern of his video installations of the late 1970s onward, in which he replaced his own presence with that of actors, mimes, and clowns.

In Nauman's early work, the human condition was examined through direct, concrete experience. First the artist and then, in his architectural installations, the viewers were subjected to physical and psychological discomfort, in rigorous performative experiments conducted over long periods of time. Informed by the 1970s preoccupation with psychology and social theory, Nauman's early perceptual methods were replaced, in the 1980s and 1990s, by circular theatrical narratives through which a more subjective anxiety and anger were expressed, making visible a previously suppressed wider political, social, and personal context.

If pieces such as *Violent Incident* (1986), and *World Peace (Received)* (1996) make these references explicit, *Raw Material—OK, OK, OK* expresses a more generalized angst. On two monitors stacked one above the other, Nauman's head revolves rapidly, shouting "Okay! Okay! Okay! Okay!" in an endlessly repeating loop. On the top monitor his head appears the right way up, while on the bottom one the image is inverted. On a large screen nearby, Nauman's head appears, projected, in an identical loop, also inverted.

Raw Material—OK, OK, OK contains many of the techniques first explored by Nauman in his early videotapes of the 1960s. In some, he used spinning and image inversion, in fixed-frame shots, to disorient both himself and the viewer. In *Lip Sync* and *Gauze* (both 1969) he focused the camera on his own face in a single close-up inverted head shot. In *Lip Sync*, he impassively repeated the words "lip sync" for one hour, moving in and out of sync with his own image. Nauman's use of repetition in sound and action was directly influenced by the work of LaMonte Young and Philip Glass. As in his other performative videotapes, in which he used singular movements, often derived from new dance, to explore the physiological and psychological effects of repetition over long periods of time, both *Lip Sync* and *Raw Material—OK, OK, OK* use difficulty, boredom, and stress as raw materials and tools of transformation.

1. BRUCE NAUMAN, "Breaking the Silence: An Interview with Joan Simon," *Art in America*, 76 (September 1988); reprinted in *Bruce Nauman: Image/texte, 1966–1996* (Paris: Centre Georges Pompidou, 1997), 114.

Plate 56
BRUCE NAUMAN,
Raw Material—OK, OK, OK,
1990, installation view.

Overleaf:

Plates 57–59
BRUCE NAUMAN,
Raw Material—OK, OK, OK,
1990, video stills.

If all Nauman's work can be said to contain an underlying aggression, the defensive shouting in *Raw Material—OK, OK, OK* is perhaps most closely related to the palpable aggression of his disturbing early sound work *Get Out of My Mind, Get Out of This Room* (1968). Viewers, on entering an empty space, are pushed out of it by a voice angrily instructing them to "get out of my mind, get out of this room." The work, which Nauman has described as "a really frightening piece,"[1] follows the same instructional pattern as *Raw Material—OK, OK, OK*, in which the artist attempts to stop the viewer from communicating or invading the artist's mental space. Yet Nauman's frustration is the expression of a more generally directed concern. As he has

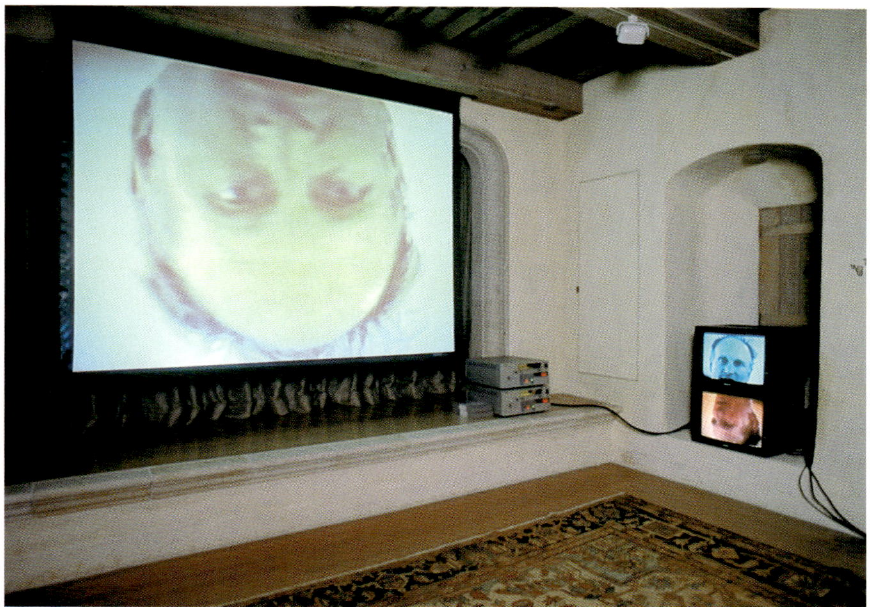

explained: "My work is basically an outgrowth of the anger I feel about the human condition. The aspects of it that make me angry are our capacity for cruelty and the ability people have to ignore situations they don't like." The monotony of the words "okay, okay, okay" and the irritation they produce in the viewer echo the frustration that Nauman feels toward the injustices of a world in which the same mistakes are endlessly repeated. Like all his work, *Raw Material—OK, OK, OK* attempts to identify the threshold, or breaking point, of the individual viewer, of the artist, and, on a deep existential level, of the collective social conscience.

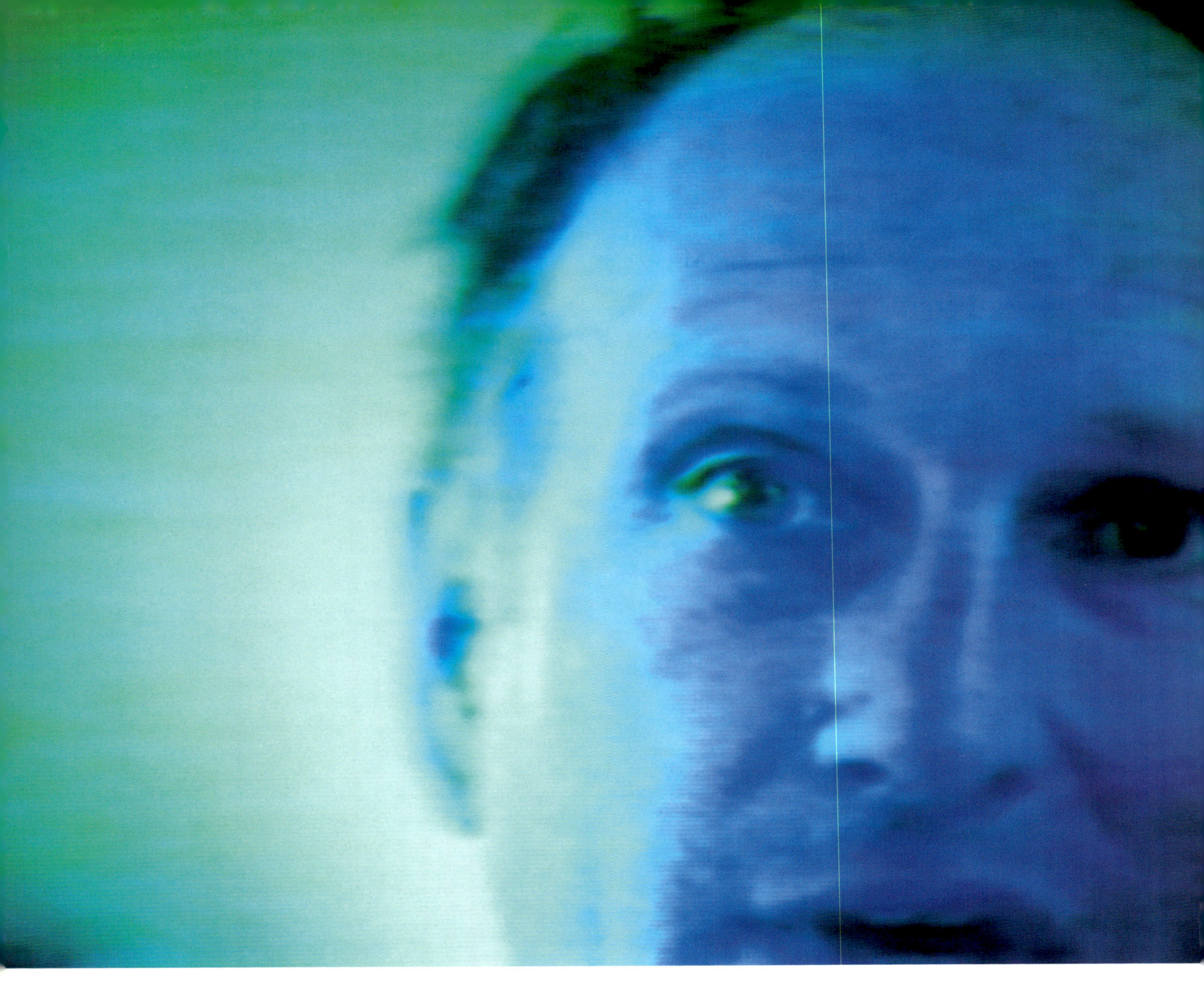

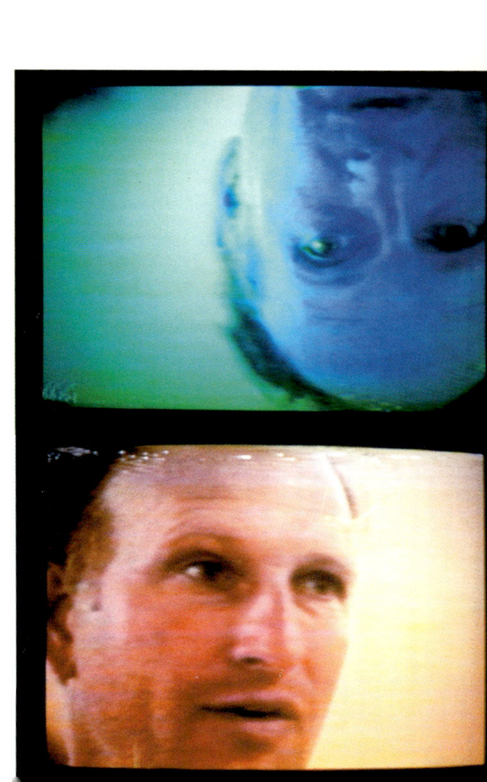

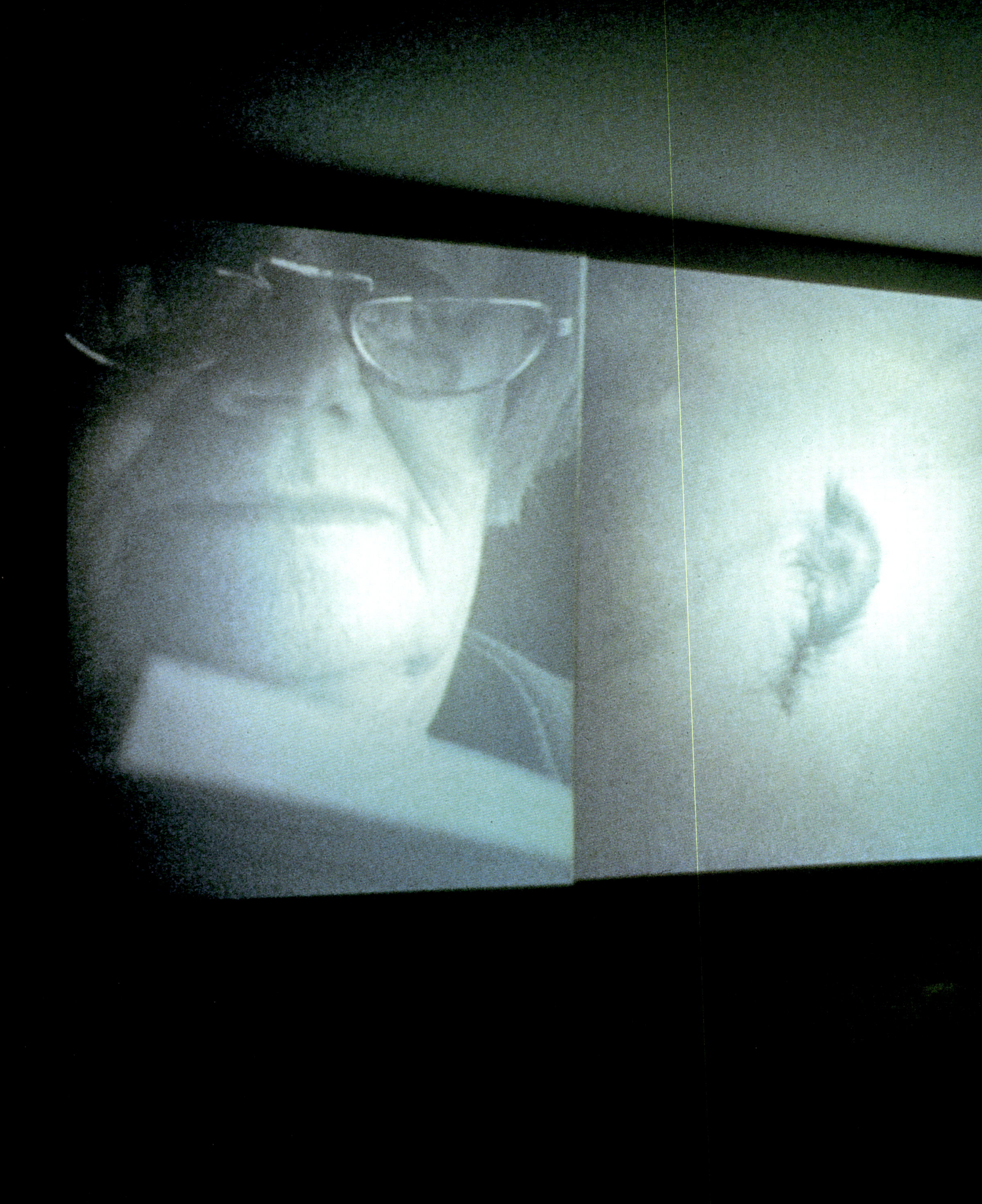

GARY HILL

CIRCULAR BREATHING (1994)

+++++

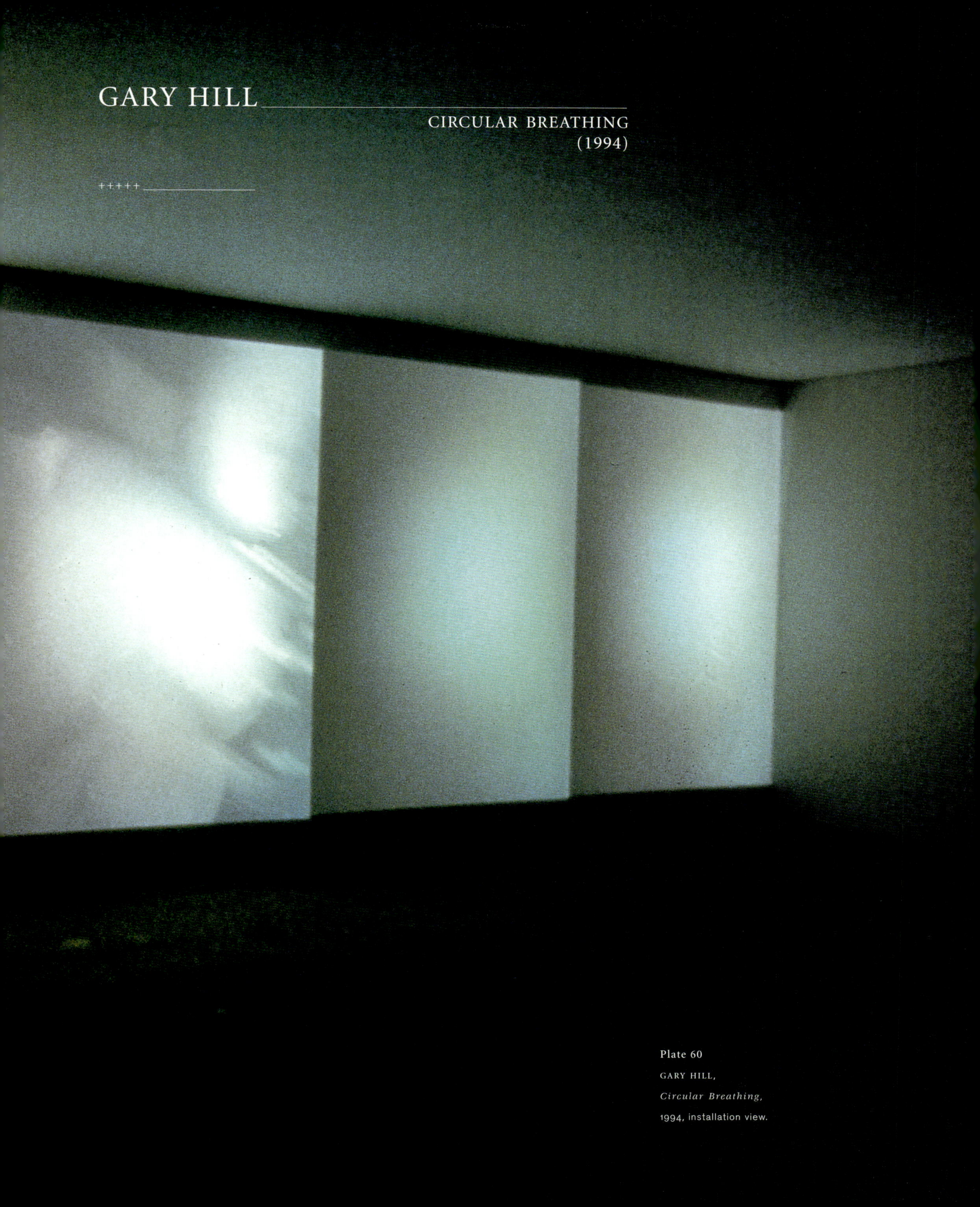

Plate 60
GARY HILL,
Circular Breathing,
1994, installation view.

+++++ Since his first experiments with video in the mid-1970s, Gary Hill has used the time-based, feedback properties of the video medium to explore the nature of perception. This inquiry takes place through an ongoing examination of the relationship between language and the image, within which the body occupies a central role, both as subject matter and, more generally, as "presence." This "presence" exists at many different levels: as image, sound, or text, and in the viewer's own physical presence.[1]

In Hill's work images appear not as literal representations of the world, but as manifestations of thinking. This reflects a deep engagement with the abstract process of working with video, in particular its specific quality of feedback, which always places the artist in a questioning role in relation to even the most basic facts of existence (for example, the perceiving of the artist's video image in relation to his or her actual presence, or to the presence of another person). Hill's work draws

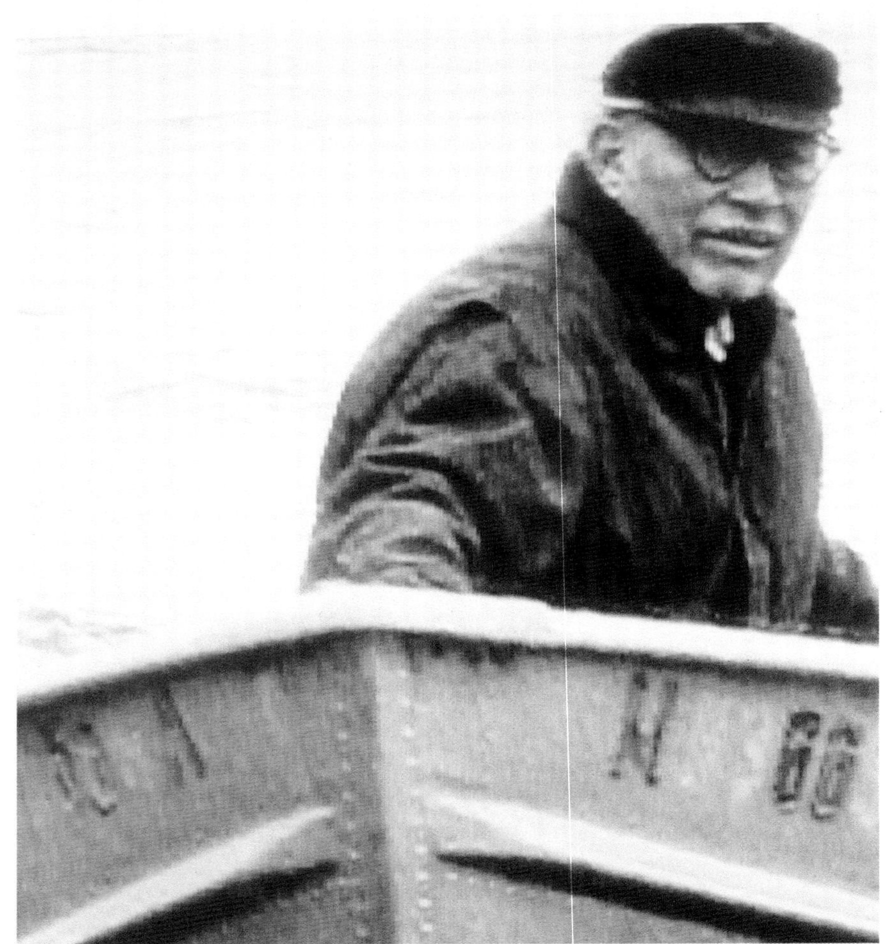

others into this mental feedback process, creating a kind of collective inquiry into the nature of seeing.

For Hill, this inquiry always involves a questioning of the predominance of the image. In *Circular Breathing*, sound is a constant presence that unites a series of fleeting images inside a visual and aural circuit. Five large black-and-white images appear sequentially, from left to right, across a wall of the gallery. As each successive image appears, its speed, and the speed of the sound, is "shared" with the previous ones, until all five images reach an almost photographic stillness, ground to a halt and blurred by the heavily slowed-down sound. As the last image slides off to the right, the sound resumes its original speed, until it is replaced by another, full-speed sound and a sharp image, both emerging from the left.

The gradual process of slowing down, followed by the rapid beginning of a new cycle, evokes the movement of breathing out deeply until no oxygen is left, followed by the rapid expansion of the lungs to inhale new air. The title refers to two kinds of breathing techniques: one adopted in the West by classical musicians who play woodwind instruments and the other practiced in the Eastern meditative discipline of tai chi. In both cases, the slow pace of deep breathing opens up the possibility for greater mental and physical clarity.

In *Circular Breathing* the reading of the images from left to right follows the structure of reading and writing. Two of the thirty-five images show reading. In one, a woman reads a book in silence; in another, a young girl reads aloud from a text by Ludwig Wittgenstein. In a third, a hand writes on a page. The indivisibility of language from the body suggested by these images is further echoed in the relationship between sound and image. In each of the seven sequences a swift action in the first image triggers the rest of the sequence to appear. Each action is symbolic of the splitting of the whole, or the ending of one phase and the beginning of another. One sequence is triggered by the turning of the page of a book; another by the emphatic writing of a period at the end of a sentence by a hand holding an ink pen. In a third, a man brings an axe down onto a log, whose splitting causes the speed of the image and sound to be split in two as the second image appears.

In each sequence, as the images begin to flicker rapidly, accompanied by a loud, agitated sound, an obscured narrative appears to build. But the sequences yield no logic, and the unrelated images slide across our vision like half-remembered fragments of a dream. The flickering and altered speed, like the slow breathing of tai chi, shift the viewer's focus from the habitual linearity that searches for a literal meaning to the deep perceptual questioning that lies at the heart of all Gary Hill's work.

1. As FRIEDMANN MALSCH argues in "The Body as Presence in Gary Hill's Videographic Work," in *Gary Hill: Imagining the Brain Closer Than the Eyes*, ed. Theodora Vischer (Basel: Museum für Gegenwartskunst; Ostfildern: Cantz, 1995), 66–74.

Plate 61
GARY HILL,
Circular Breathing,
1994, video still.

GARY HILL

CUT PIPE
(1992)

+++++ The video work of Gary Hill always engages the viewer spatially. In some cases, this spatiality is expressed in a physical, sculptural form, either in the treatment of the video monitors themselves—stripped of their casing, turned on their sides, flattened to the wall—or by enclosing video images within metal structures that have a physical presence within the gallery space, echoing an early engagement with metal sculpture and sound, out of which Hill's first experiments with video emerged.

Cut Pipe (1992) is perhaps the most literally sculptural of Hill's video objects and his most complex inquiry into the relationship between physical surface and the electronic image. A large, hollow aluminum pipe lies on the floor, cut in two. Its physical density contrasts sharply with the delicacy of a small circular video image, projected onto a speaker cone inserted into one of the cut surfaces. The black-and-white image, which appears to form an electronic membrane over the hollow gap in the pipe, shows two hands moving sensuously across an image of a circular speaker cone, creating a third reality from a three-layered image, fusing real and electronic surfaces.

This third reality is described in a spoken text emitting from the actual speaker cone beneath: "my skin, its skin, forming another skin." The boundaries between imaged and real, physical substance and energy, become permeable. Hill speaks of moving across these boundaries and "touching" his own voice, for which the speaker cone is a metaphor, both of its physical structure, and the sounds it produces: "stretching the skin taut . . . touching sound . . . touching image . . . touching, touching . . . I want your mind for the skin space . . . I want to spread the skin . . . I want to cover my voice with the skin."

Marshall McLuhan has argued that, unlike film and photography, television and video are an extension of touch rather than of sight. Since the video image is low definition, viewers complete the picture with their eyes, which induces a more intense involvement with the screen. This tactility results in an osmosis, or what McLuhan describes as a tattooing of technology directly onto our skin. Hill's questioning of where the skin (of the body, speaker cone, sound, and image) ends and begins, explores, in philosophical and linguistic terms, McLuhan's argument that electronic media, like all media, are an extension of our physical and psychic selves, forming a kind of total field awareness, or simultaneity. In *Cut Pipe*, this simultaneity is expressed in the implication that language comes into being through the body, represented here both in literal terms and associatively: the body, the speaker cone, and the pipe are all conductors of the voice.

Plate 62
GARY HILL,
Cut Pipe,
1992, installation view.

Overleaf:

Plate 63
GARY HILL,
Cut Pipe,
1992, installation view.

The fusion of material and electronic surfaces inside the cut pipe contrasts with the space between the pipe's two external sections. This space could be argued to represent the unbridgeable gap between the viewer and the imaged—expressed in Hill's silent projection pieces, such as *Tall Ships* (1992)—which symbolizes the impossibility of achieving complete union with the "other." *Cut Pipe*'s tactile sensuality expresses an intense desire for union with the other, and with the self, at the deepest level (in psychoanalytic terms, a desire to return to a fusion with the maternal body): by a fusion of one skin with another, through touch, through seeing, and through thinking.

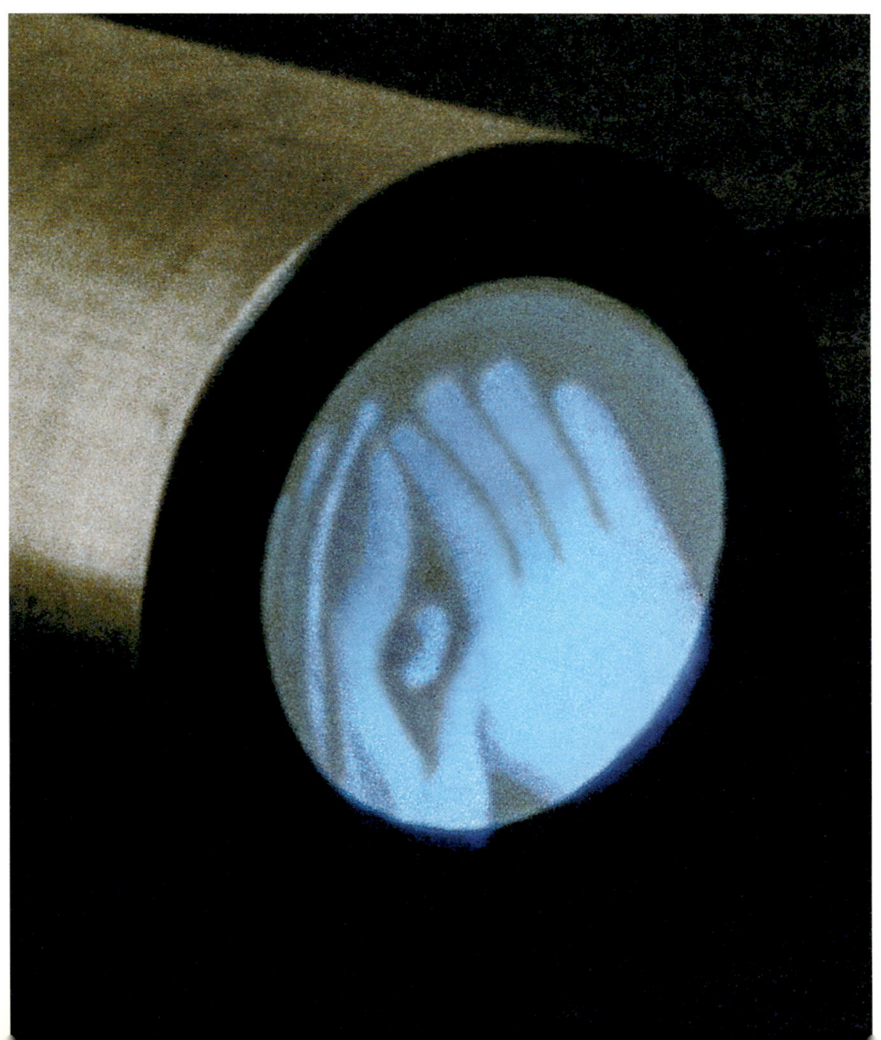

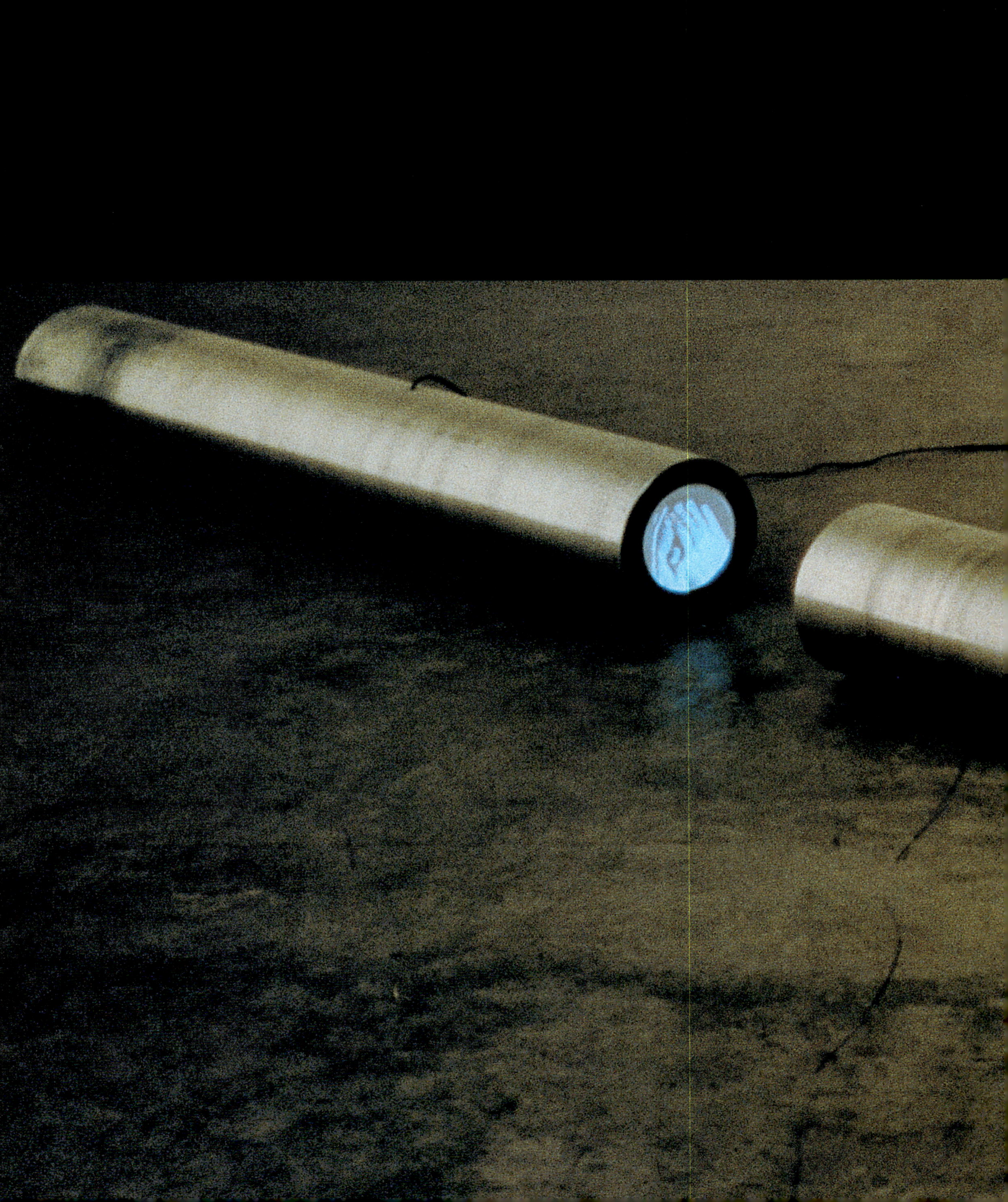

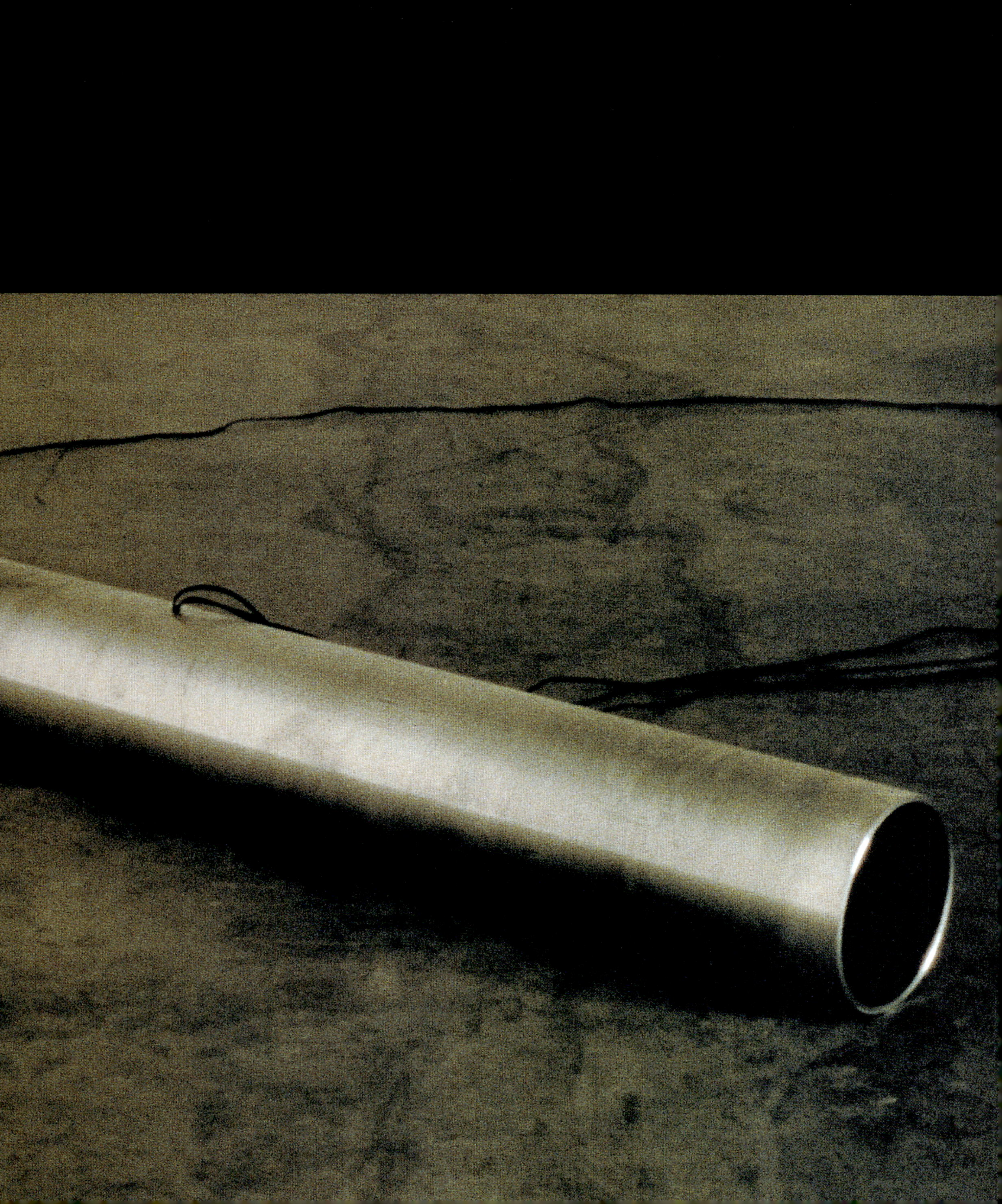

MARIKO MORI

MIKO NO INORI (1996)

1. MARIKO MORI, "Artist's Statement," in *XLVII esposizione internazionale d'arte: Futuro presente passato*, ed. Germano Celant (Venice: Biennale de Venezia; Milan: Electa, 1997), 424.

+++++ The work of Mariko Mori describes the nexus between spirituality and technology at the end of the twentieth century. In Mori's futuristic video installations and photographs, the female cybernetic body becomes the embodiment of a transmutation of the physical world into a fantastical space of hyperreality. Mori's vision has been forged within the context of the futuristic, high-tech world of modern Tokyo, her hometown, and filtered through the fast, sophisticated cultural environment of New York, where she is now based. She was once a fashion model, and her work reflects the growing interaction between fine art and fashion, first seen during the 1980s in the work of artists such as Cindy Sherman and reflected more recently in the stylized installations and films of another ex-fashion model, Matthew Barney (see pls. 83–94).

The extent to which Mori's futuristic vision establishes a new level of artifice can be seen by comparing the ephemerality of her cyborg women with the cinematic physicality of Sherman's feminine personae. Although both artists reconstruct iconic female roles drawn from popular culture, Mori's hyperreal figures reflect the increasing dominance of cyberspace over the traditional medium of cinema as an important influence on contemporary art. Within the futuristic world of global cyberspace, Mori (like Pipilotti Rist, in a European context) combines references to techno-pop, spiritual transformation, utopianism, science fiction, and kitsch to create a strangely detached world of synthetic hypervisuality.

The transformation from physicality to virtuality effected by new technology, and the disintegration of the corporeal that accompanies it, becomes, in Mori's work, a direct metaphor for spiritual enlightenment. In *Miko no inori* (The shaman girl's prayer), Mori—dressed in a white, iridescent costume and caressing a large crystal ball—appears as a pale, cosmic presence inside the futuristic environment of Renzo Piano's new Kansai International Airport in Osaka, while a haunting Japanese song plays in the background. Mori's digitally re-created eyes, traditionally the windows of the soul, radiate an unnatural glow, implying that technology has subsumed consciousness itself. Both her eyes and the crystal ball reflect the airport interior, distorting the architectural curves into a surreal prism through their elliptical surfaces and the fish-eye video camera lens used to film the scene.

Plate 64
MARIKO MORI,
Miko no inori,
1996, production still (detail).

Overleaf:

Plate 65
MARIKO MORI,
Miko no inori,
1996, production still (detail).

Mori's choice of a futuristic site of departure on a long journey suggests the transition from earthbound human life to this artificial nirvana. Her cybernetic spiritual metaphor is underlined in the title of an accompanying photographic work, *The Last Journey* (1996), also set in Kansai Airport, in which Mori appears in a triadic form, her central figure flanked by two ghostly reflections, evoking an otherworldly presence informed by images from Japanese video games, comic books, and techno-pop. In *Miko no inori*, the mesmerizing power of Mori's crystal ball evokes the Nintendo screen as much as a soothsayer's globe. The future is framed in terms of a synthetic spirituality, in which the principles of Buddhism play a major role. Mori focuses on their most utopian aspects: "All living beings are connected at every moment in inner space. Every life form with its own life cycle is part of the outer universe and there is only one planet earth. In the next millennium, the power and energy of the human spirit should unify the world in peace and harmony without any cultural or national borders."[1]

Mori's idealistic statement (which could also describe an internet philosophy) reflects a desire to transcend her own cultural boundaries, and link Japan, where she is now considered to be an outsider, with the West, which still regards Japan with some ambivalence. The spirituality that increasingly pervades her recent work also reflects the anxiety of a generation on the brink of the new millennium, looking for stability and meaning in the face of a disappearing physical world. In Mori's universe, the instantaneousness with which different geographical and temporal zones can be traversed is translated into another kind of transcendence of time and space, in which the transformation from corporeal into cyber is interpreted as a process of spiritual renewal.

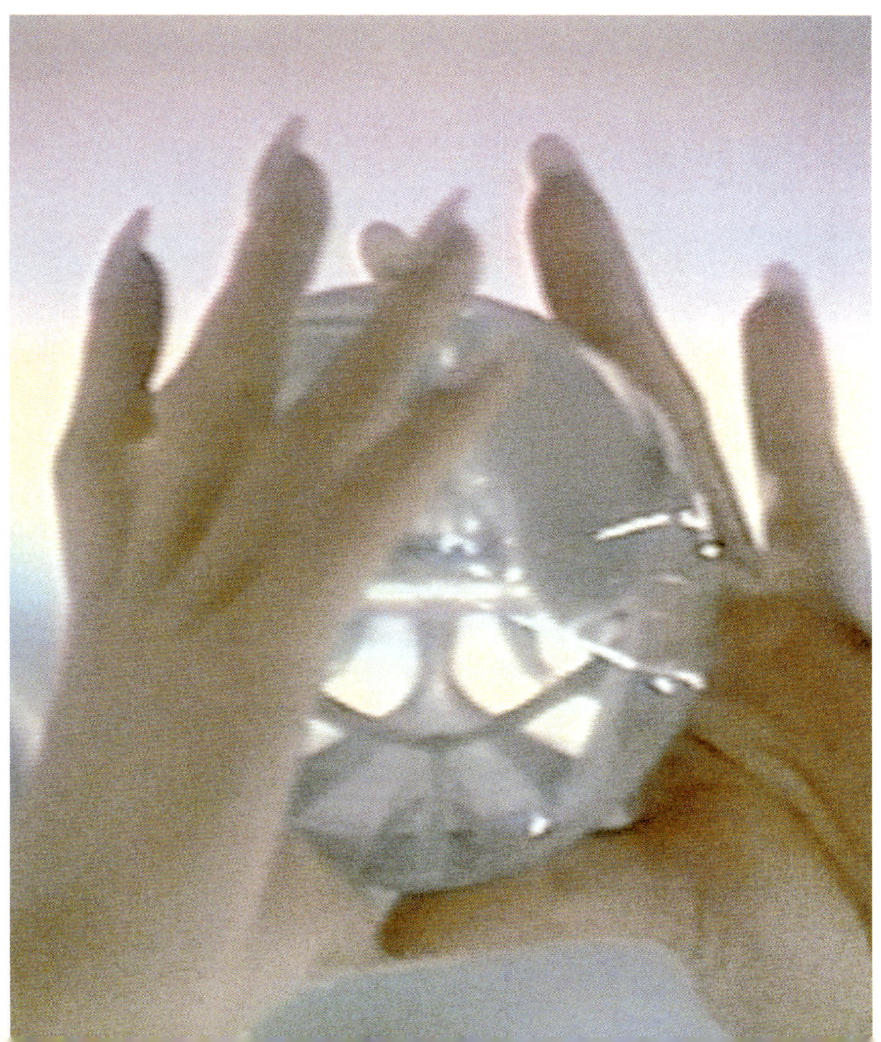

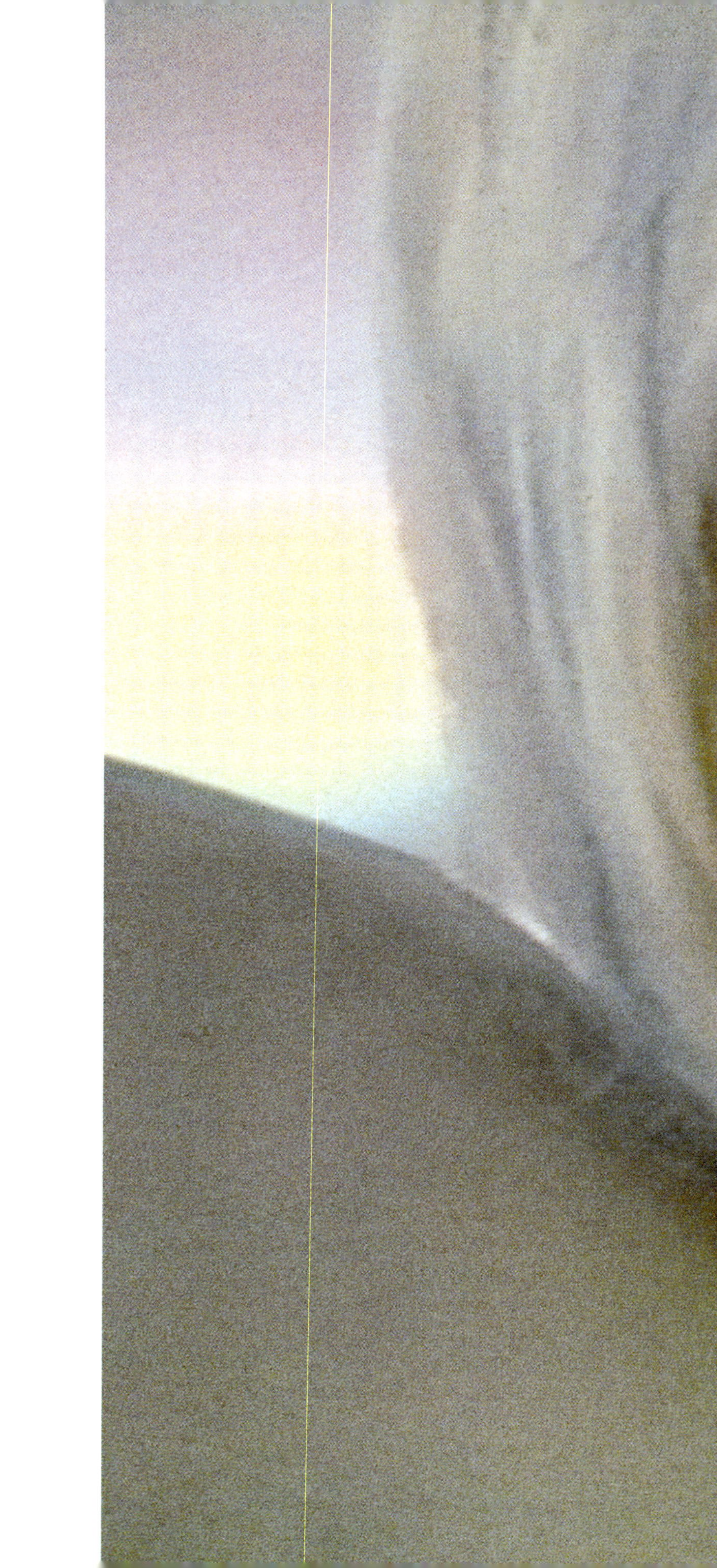

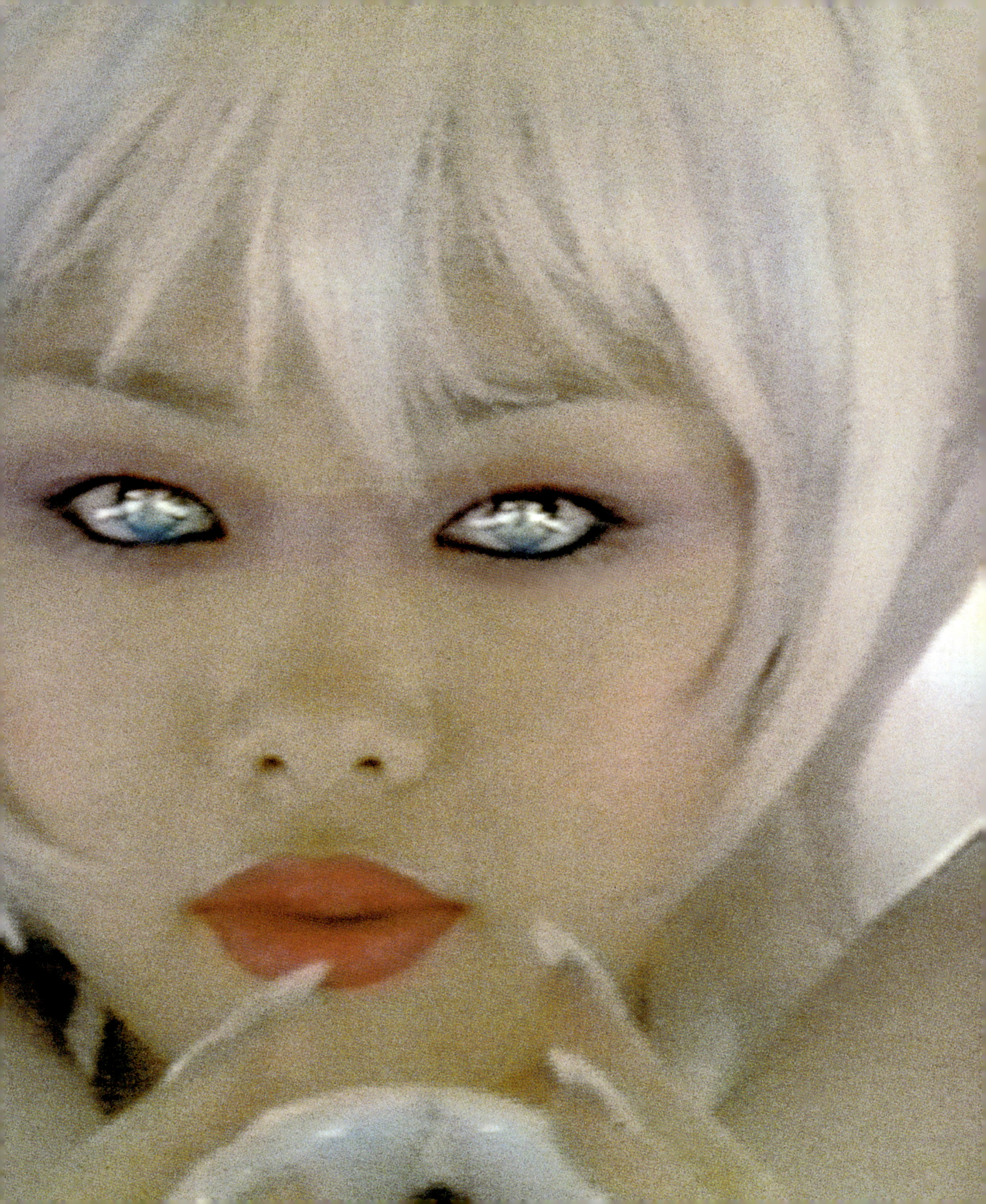

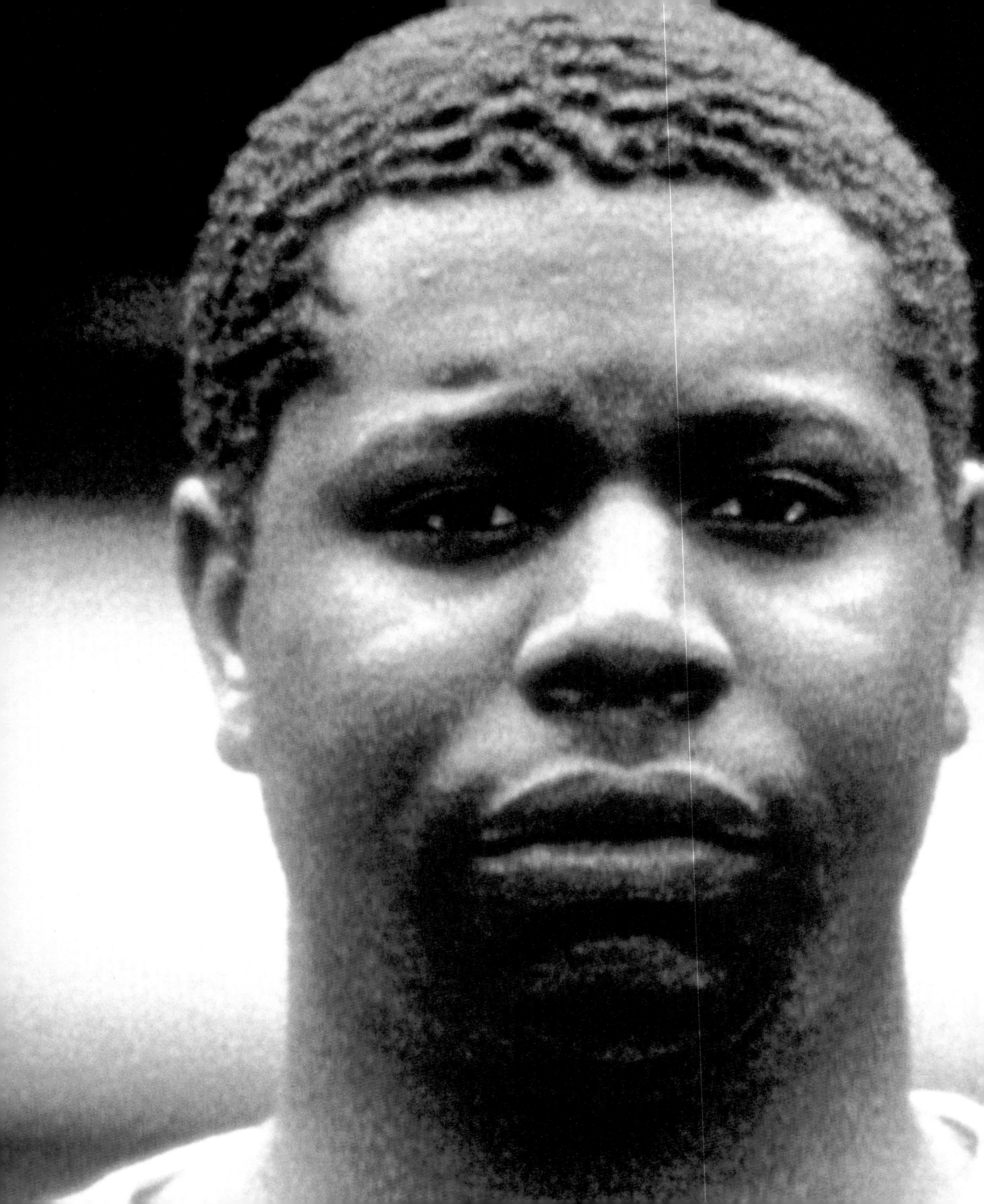

STEVE MCQUEEN

DEADPAN
(1997)

+++++

Plate 66

STEVE MCQUEEN,
Deadpan,
1997, film still.

+++++ The work of Steve McQueen insists on the physicality of the cinematic experience. Single banal or incidental fragments of film narrative are restaged and given new prominence, edited together into pieces that occupy a position somewhere between film and installation. McQueen's emphasis on process—filming, editing, and presentation—draws attention to the importance of movement in the construction of the film image, with a tactility reinforced by its relation to physical space.

In all of McQueen's pieces, a film is projected onto the back wall of an enclosed, dark space, its large image framed by the edges of the walls, ceiling, and floor. The black walls identify the space as cinematic, yet the connection of the bottom edge of the moving image to the floor removes it from the abstract space of the "screen" and connects it concretely to the shared space of the viewer, suggesting the expanse of the gallery rather than the confined environment of the cinema. This dichotomy locates McQueen's film narrative as a phenomenological inquiry in which the singular action becomes the subject.

In *Deadpan* this focus on singular action evokes the structure of early silent film. In contrast to the more complex narratives of 1920s silent cinema, early silent films were strongly connected to vaudeville and penny arcade entertainment, focusing on a single dramatic action (the firing of a cannon, the demolition of a wall), rather than a complex story. As Tom Gunning has argued, "the interaction between characters on screen and audiences was frequently based on the performer's self-conscious ... exhibitionism, rather than, as in 'classical' cinema, determined by the spectator's unacknowledged voyeurism."[1]

McQueen restages the "self-conscious exhibitionism" of early silent cinema in *Deadpan* by isolating and repeating, in a continuous loop, a moment from an American silent film of the 1920s. Playing the central character, he reenacts a shot in a Buster Keaton comedy, *Steamboat Bill Jr.*, in which Keaton stands immobile as four walls of a house come crashing down around him, then emerges unscathed. A moment from a later phase of silent film, in which a more complex narrative has been developed, is extracted and recast as a short, pre-1900, single-action film. If narrative is constructed in order to disguise discontinuity, McQueen reverses this process. The loop, replaying the same moment, shot from different angles, repeatedly for four minutes, refuses the forward movement of narrative continuity and exposes the discontinuous fragmentation of reality.

The speed at which the frame house collapses around McQueen increases toward the end of the film, suggesting a dramatic climax that is never realized. The looped action's suspension of the dramatic moment evokes the repetitive performative actions in artists' films and videotapes of the late 1960s and early 1970s. Using non-studio film equipment and the newly emergent video technology, artists

1. THOMAS ELSAESSER, "Introduction: Early Film Form: Articulations of Space and Time," *Early Cinema, Space, Frame, Narrative*, ed. Thomas Elsaesser (London: British Film Institute, 1990), 14.

Plate 67
STEVE MCQUEEN, *Deadpan*, 1997, film still.

recorded repetitive actions, staged for the camera over a long period of time, which questioned the traditional cinematic relationship of subject to camera, and of viewer to moving image. McQueen's impassive insertion into the silent movie sequence asserts his own performative presence, further undermining the illusionism of the cinematic sequence. *Deadpan*'s fusion of two approaches to the single action—one theatrical and dramatic, the other banal and conceptual—creates a kind of perpetual present. The viewer is caught somewhere between the past memory of the original silent film, the phenomenological time of the sequence's reconstruction, and the time and space of the viewer's own physical reality.

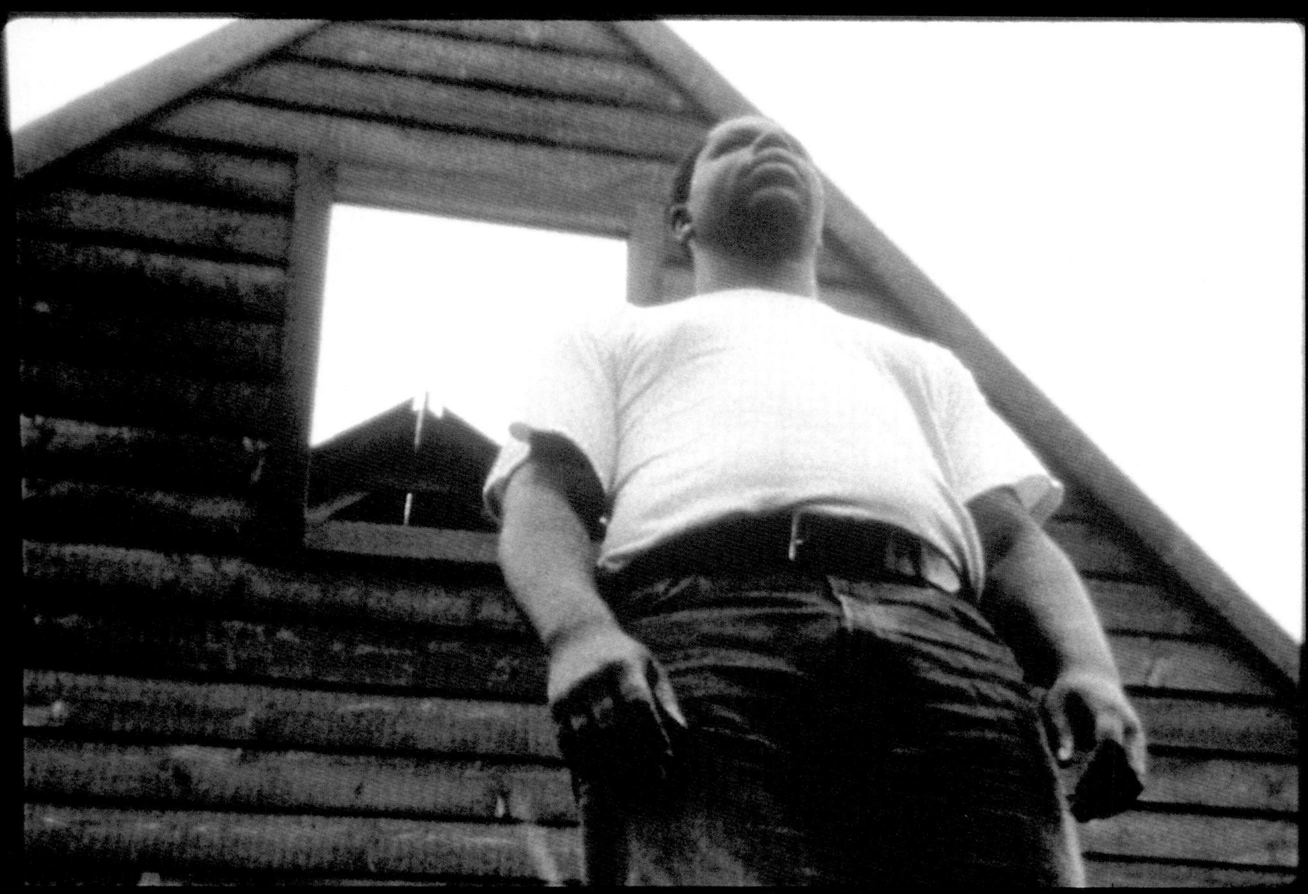

EIJA-LIISA AHTILA

ANNE, AKI, AND GOD (1998)

+++++ The work of the Finnish artist Eija-Liisa Ahtila is infused with the themes of interiority, madness, and melancholy, which have traditionally characterized Nordic filmmaking and art. The spatial and filmic composition of the installation *Anne, Aki, and God* draws on Ahtila's work in film and performance, combining documentary and fictional narrative to create a complex inquiry into the nature of reality and insanity.

The installation emerged out of research into a true story, from which Ahtila planned to make a film. In the story, a young Finnish telecommunications engineer named Aki suddenly becomes reclusive and is eventually unable to leave his apartment. He begins to display the classic symptoms of schizophrenia, experiencing hallucinations and voices and seeing God in a vision above his bed. The central character in a series of imaginary people, places, and events he experiences daily is a fictitious girlfriend named Anne. In the blurring of reality and illusion, Aki imagines that Anne is real, and the relationship becomes the center of his life. The voices in Aki's head explain that all these events have already been filmed in his brain and that he is now watching them and should act according to the events he sees taking place.

The disjunction between hallucination and reality in Aki's experience is clearly demonstrated in the space of the installation, which is divided into two parts, one active, the other passive. In the passive space, an empty bed, a reading lamp, and five monitors are contained inside a large wooden structure symbolizing the boundaries of a domestic space. A large projection screen towers overhead, projecting two actors—one female, the other male—playing the role of God. The space, an abstraction of Aki's one-room apartment, becomes the symbolic site of his delusionary experiences, of which the large screen becomes the focus. The dual gender of God and the theatricality of the staged monologue emphasize God's metaphorical status. Aki's God has delusional thoughts, encourages Aki to see Anne, describes Aki's fate, and reflects on his/her existence.

The large projected image looks down onto the monitors around the bed, on which different actors deliver Aki's confessional dialogue with an unseen therapist, as he describes in lucid detail his hallucinatory relationship with Anne. Aki's presence is brought into the room at one theatrical remove, as a group of multiple personalities. The simultaneous delivery of the same lines by different voices, preventing the viewer from attaching identity to any single young man, underlines his schizophrenic state. The actors' pensive delivery—as well as the barely furnished, sparsely lit room in which they sit—evokes the psychologically charged interiority of Ingmar Bergman's films. The empty bed suggests the nineteenth-century Nordic leitmotiv of sickness, depicted by artists such as Edvard Munch, which

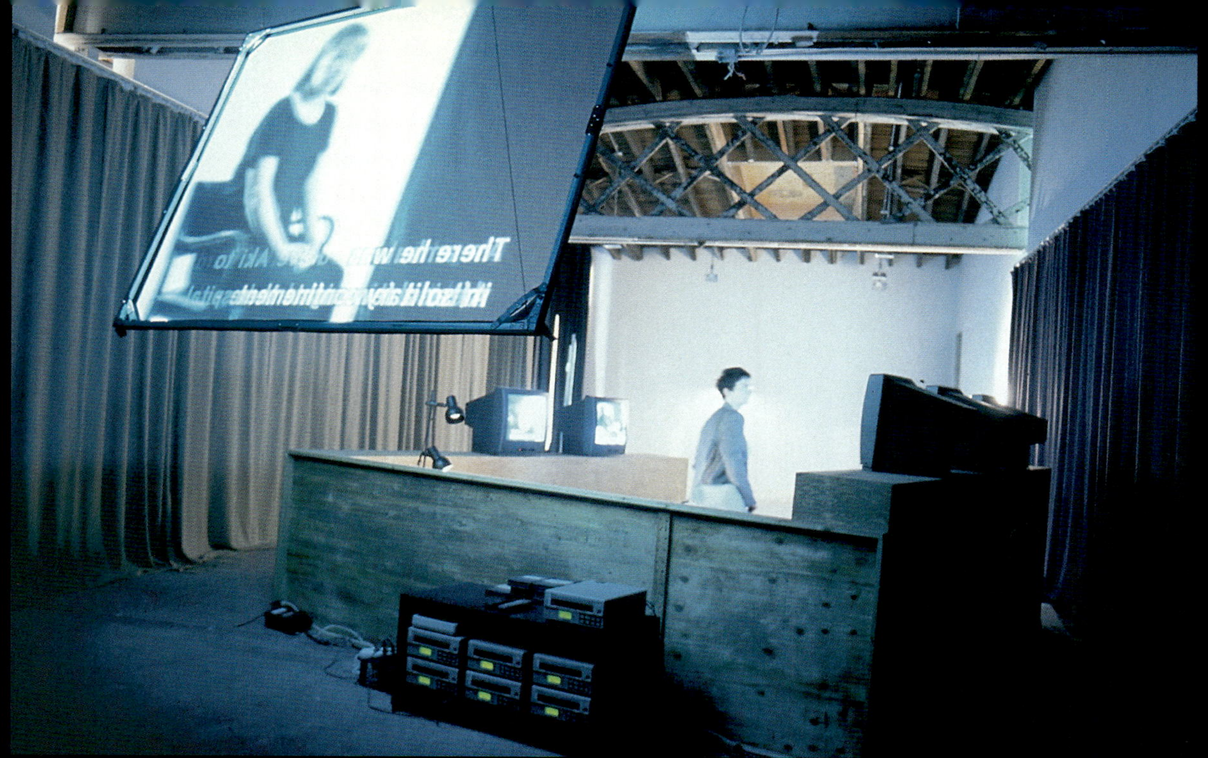

became associated with hallucination, delirium, and spiritual experiences. It also invites the passive, psychoanalytic receptiveness that allows the patient to verbalize repressed thoughts.

In the second, "active" space of the installation, a domestic chair, reading lamp, and side table are placed opposite a large, freestanding projection screen, showing segments of real interviews with young Finnish women applying to play the role of Aki's imaginary girlfriend, Anne. The documentary nature of these interviews, in which the women outline their reasons for wanting to play the role and give their interpretations of Anne's personality, ground this space in everyday reality, in stark contrast to the fictional, hallucinatory space of the adjacent area. In a reversal of the classic stereotype of the female as hysteric, the unstable, delirious male is placed in opposition to the stable, caretaking female.

In contrast to the fragmentation between bed, monitors, and screen in Aki's symbolic room, this "female" space is unified; there is one single image of different voices saying different things, rather than several voices representing the same person. The position of the seated women being interviewed, one by one, on the screen is mirrored by the live presence of the woman who was finally chosen to play Anne, who sits in the chair opposite for the duration of the piece's presentation and answers viewers' questions. The unusual experience of a live presence as part of an installation emphasizes both the reality of the women on screen and the documentary basis of this part of the installation. Ahtila interweaves the charge of live performance with the fictional and documentary modes of filmmaking, creating a multilayered spatial narrative that deconstructs both the anguish of insanity and the thin line between imagination, hallucination, and reality.

Plate 68
EIJA-LIISA AHTILA,
Anne, Aki, and God,
1998, installation view.

Overleaf:

Plate 69
EIJA-LIISA AHTILA,
Anne, Aki, and God,
1998, installation view.

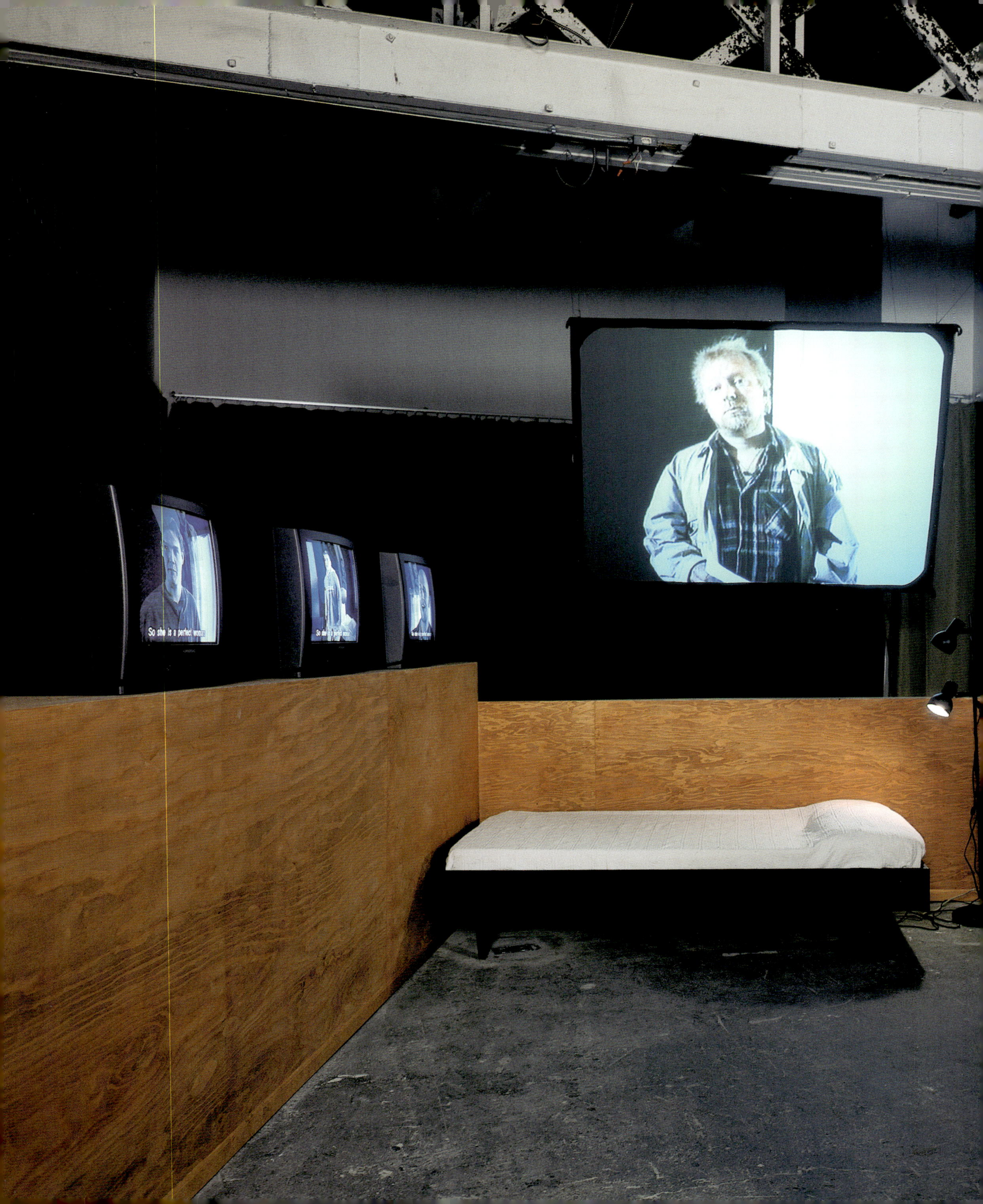
So she is a perfect

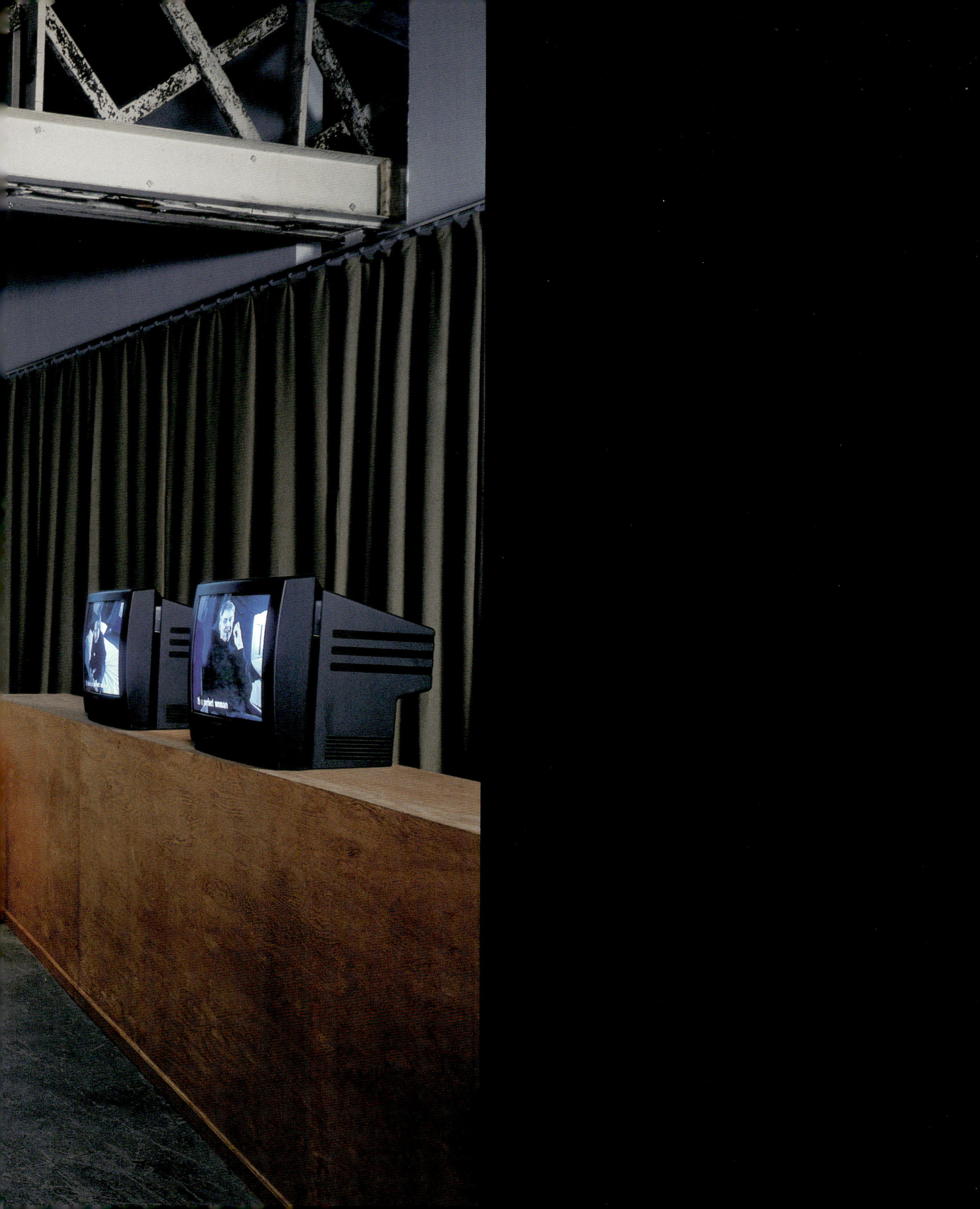
perfect woman

LARRY CLARK

NATE, G-STREET LIVE (1992)

+++++ For nearly thirty years the raw emotion and disturbing narratives of Larry Clark's photographs and films have created a painful portrait of an American teenagehood that appears to have changed little since his first images, made in the early 1960s and published in his first black-and-white photographic series, *Tulsa*, in 1972. The violence, drugs, and precocious sexual permissiveness that Clark portrays reflect his own unhappy late childhood and adolescence, which have sharpened his acute understanding of the vulnerability of the teenage mind.

Clark encountered the photographic possibilities of transference at an early age, when he became involved in his family's child photography business. During this early formal training, as Neville Wakefield has observed,[1] he learned how to make young people feel at ease in front of the camera. In his subsequent photographic series, his understanding of formal composition and lighting was used to capture the sadness, debauchery, and pain of a group of teenagers whose lives reflected the problems and abjectness of his own. Clark's subjects have always included boys and girls, but it is his portraits of teenage boys that exude the greatest intensity.

Nate, G-Street Live is the latest of a series of works involving groups of adolescent boys, pictured in all their awkwardness, uncertainty, and immaturity. In contrast to Clark's previous work, this piece presents a less extreme, more ordinary teenage angst, juxtaposing it with an example of the civilized veneer adopted by a teenager in polite, public conversation with an adult in a position of authority. Clark has taken both these aspects of contemporary teenagehood directly from television, and re-presents them in the gallery in a casual format that—like his other work made after 1990, which includes presentations of newspaper and teen fanzine clippings and television images—marks a radical shift from his earlier, more formally composed black-and-white photographic portraits. *Nate, G-Street Live* operates in sharp contrast to his more recent film, *Kids* (1996), in which the extremes of his earlier photography are brought to a disturbing new level in a radical cinematic narrative.

In *Nate, G-Street Live*, thirty-six domestic color photographs of a young teenager named Nate are attached to the wall, unframed, as if they had just been collected from a one-hour photo shop. The structure of the piece reflects Clark's interest in moving away from the single, crafted image, not only toward the cinematic but also toward a more general engagement with popular culture media consumed by adolescents, in this case, public-access television. The crudely made and presented images have all been taken directly from a television screen, showing a local New York public-access television program, *G-Street Live*.

Nearby, a monitor on a pedestal shows a videotape of one program, in which a group of adolescent boys in the television studio field questions, insults, invitations for dates, messages of support, and aggressive comments from an unseen audience of peers, mainly male, telephoning in live. Clark has edited the tape to focus on Nate, who sits awkwardly in the front row, one of four boys who receive the majority of the viewers' attention. By focusing on his image in close-up, Clark breaks down the already poor-quality television image even further, creating a blurred electronic surface. The four boys respond passively to the jibes and jokes, laughing awkwardly. Both sides know that the mediating device of live phone-in television allows everyone a degree of protection that a direct confrontation would not.

In the second part of the tape, a short loop shows a teenage boy being interviewed by a local Los Angeles newscaster, who asks him about his career ambitions. In an oblique reference to an unknown event, the newscaster begins by saying, "So, good things have come from misfortune," to which the boy replies, "Yes." In contrast to the previous crude and often insulting footage, the boy responds politely to the newscaster's questions, explaining that he has been accepted by an all-star wrestling team and is applying to college. This redemptive sequence suggests a depiction of Clark's other, teenage self—a glimpse of the direction he could have taken, and perhaps could still take. In Clark's role as what Wakefield has described as unofficial spokesman for an age group from which he is separated by a generation,[2] his most revealing statement is that of his own desire for self-transcendence.

1. NEVILLE WAKEFIELD, "Lost Youth," *Vogue*, October 1993, 258.

2. Ibid.

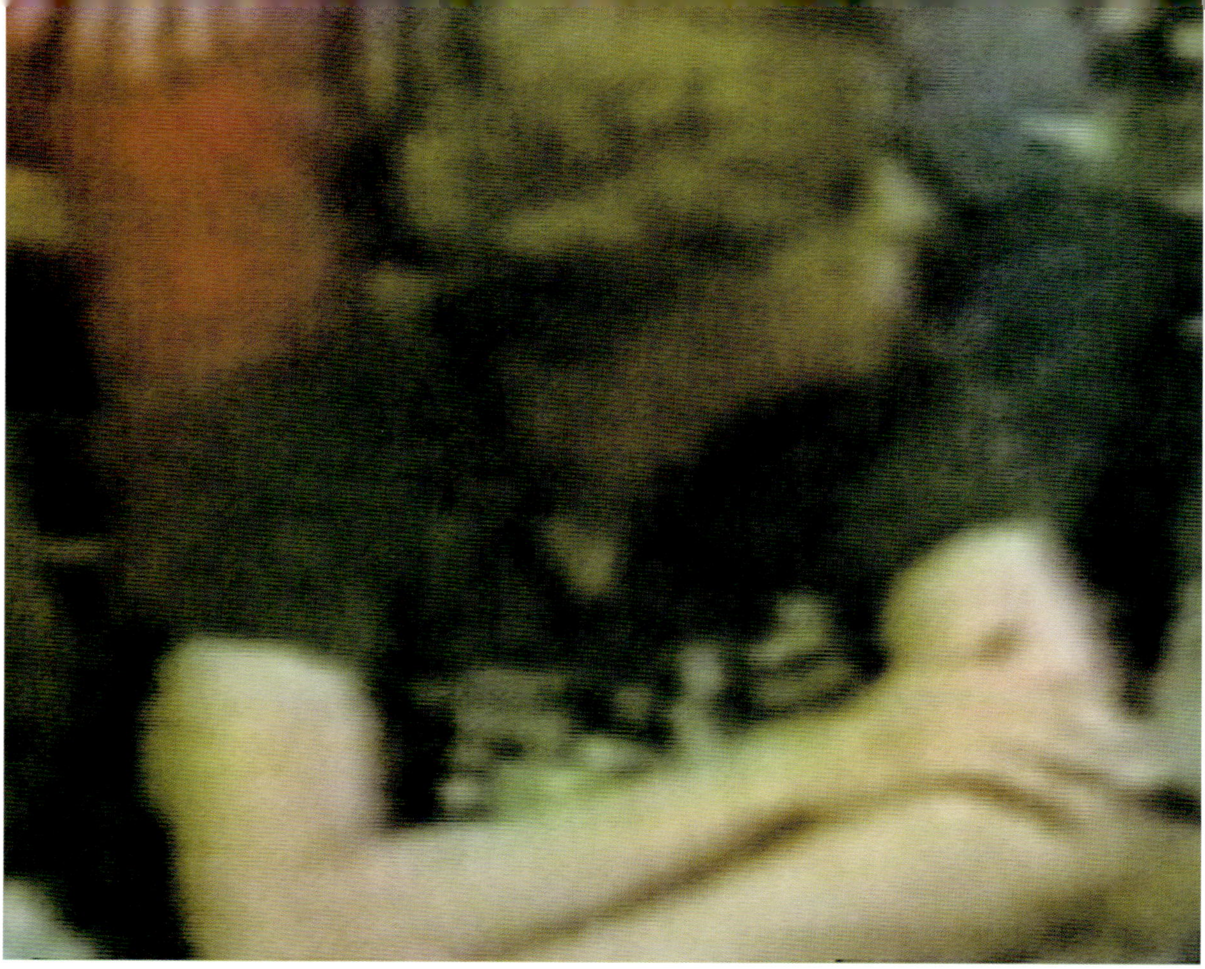

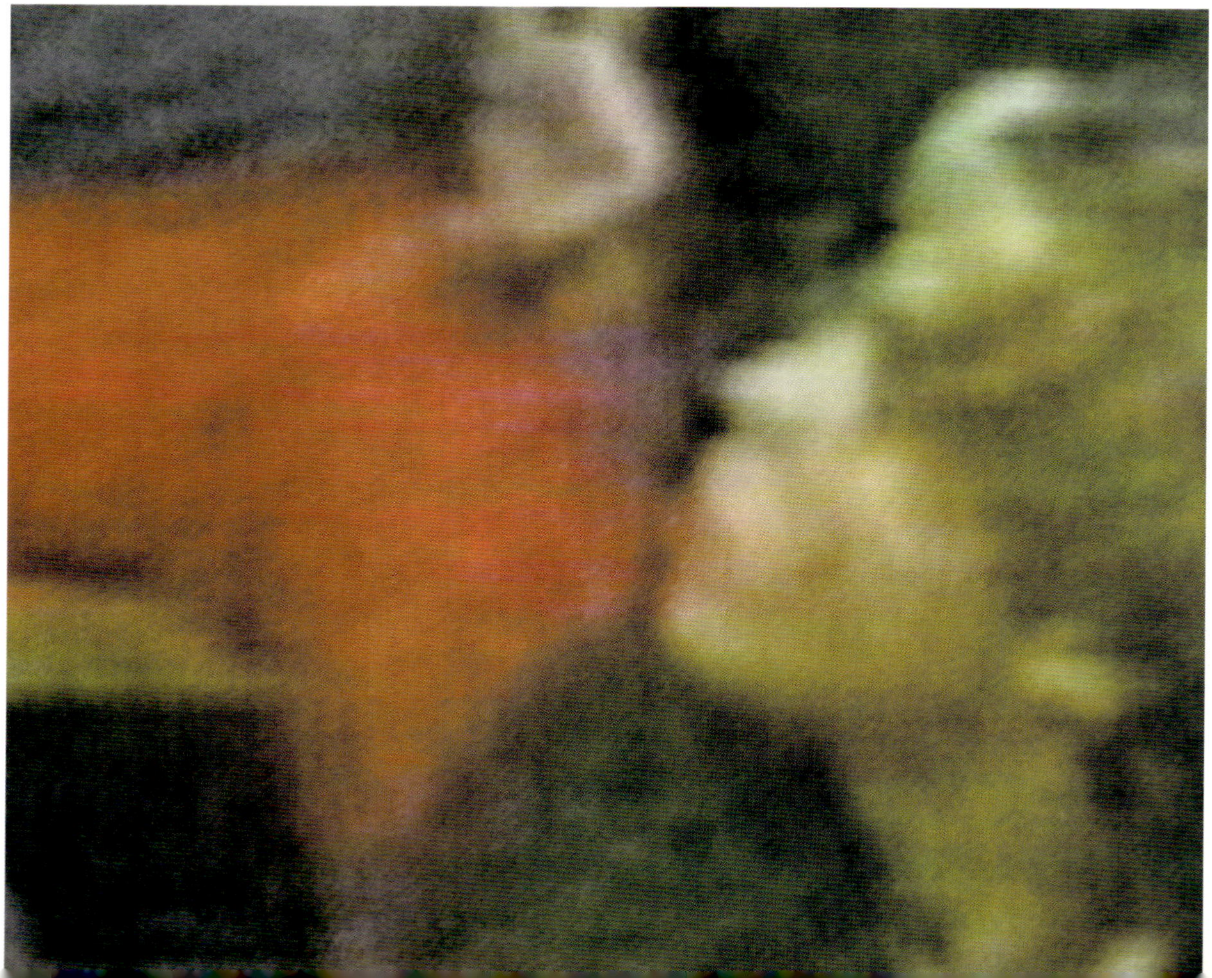

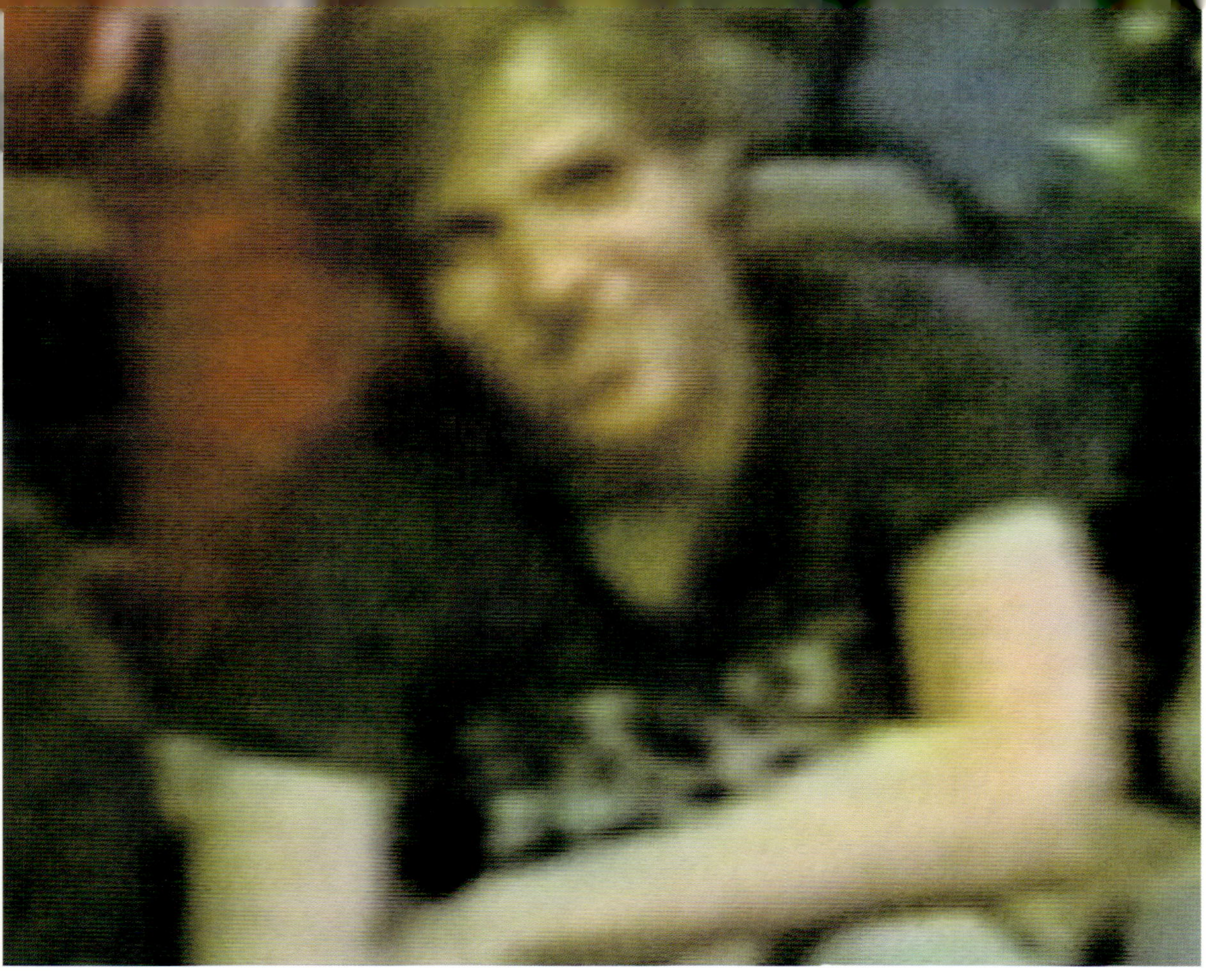

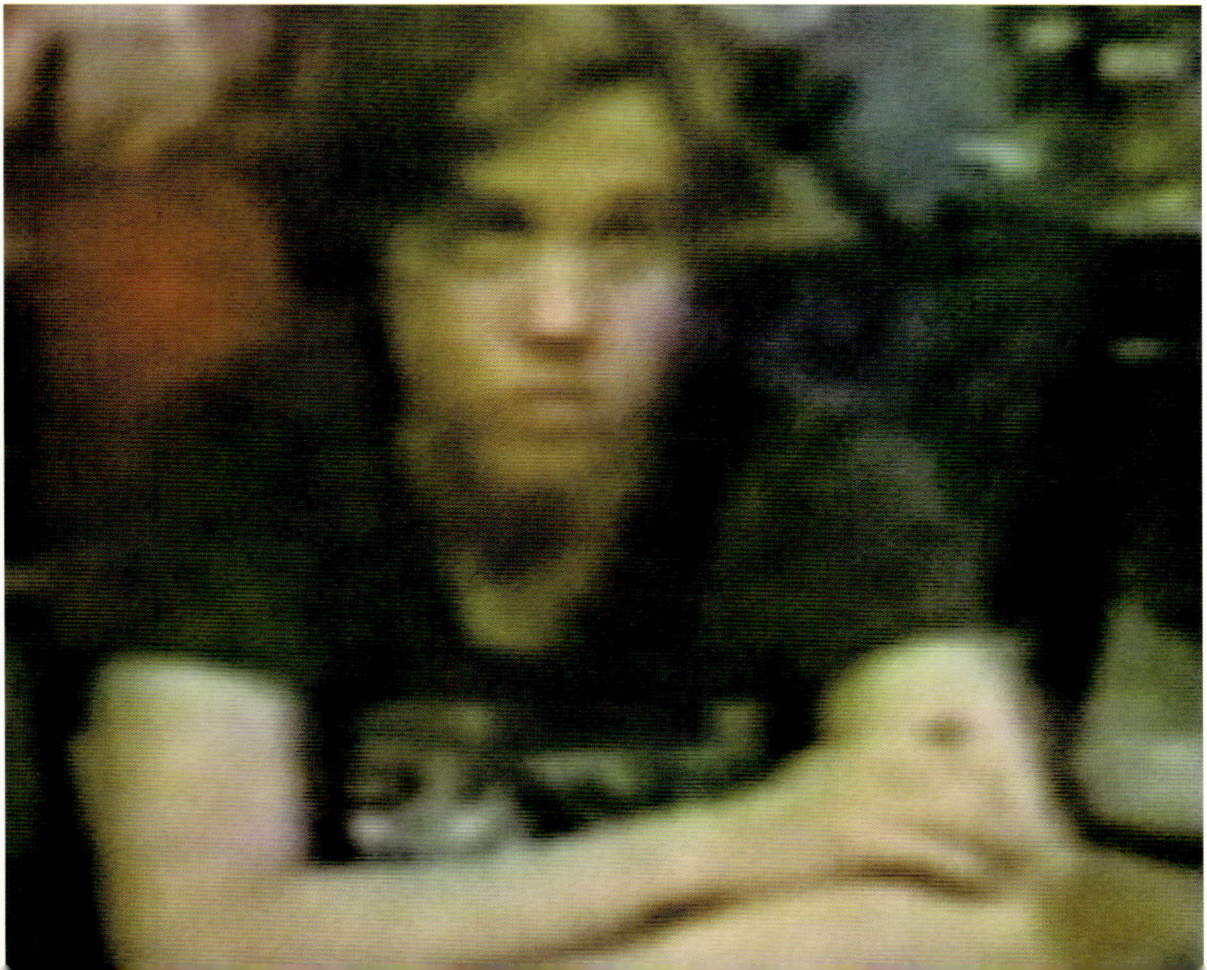

Plates 70–73

LARRY CLARK,

Nate, G-Street Live,

1992, video stills.

VITO ACCONCI

PORNOGRAPHY IN THE CLASSROOM (1975)

+++++ During the 1960s and early 1970s American art was transformed by a climate of radical experimentation, influenced by new psychological and social theories, sexual liberation, and political rebellion. Vito Acconci was a pivotal figure in a group of artists whose work in performance, body art, video, sound, and installation during this period redefined the parameters of art.

Pornography in the Classroom belongs to a group of installations Acconci made in the mid-1970s, after he stopped working with performance. Its title refers both to the grounding of Acconci's work in writing, literature, and language and to his subversive use of sexual content to destabilize the viewer and disrupt the repressive social order, for which the classroom functions as a metaphor. Acconci's mutation of the classroom into the gallery—which, for him, operated as a "general structure," "training room," or "framework for meaning"—suggests the construction of an alternative social structure.

Language, in spoken and written form, is inserted into the gallery "framework" as a parody of the ordering system.[1] Eighty slides are projected into one corner of the darkened gallery, showing a blackboard on which titles of books appear one after the other, in alphabetical order, written in white chalk capital letters. The books cover topics that were of deep importance to Acconci's thinking and to the countercultural climate of the 1970s: psychology and social science (*Transcultural Psychiatry*, *Sociology as a Skin Trade*, *Identification and Projection*), philosophy (*The Dialectical Imagination*, *The Negativity of Reality*), radical politics (*A Manual for Direct Action*, *Society against the State*), and linguistics (*Language as a Symbolic Action*, *The Sociology of Mass Communication*). These titles represent a body of thinking about the redefinition of the self and society. Their collective presence, a kind of alternative syllabus for the classroom, reflects Acconci's deep interest in semiotics and the role of language in the production of meaning.

Inserted after every nine titles are single words in red, expressing strong emotions—*fear*, *desire*, *frustration*, *envy*, *anger*, *hate*, *detachment*, *will*—all indirect subjects of many of the book titles. Projected in the opposite corner of the room are large color close-up images of naked women's bodies, resembling stills from a pornographic movie, which are arguably the focus of the conflicted emotions expressed in red on the opposite wall. In front of the projected images, a small monitor on the floor displays an erect penis in black-and-white, which appears every thirty seconds, rising vertically toward the image, as Acconci's voice shouts, "Help me, I'm drowning.... Land ho!"

The conflicted emotions expressed by the words in red, the comical presentation of the small male organ encountering the large erotic image, and

1. KATE LINKER, "Locating the Self: Installation Art in the 1970s," in *Vito Acconci* (New York: Rizzoli, 1994), 72.

2. Ibid., 15.

Plate 74
VITO ACCONCI, *Pornography in the Classroom*, 1975, video still.

Overleaf:

Plate 75
VITO ACCONCI, *Pornography in the Classroom*, 1975, sampling of projected images.

the ambiguous fear and pleasure in Acconci's sensation of drowning in the erotic, maternal body, all suggest a sense of emotional and sexual confusion and inadequacy before the female. Acconci's relationships with women, and his often disturbing feelings about intimate emotional and sexual issues, became subject matter for his work. The projection of his inner anxieties outward became a strategy for defining the self, using the personal for impersonal ends.

The juxtaposition of sexual space with a space of learning also suggests a blurring of the boundary between public and private (domestic, intimate, erotic) space, a theme that many artists explored during this period. (Acconci's provocative performance *Seedbed* [1972] became a landmark of this genre.) The late 1960s saw a reform of censorship laws, which brought pornographic film into the open for the first time. Acconci's reference to pornography reflects both the importance of sexual freedom in 1970s counterculture and his interest in the increasing power of the media, of which pornography was rapidly becoming a part, in shaping American identity.

On a more abstract level, the symmetry of the piece underlines Acconci's analogy between the body and a word system. The spatial split between the body and language reflects the underlying semiotic nature of much body art. The gallery space was regarded as a perceptual field, onto which, as Kate Linker has observed, the human subject was mapped in space and time.[2] Within this structure Acconci reveals the self to be fragmented, split, divided. *Pornography in the Classroom* epitomizes the profound transition in American culture that took place in the 1960s and early 1970s, from the coherent unity of the heroic modernist "I" to the decentered, fragmented, postmodern self.

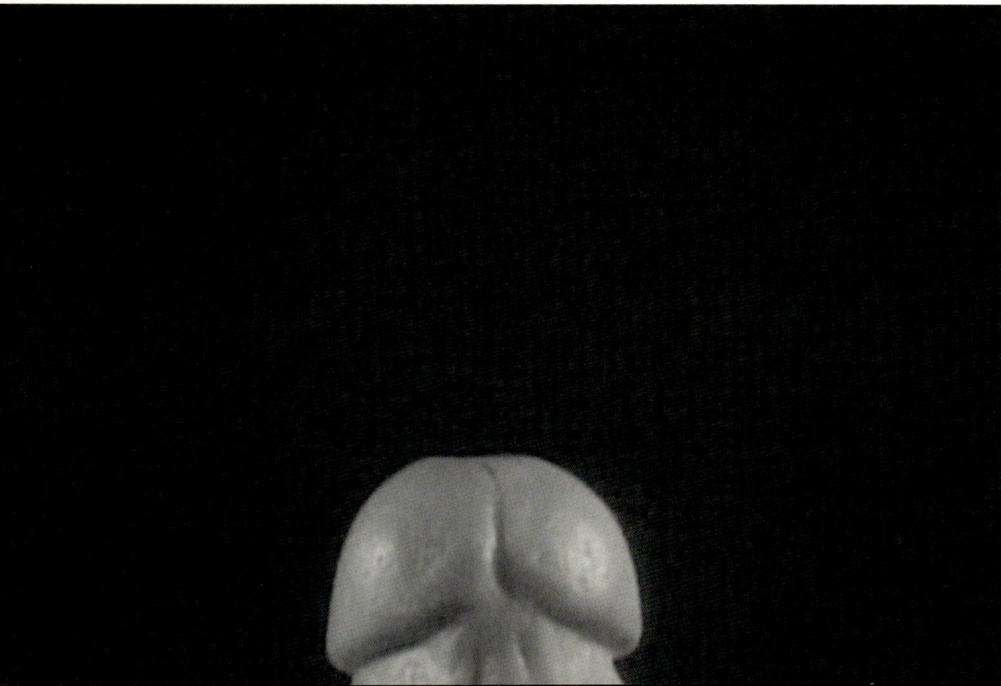

AT THE EDGE OF HISTORY

AWARENESS AND EMANCIPATION

BODY IMAGE AND PERSONALITY

THE BODY POLITIC

THE CIVILIZING PROCESS

CONFLICT IN MAN-MADE ENVIRONMENT

CONFLICT IN MAN-MADE ENVIRONMENT

CRITICAL THEORY AND PUBLIC LIFE

CRITIQUE OF TASTE

FEAR

CULTURE AND COMMITMENT

DESIGN FOR A BRAIN

DESIGNS AND DEVICES

DESIGNS AND DEVICES

DESIGNS AND FABRICATIONS

THE DIALECTICAL IMAGINATION

DRAMAS, FIELDS & METAPHORS

THE ECLIPSE OF REASON

ESTRANGEMENT AND EMBODIMENT

DESIRE

EXPERIENCES IN GROUPS

THE EXPRESSION OF EMOTIONS IN MEN & ANIMALS

THE GOVERNMENTAL ARM

THE GRAMMAR OF MOTIVES

GUERILLA STRATEGIES

THE HISTORY OF BOURGEOIS PERCEPTION

A HISTORY OF THE END OF THE WORLD

OBJECTIVE REVOLUTIONARY SITUATIONS
ORGANIC SOLIDARITY
PERCEPTION AND ACTION
ANGER
THE PRESENTATION OF SELF IN EVERYDAY LIFE
THE PHYSICAL BASIS OF INTELLIGENT LIFE
THE POETICS OF MURDER
PRIVATE TROUBLES & PUBLIC ISSUES
A MANUAL FOR DIRECT ACTION
ENVY
THE MIND OF A MNEMONIST
THE MOLECULAR REVOLUTION
THE MYTH OF MENTAL ILLNESS
THE NAVEL OF THE WORLD
THE NEGATIVITY OF REALITY
NORMATIVE RATIONALITY
LANGUAGE AS SYMBOLIC ACTION
LEGITIMATION CRISIS
THE LIMITS OF INFINITY
LOGIC MACHINES
IDOLS OF THE TRIBE
INTERACTION RITUAL
KNOWLEDGE AND HUMAN INTERESTS
THE LANGUAGE OF THE SELF
IDENTIFICATION AND PROJECTION
FRUSTRATION
HUMAN TERRITORIES

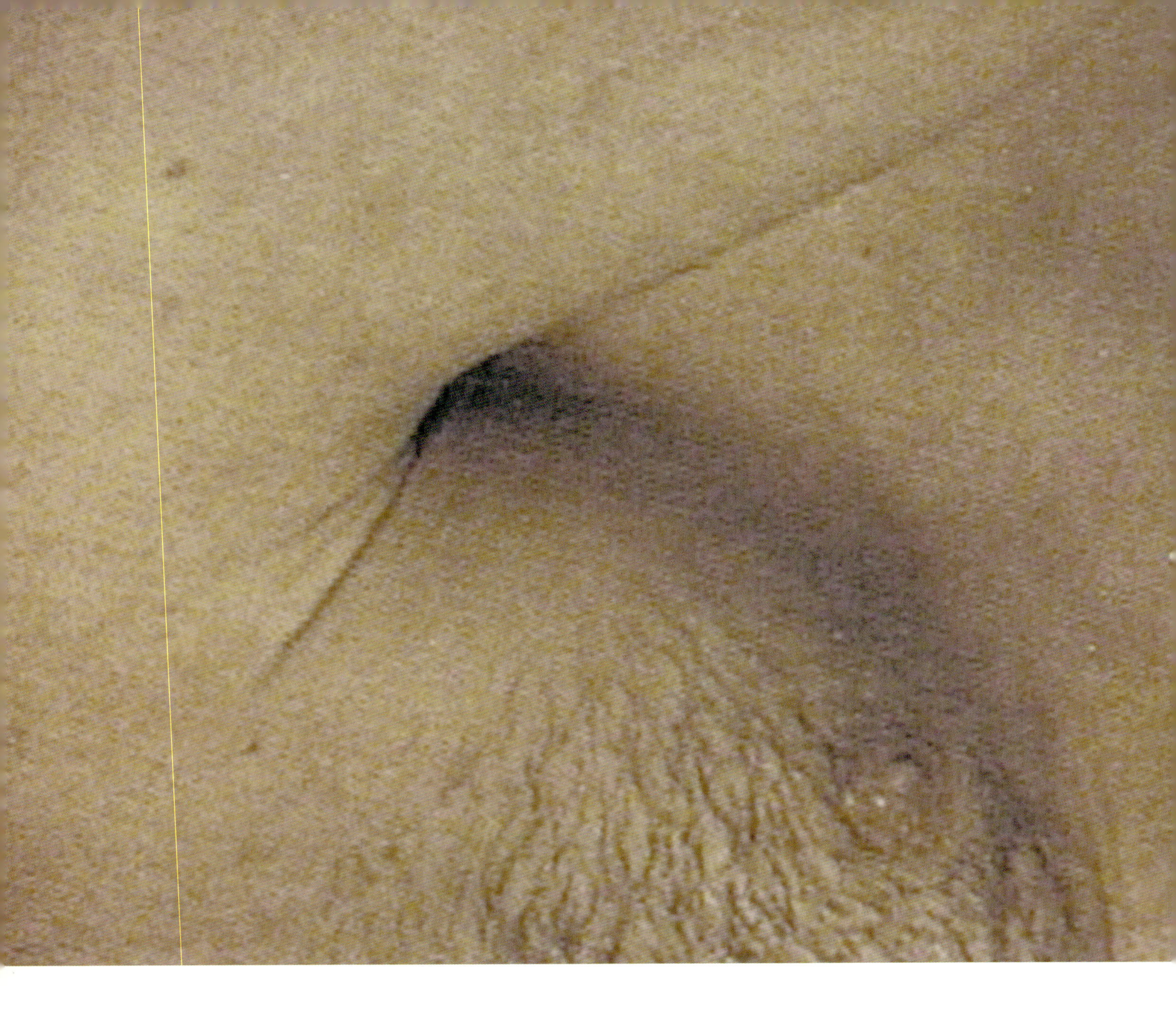

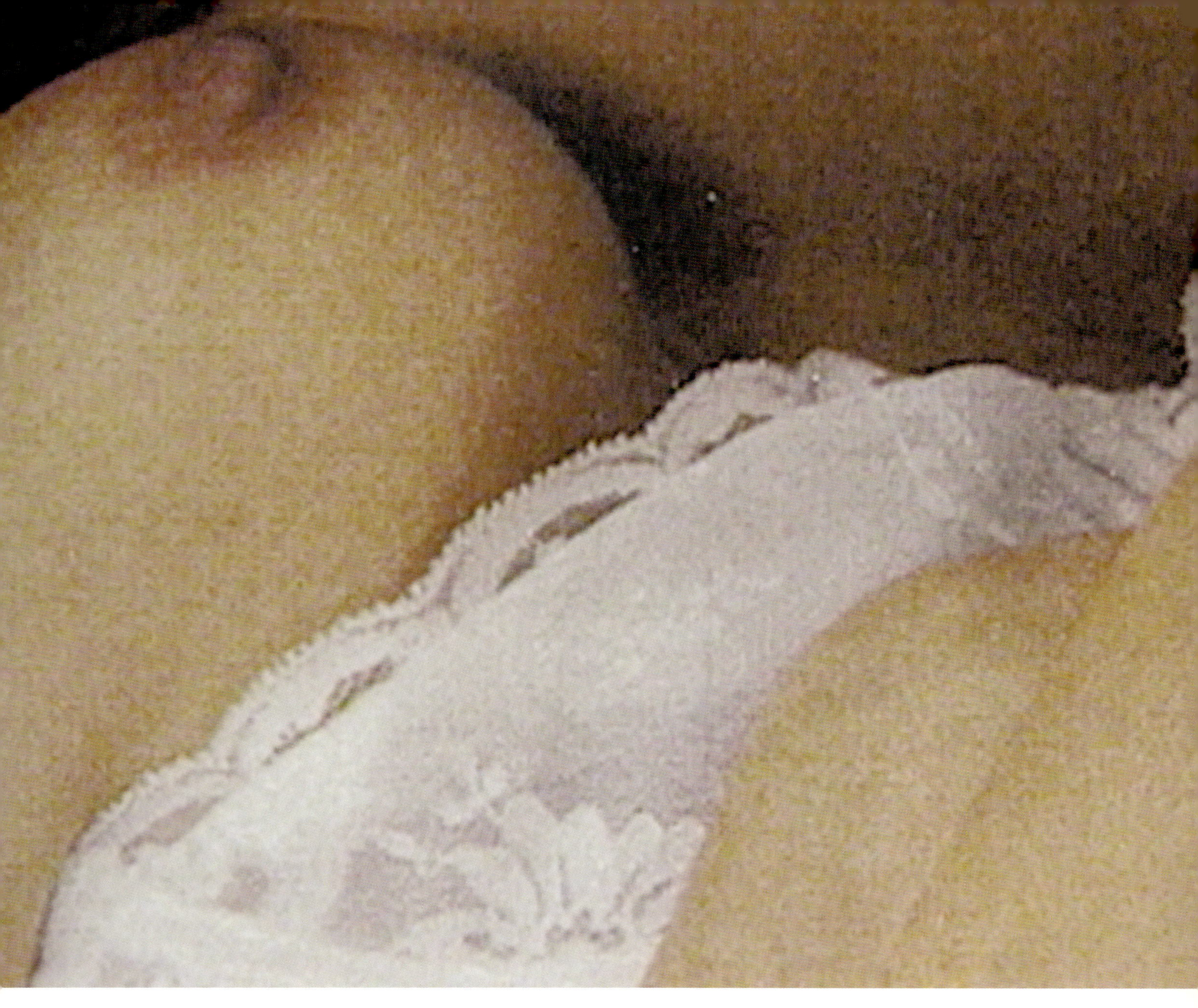

Plates 76–77

VITO ACCONCI,

Pornography in the Classroom,

1975, video stills.

STEPHANIE SMITH AND EDWARD STEWART

INTERCOURSE (1993)

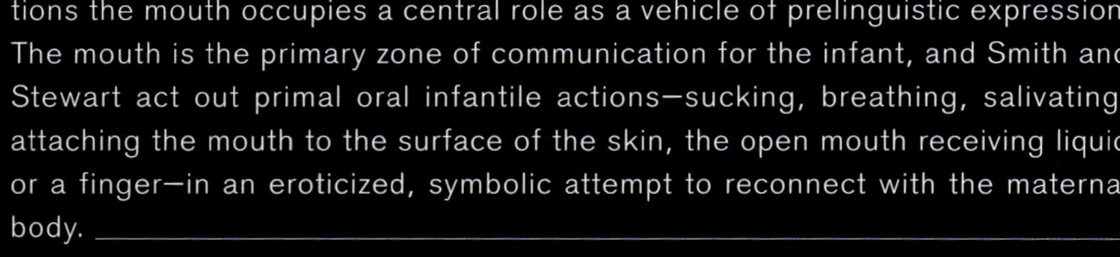

Plate 78

STEPHANIE SMITH AND EDWARD STEWART, *Intercourse*, 1993, installation view.

Overleaf:

Plate 79

STEPHANIE SMITH AND EDWARD STEWART, *Intercourse*, 1993, installation view.

+++++ In Smith and Stewart's video installations the mouth occupies a central role as a vehicle of prelinguistic expression. The mouth is the primary zone of communication for the infant, and Smith and Stewart act out primal oral infantile actions—sucking, breathing, salivating, attaching the mouth to the surface of the skin, the open mouth receiving liquid or a finger—in an eroticized, symbolic attempt to reconnect with the maternal body.

Smith and Stewart's emphasis on the mouth also reflects their strong interest in the work of Samuel Beckett, in particular pieces such as *Not I*, in which the mouth is the only visible part of the body, looming out of the darkness. Beckett's emphasis on the physicality of language, and its emanation from the body, is echoed in Smith and Stewart's focus on language as the starting point for each one of their pieces. Double-screen video projections such as *Intercourse* deal with the nonverbal language of sex and aggression. In *Intercourse*, Edward Stewart gathers spittle in his mouth on one screen, which is propelled into the open mouth of Stephanie Smith on the other. In this mimicking of sexual intercourse, both mouths become symbols of the male and female genitalia, engaged in the timeless erotic expression of submission and domination.

This expression is not only erotic; spitting at someone, in any culture, is one of the strongest acts of hatred and contempt. In many cultures spitting is also used as a sign of blessing and marking, and spittle is regarded as an internal bodily substance, which, like other internal corporeal liquids, can be put to ritual and magic use. In *Intercourse*, the mouth willingly held open shifts the meaning of the act into a binding erotic metaphor. The gap between the two screen images—and also, by implication, between the two bodies—suggests the artifice of a lovers' game, in which desire is sustained through withholding. As in *Sustain* (1995; pls. 80–82), *Mouth to Mouth*, *Breathing Space*, *Gag*, *Vent*, and *Finger*, the rhythm of regular breathing is interrupted by a repeated performative action by, or within, the mouth. *Intercourse* is perhaps the most gentle manifestation of this repeated intervention, which in other pieces contains a violent edge: a finger is stuffed into the mouth over cloth; both artists struggle to breathe inside plastic bags placed over their heads; one lies underwater, breathing out until the other replenishes him with new breath. The flirtation with obliteration implied by these extreme actions, repeated over time in each looped installation, suggests a resonance with the thinking of the French writer Georges Bataille, and a desire to push the erotic symbiosis of both artists to its farthest limits—beyond verbal language and beyond the boundary of conscious thinking.

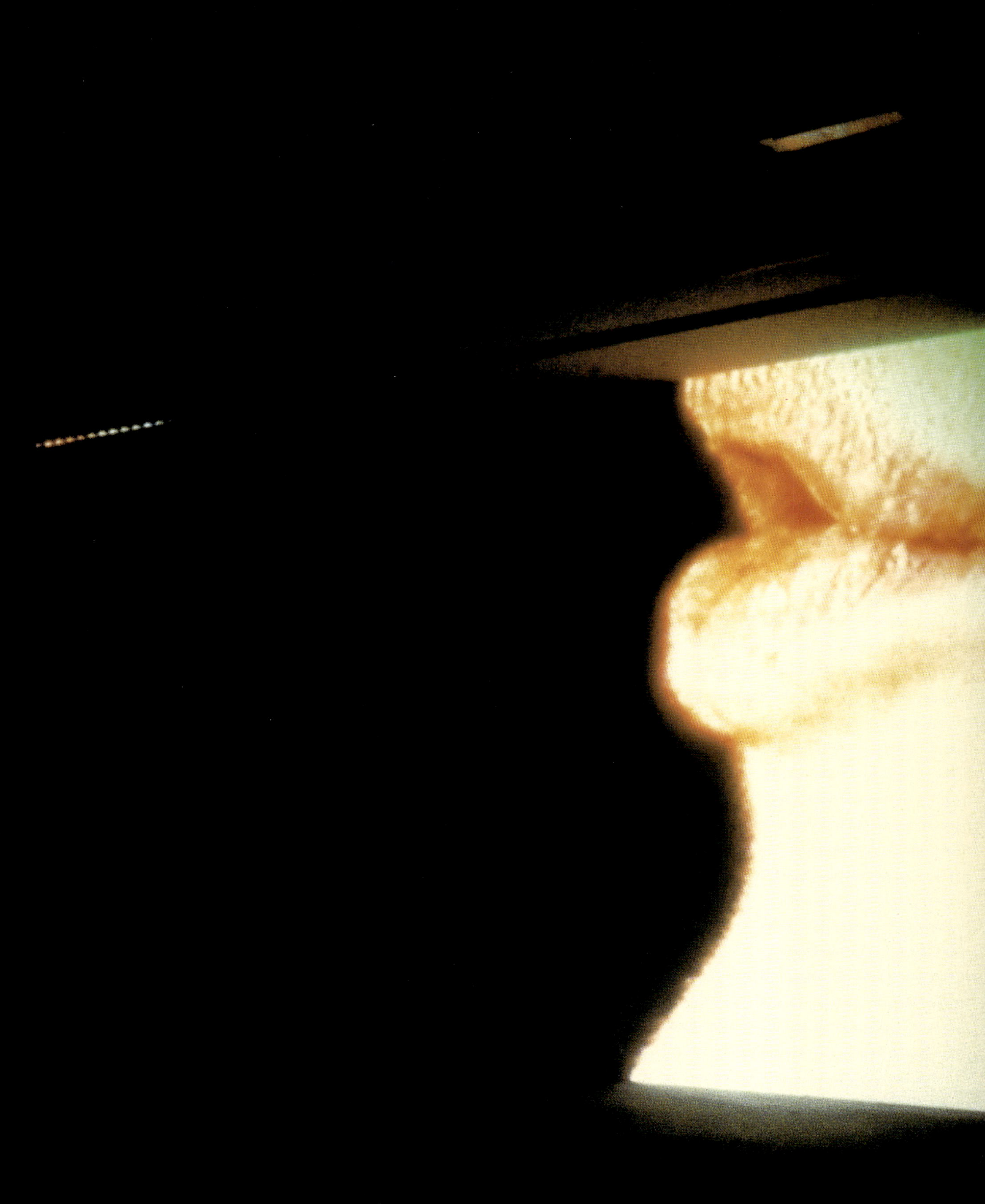

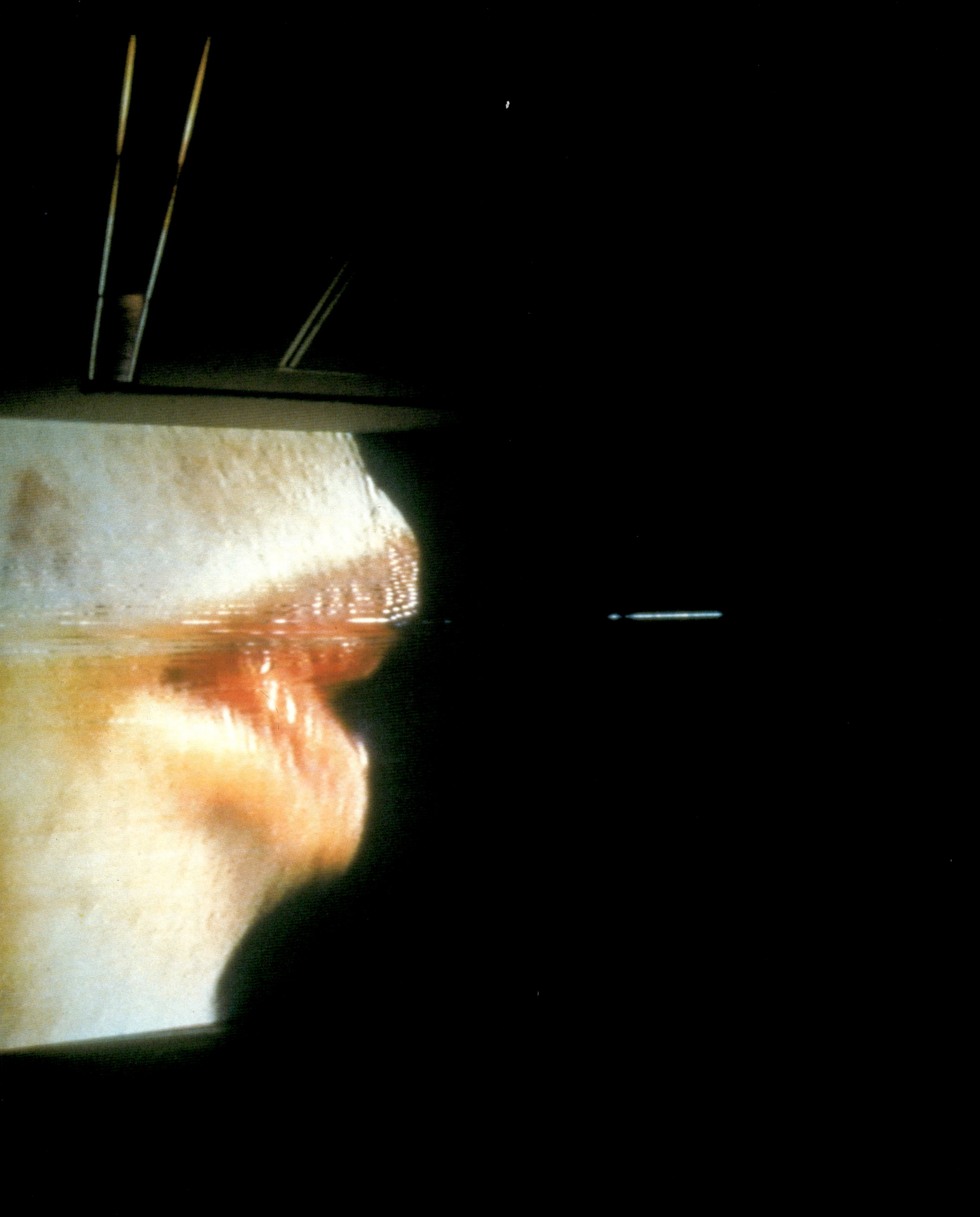

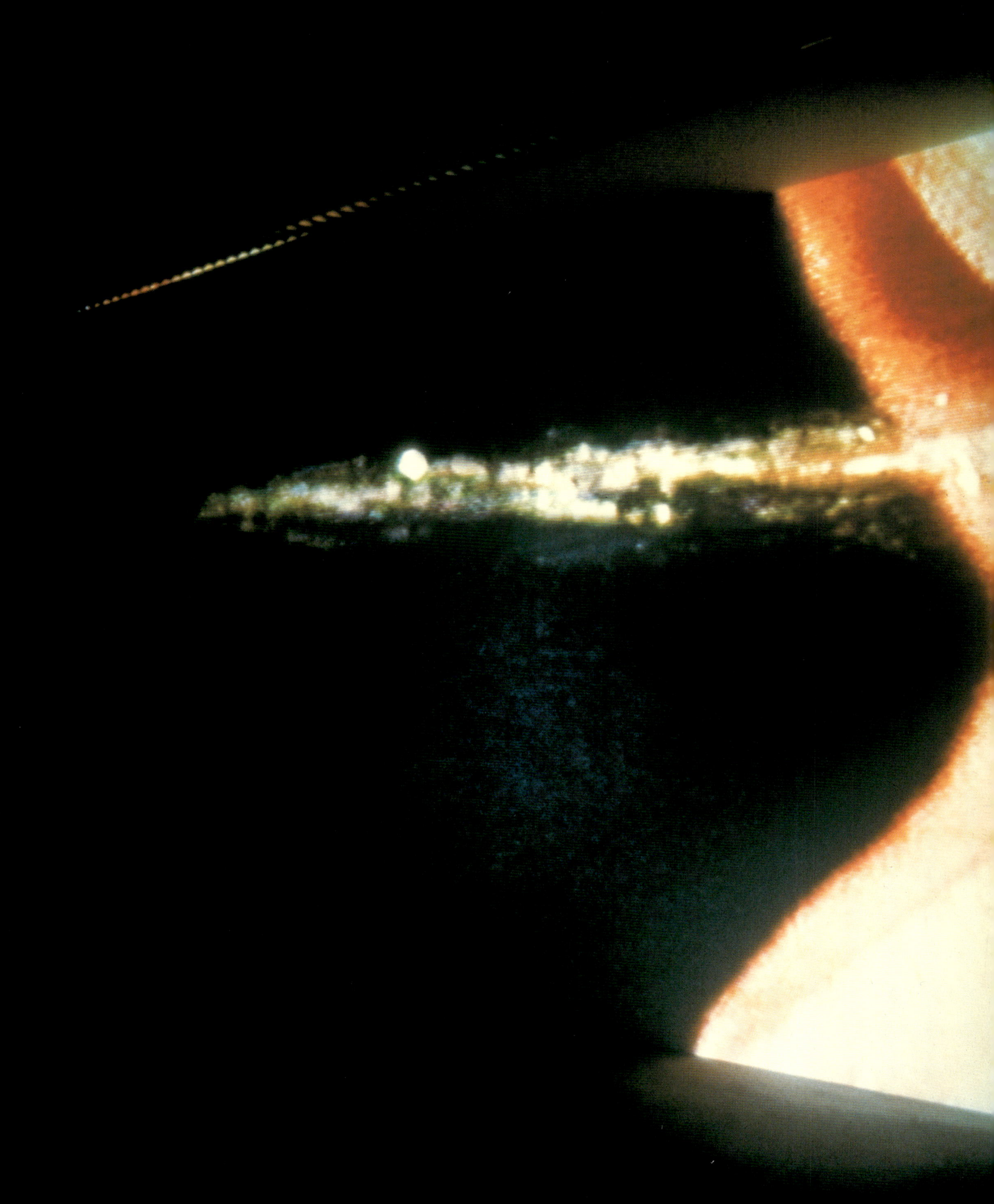

STEPHANIE SMITH AND EDWARD STEWART

SUSTAIN (1995)

+++++ Sigmund Freud described the double as insurance against the loss of the ego and a denial of the power of death—in other words, a narcissistic attempt to attain immortality. The work of Smith and Stewart, who have collaborated professionally and personally since 1992, is constructed around the axis of the double, or mirror image. In a series of double-screen performative video projection pieces, they use their own bodies, in particular the mouth, engaging in sadomasochistically inflected actions involving physical pain, emotional intensity, and duration.

In Smith and Stewart's work, video, which Rosalind Krauss famously described as intrinsically narcissistic because of its mirroring properties,[1] functions as a silent, voyeuristic witness to intimate acts. In *Sustain*, on one screen, Edward Stewart covers Stephanie Smith's body with lipstick kisses, while she covers his with painful love bites. This action evokes performative works of the 1970s, such as Vito Acconci's *Applications* (1970), in which Kathy Dillon, Acconci's partner and collaborator in many of his performances, lipstick-kisses Acconci's naked body, which he then rubs against a third party, Dennis Oppenheim, in a deflection of her affection. By contrast, Smith rewards Stewart's kisses with love bites, an aggressive, eroticized form of the same gesture, creating a circular structure of feedback. The power relationship expressed in *Applications* is reversed in *Sustain*, in which the female is the recipient of lipstick kisses from the male and is the deliverer of a painful erotic response.

On an adjacent screen, the reversed power relationship is echoed in a disturbing sequence in which Stewart lies, fully clothed, underwater in a bathtub, exhaling. When he reaches the limit of his oxygen, Smith leans over him and breathes new oxygen into his lungs. Smith and Stewart's exchange of breath evokes Marina Abramovic and Ulay's collaborative performance *Breathing In, Breathing Out* (1976), in which each artist breathed into the other's mouth until the oxygen was exhausted, creating a single, circular breathing action. There are superficial parallels between the collaborative work of Smith and Stewart and that of Marina Abramovic and Ulay, whose cathartic performances of the early 1970s—involving painful physical duration and an exchange of energy, breath, bodily fluids, and psychic concentration—attempted, through repeated doubling actions, to connect with the live audience and heal the alienated self. Yet pieces such as *Sustain* have a different temporal structure and meaning than the videotapes of these performances, which serve as documentation. In the color video installations, performative actions have been "staged" for the camera and can be experienced at any point by a viewer entering the space. In Smith and Stewart's work, sustained physical intensity is used to build an erotic charge, which becomes the subject of the piece, rather than moving viewer and artist live, at the same rate, through an extended temporal experience.

tes 80–81
STEWART,
Sustain,
ideo stills.

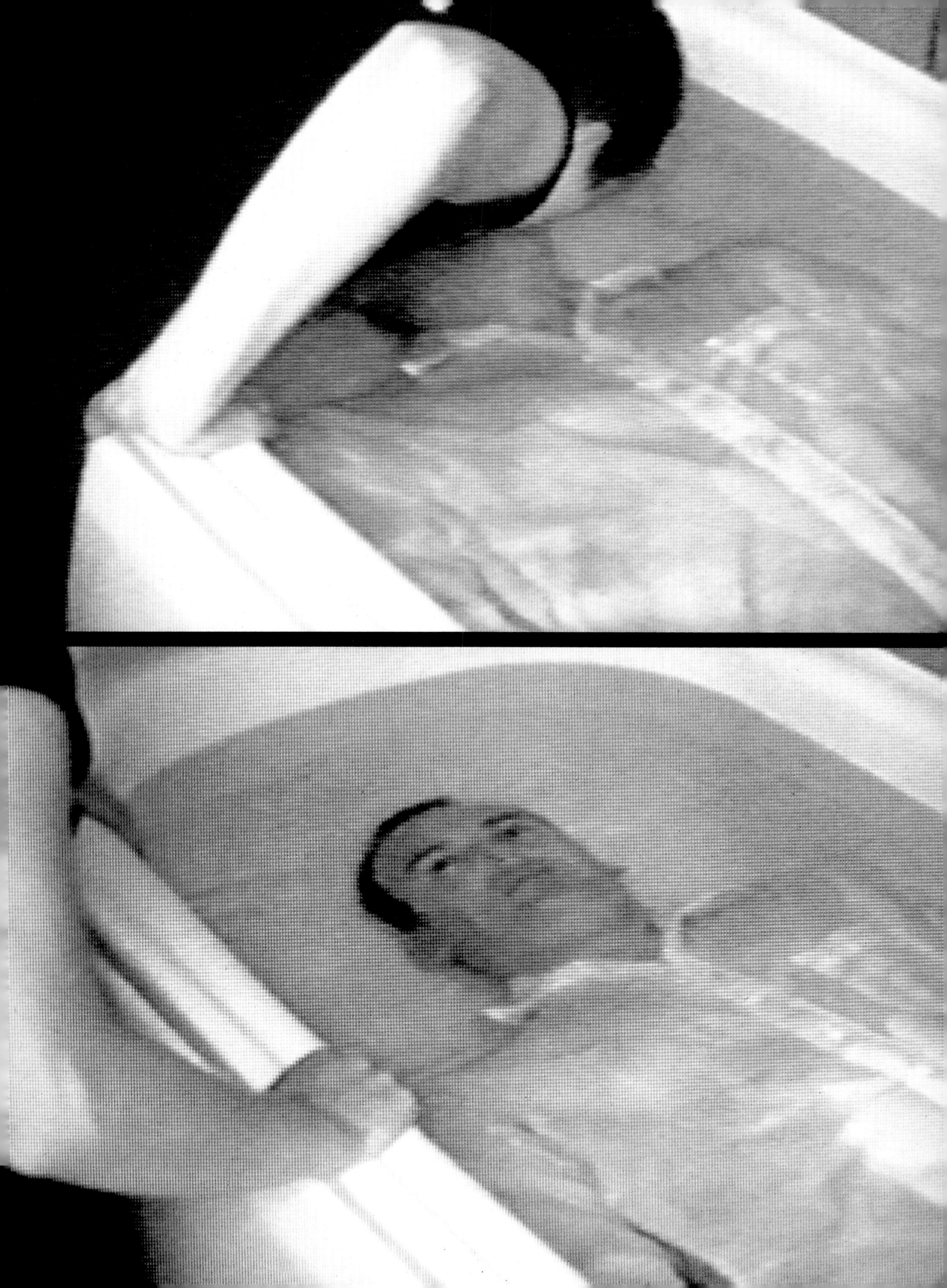

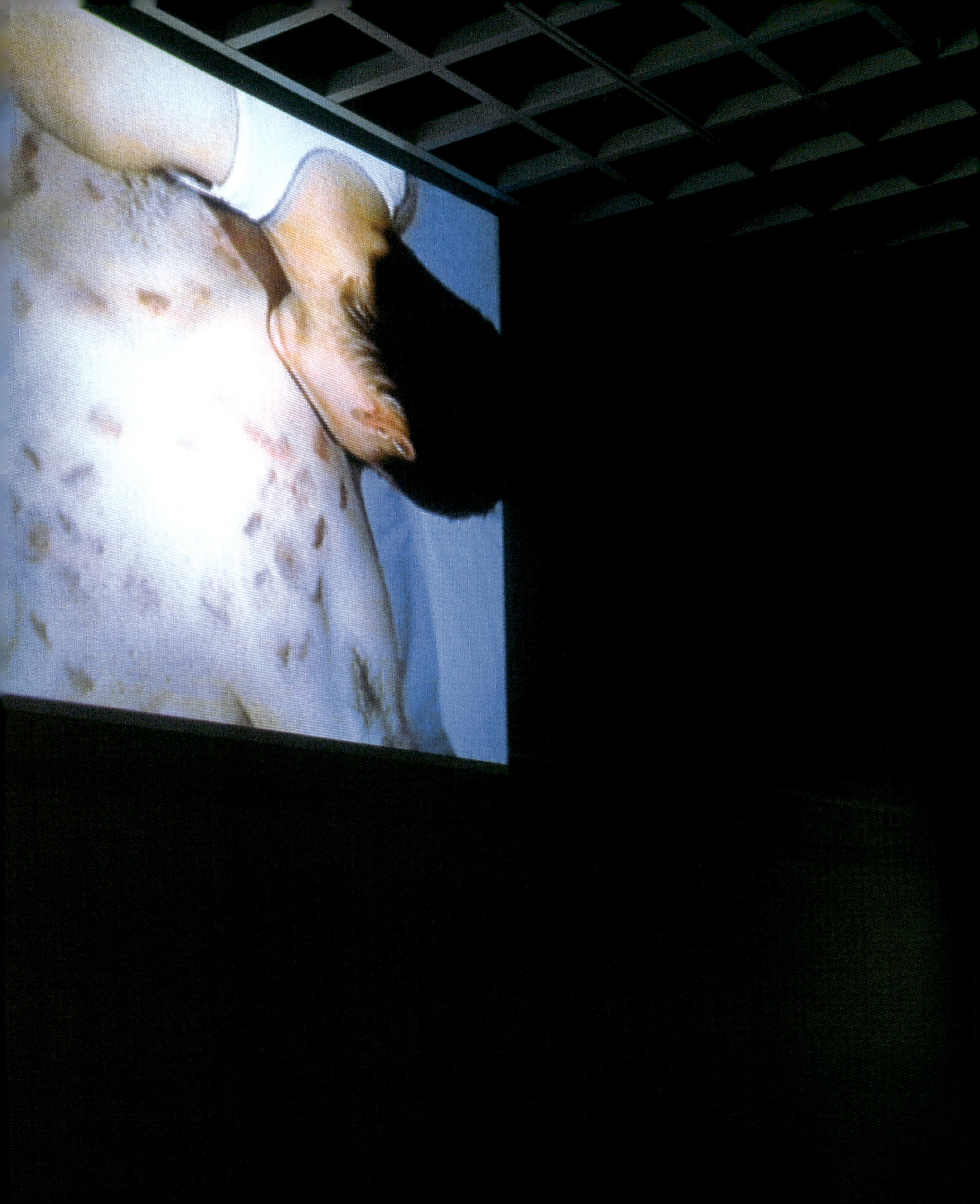

The title of *Sustain* addresses both Smith and Stewart's actions in kissing and breathing. In the repeated act of kissing, each literally and metaphorically smothers the other's body with lipstick and love bites, marking it, as if attempting to defy the ephemerality of desire. In Acconci's performance *Trademarks* (1970), he bit his body all over in an attempt to claim it for his own. The transference of this self-lesion to another in Smith and Stewart's work places the emphasis on the relationship to the other. The marking of the skin is a possessive act; the body becomes a page onto which the language of desire is written. The mouth becomes the pen, and the body the conduit of language, a word system of flesh. The masochistic tolerance of pain, and the sadism suggested by its infliction in return for gentle kisses, demonstrates the erotic underpinnings of all Smith and Stewart's work, in which the dualism of their doubled performative actions coheres into a kind of durational *petite mort.*

1. See ROSALIND KRAUSS, "Video: The Aesthetics of Narcissism," in *New Artists' Video: A Critical Anthology*, ed. Gregory Battcock (New York: Dutton, 1978), 43–63.

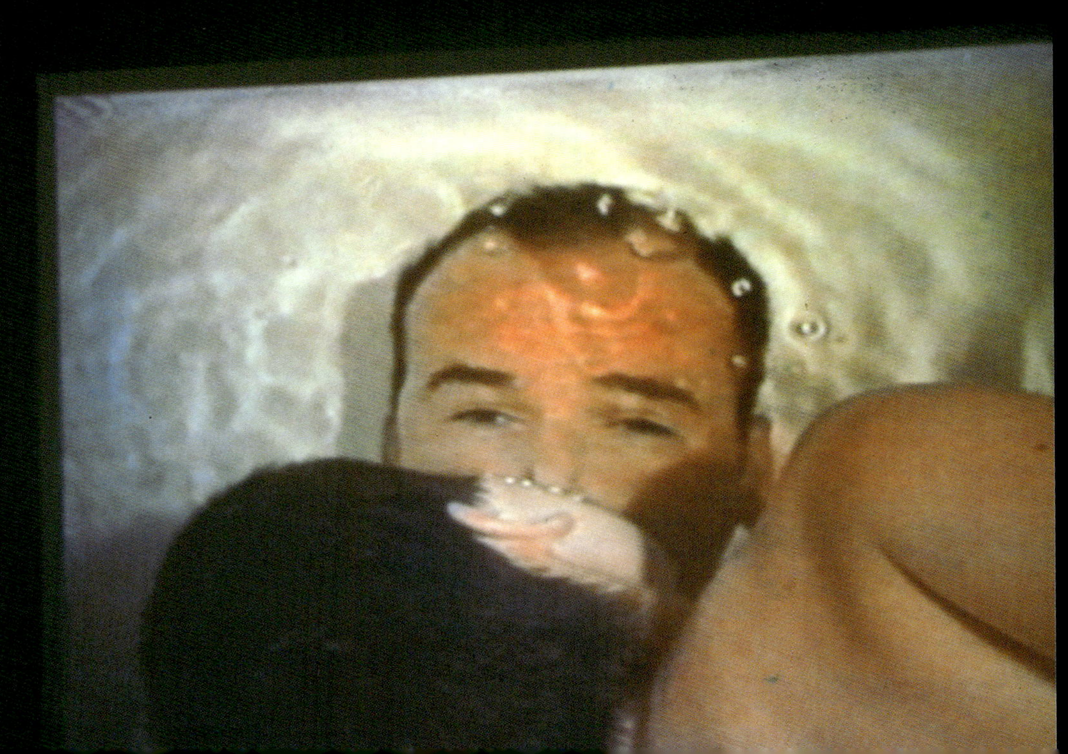

Plate 82
STEPHANIE SMITH AND EDWARD STEWART, *Sustain*, 1995, installation view.

MATTHEW BARNEY

SCABACTION
(1988)
CREMASTER IV: MANANNAN
(1994)
CREMASTER IV
(1994–95)
CREMASTER I
(1995–96)
CREMASTER V
(1997)

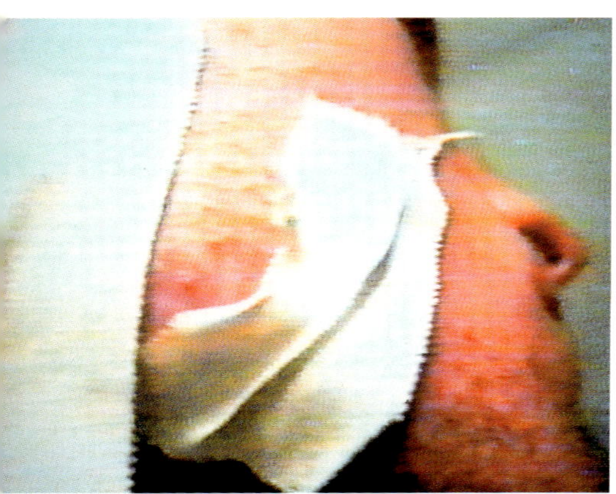

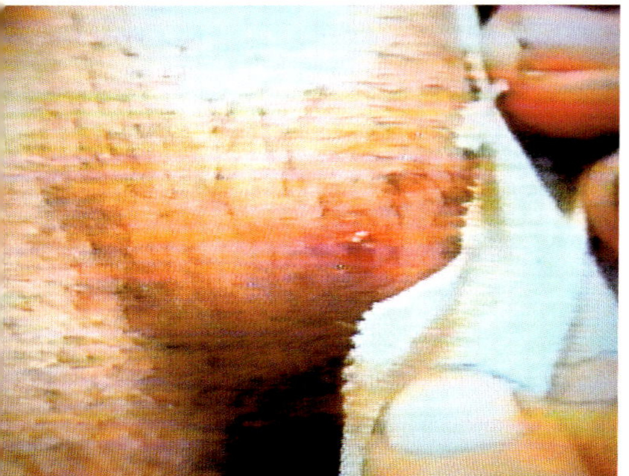

+++++ From his earliest work to his most recent *Cremaster* project, Matthew Barney has framed his desire to overcome the physical limitations of the body within an ambiguously erotic, artificial personal world, constructing a dreamlike, fantastical iconography drawn from Hollywood cinema, sport, science fiction, fetishism, cyberspace, medicine, and ancient mythology. Barney's preoccupation with the viscerality of the body transforms the earlier preoccupations of 1970s body art into a posthuman performative cinema, through the basic tenets of Mannerism: artifice, complexity, caprice, abstraction from natural behavior, "difficulta" (the notion of difficulty overcome), and bizarre fantasy. These sixteenth-century principles are given postmodern, cinematic form in a series of installations, sculptures, videotapes, and films deeply influenced by Hollywood, in particular the work of Busby Berkeley, David Cronenberg, and, most profoundly, the transformative, cosmic fictions of Stanley Kubrick.

Barney's Mannerist approach is made clearly evident in *Scabaction* (1988), an early installation in which the artist, as always, performs for the camera. A video monitor chronicles Barney in close-up, identifying an irritation on his skin, carefully making an incision with a razor, and treating the wound with Vaseline and a gel pack. Intercut with this imagery, a parallel narrative shows a bag of water, attached to a metal plate and filled with oxygen, being opened by a blowtorch and welded closed. In twelve drawings presented in a vertical row opposite the video monitor, the gradual formation of Barney's scab is charted.

Plates 83–84
MATTHEW BARNEY,
Scabaction,
1988, video stills.

Opposite:

Plates 85–88
MATTHEW BARNEY,
Scabaction,
1988, mixed-media drawings.

The *Scabaction* sequences mark the beginning of a recurring metaphor that dominates Barney's subsequent *Cremaster* series: opening (penetration) and closing (thin membranes covering an orifice, rupture, or hole, sometimes containing liquid or bodily fluids), suggesting simultaneously an erotic, aggressive, and regenerative impulse. The real and symbolic open wounds and slippery, oozing surfaces, which have become a signature element in Barney's work, transform an earlier, Beuysian performative symbolism of shamanic healing, using natural substances such as fat and honey, into a pseudo-medical act in which the natural body becomes an artificial, permeable surface. The body is rendered machinelike through the analogy between the skin and plastic or, in the surface of the drawings, steel. By implication, the body could transcend its physical limits by moving beyond the boundaries of human flesh into a robotic immateriality evocative of HAL, the computer in

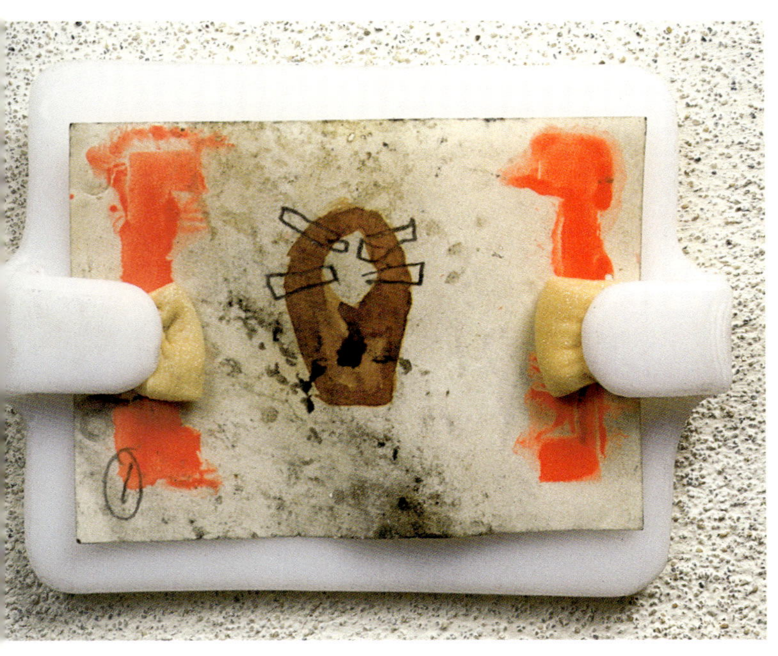

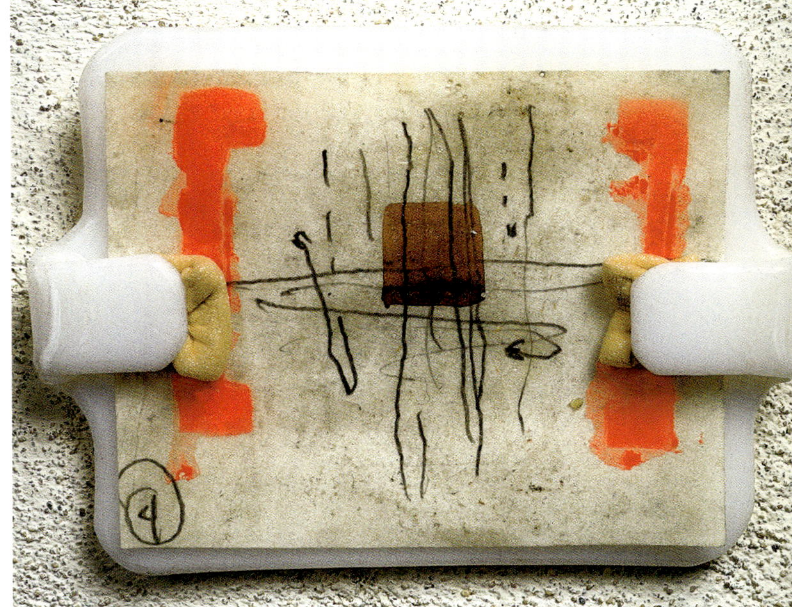

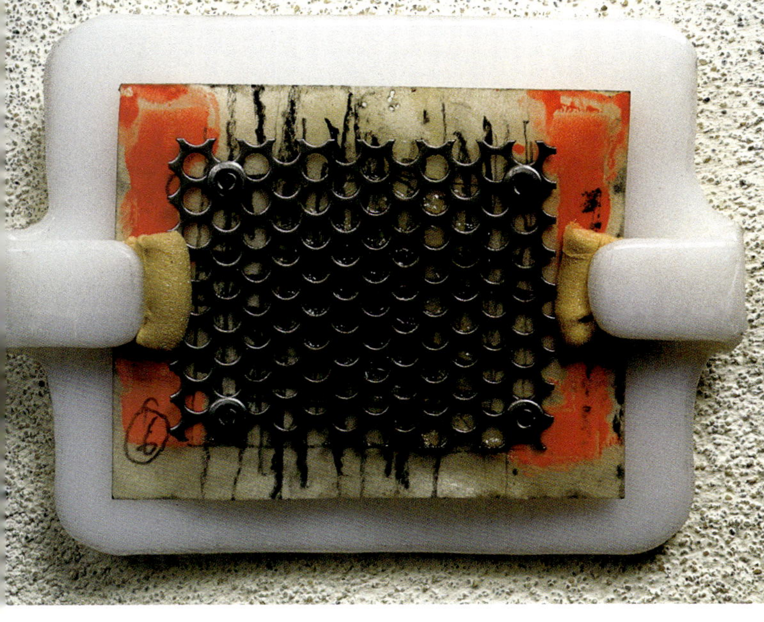

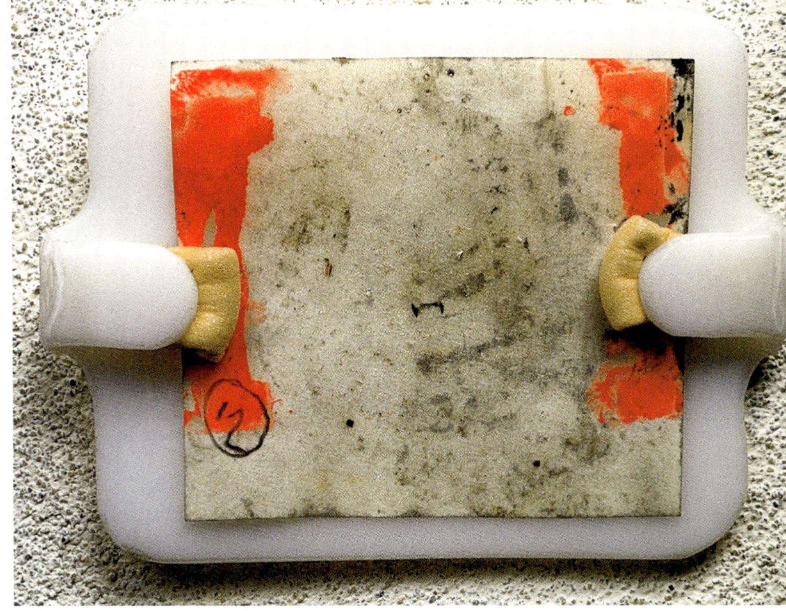

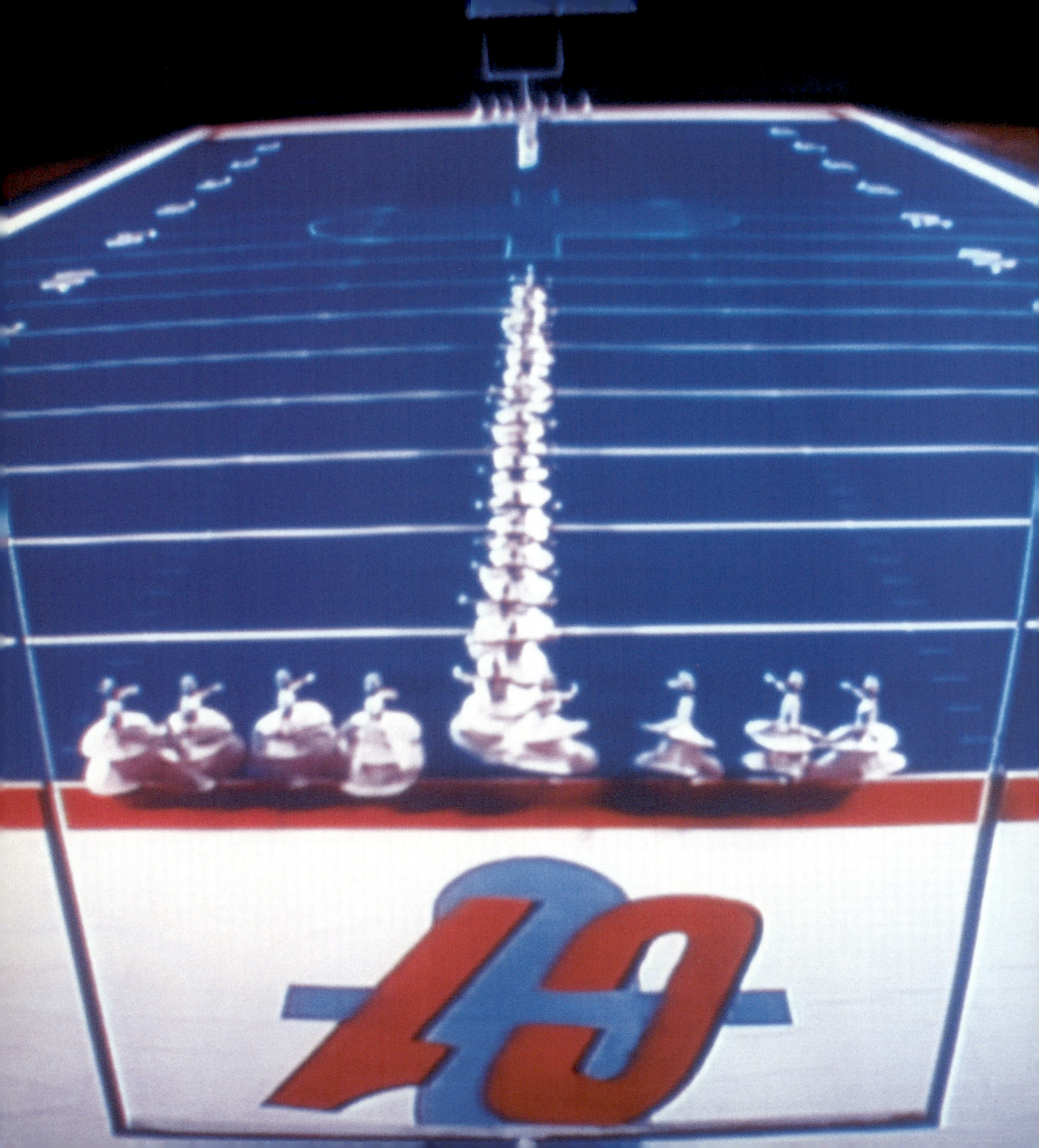

Kubrick's *2001: A Space Odyssey*, whose existence exclusively as voice, brain, and intelligence prefigures the cyberspace to which, Hansmartin Siegrist has argued, Barney's posthuman sensibility ultimately belongs.[1]

The physical pain, self-lesion, and healing described in *Scabaction* were central themes of body art during the 1970s, in the work of artists such as Marina Abramovic and Ulay, Vito Acconci, Chris Burden, and Gina Pane. If, as Siegrist has suggested,[2]

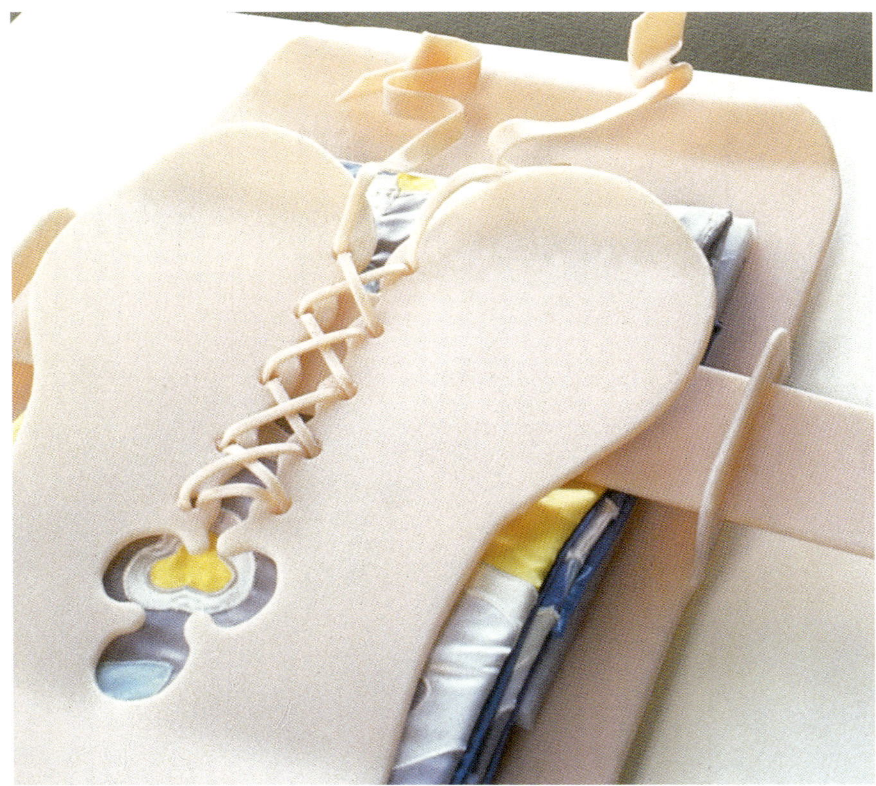

there is a strong connection between Barney's films and the sensibility of Cronenberg's surgical horror film *Dead Ringers* (1988), a parallel could also be drawn with the extreme performances of male catharsis by Viennese Actionists Günter Brus and Rudolf Schwarzkogler, whose bandaged bodies, sexual organs, bodily fluids, and medical instruments arguably prefigure Barney's use of specula, anuses, prosthetic armature, Vaseline, and, most directly, the cremaster itself.[3]

This set of muscles, which regulates the temperature of the testicles by adjusting their position in relation to the body, presents the most tangible evidence of male corporeal vulnerability. In naming a series of films and accompanying artworks after this most sensitive part of the male anatomy, Barney positions the body, and the construction of male sexual identity, as the central subject of his work.

Plate 89
MATTHEW BARNEY,
Cremaster I,
1995–96, video still.

Plate 90
MATTHEW BARNEY,
Cremaster IV,
1994–95, installation view.

The *Cremaster* series, conceived as a single drama in five acts,[4] comprises five thirty-five-millimeter films and a group of related sculptures—within which the films are also included as videodiscs—drawings, and photographs. In the final shot of the film *Cremaster IV*, a surreal narrative set on the mysterious Celtic Isle of Man, off the coast of Britain, an extreme close-up between-legs shot of Barney as the central character—the Loughton Candidate—shows his naked scrotum (a direct reference to the series' title), pierced by clumps of pseudo-medical tubes from which wires

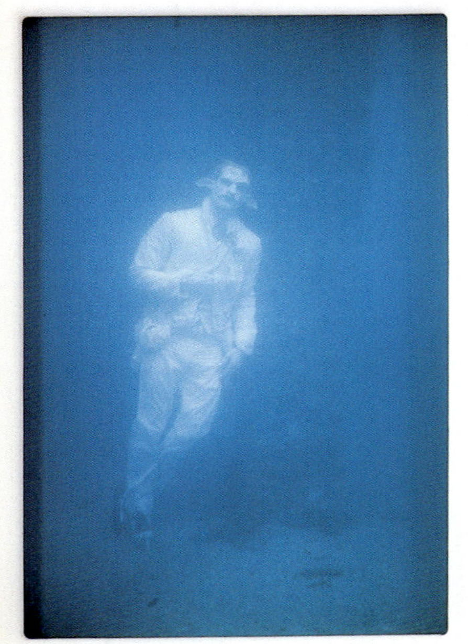

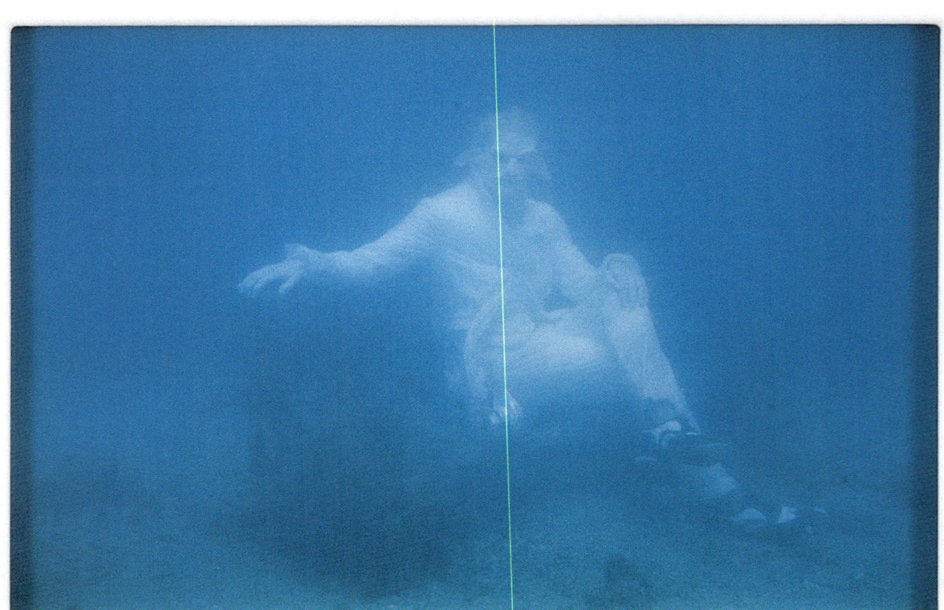

dangle down, as though either pumping the testicles with gas or draining them. The body is, once again, aligned to a machine, in this case the motorbike, a famous symbol of the Isle of Man through its annual T.T. motorbike race, parodied in *Cremaster IV*, in which all the film's characters are attempting to win the race. The oblique reference to the extremes of 1970s body art is diffused by the white and green plastic shapes, which shift the masochism of physical suffering into a surreal, sculptural territory.

As in *Cremaster I* (1995–96), in which the action takes place on a football field, Barney chooses a traditionally male sport for his location and subject, then undermines its macho presumptions. In his surreal tableaux, the sharp corners of male testosterone are molded into smooth, slippery curves and tamed by the opened orifice. In the sculpture *Cremaster IV*, a flesh-colored, corset-shaped object made from prosthetic plastic contains the rest of the sculpture's contents, packed flat inside its two stiff sides and tied together with plastic cords. The corset's shape reiterates,

Plate 91
MATTHEW BARNEY,
Cremaster IV: MANANNAN,
1994, installation view.

in abstract terms, *Cremaster IV*'s many filmic references to testicles, orifices, fetishism, the eroticism of restrictive clothing, and the vulnerability of the male body implied by the corset's medical and athletic associations of protection and support. ___

___The anxiety of castration is suggested by the corset's ambiguous sexual identity. The roundedness of its two lower edges suggests the curves of female hips, yet also the double curve of the male testicle sac. This hybrid sexuality is echoed in a trefoil shape cut out of the top of the corset above the laced cords. At first glance a feminine decorative detail, the trefoil cutout makes visible from underneath a triadic orifice pattern, printed onto a "bridal banner" folded inside the corset. This triadic shape is positioned at the center of a heraldic design of three armored, running legs, an adaptation of the ancient symbol of the Isle of Man, which appears, spinning, throughout the *Cremaster IV* film and is stamped onto the videodisc. The position of the orifice in the center of the three-legged torso suggests a castrated phallus, and its egglike yellow and white colors, its replacement by a fertile female egg. The spurs and armor of the three-legged torso, reminiscent of protective football gear or motorcycle wear, do nothing to protect the vulnerable soft center of ambiguous gender, whose exposure appears to invite penetration. ___

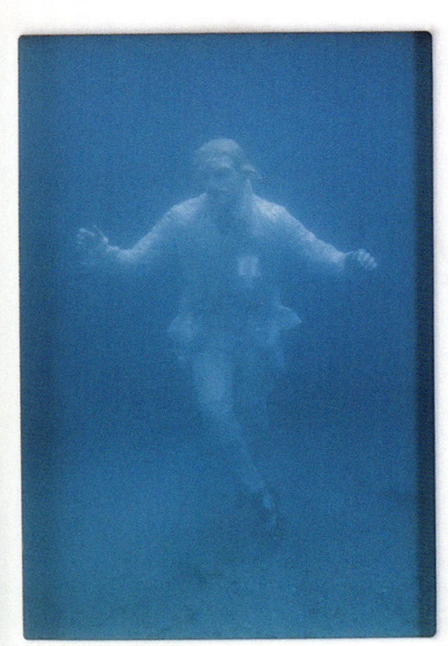

___The title of *Cremaster IV: MANANNAN* (1994), three Cibachrome prints in self-lubricating plastic frames, refers to Manannan, the Celtic god of the sea after whom the Isle of Man was named. In all three photographs, Barney appears as the satyrlike central character, the Loughton Candidate, walking along the seabed as though he were Manannan himself. The photographs present moments from the film, in which the Loughton Candidate (named after a rare breed of sheep found only on the Isle of Man) falls into the sea and moves along the seabed, toward an internal passage. Barney's dyed-red hair and bizarre horns pay homage to the Loughton sheep's distinctive red fleece and downward-drooping horns. The photographs capture Barney's character at its most omnipotent, moving with ease in the womblike water, before he enters a narrow, Vaselined passage. Both the sea and the island represent a kind of giant body, or organism, in which, as James Lingwood has observed, mythology and topography become one.[5]

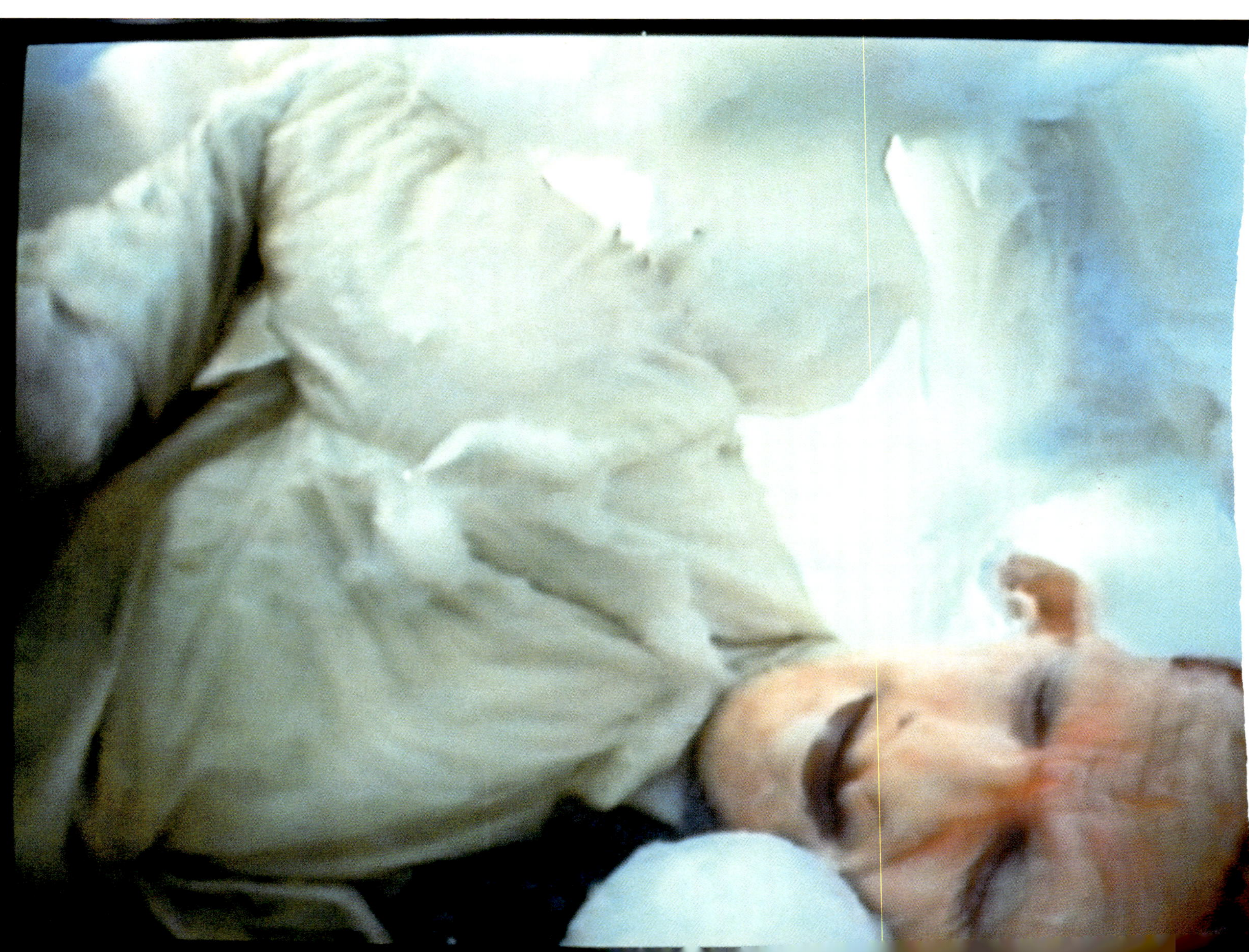

Barney's erotically ambiguous performing body, moving through the water and the slippery caves of *Cremaster IV*, undermines the cliché of the athletic, macho American male, which, as a football player and pre-med student, he experienced firsthand. The softness and fluidity of his membrane shapes recall the sensuous sculptures of Lygia Clarke, in particular *Ar e pedra* (Air and stone, 1966), in which a stone ball sits on the surface of an air-filled bag, which is softly squeezed between the hands. The feminine sensuality of Clarke's participatory organic forms is echoed in Barney's tactile desire to experience the inner surfaces of the body from the inside out.

Yet, as Richard Flood has suggested, all is not well inside the body. The American football field location of the *Cremaster I* film and the island location of *Cremaster IV* "function as organisms which have been infected with a virus that, in the convoluted elegance of its construct, threatens to dominate the host in which it has taken shelter."[6] Just as Kubrick's *The Shining* suggests a radical disruption of the social body, the extreme symbolism and high artifice of Barney's *Cremaster* series reflects a posthuman age of AIDS, in which the body is experienced synthetically, in fragments and at one remove.

The objects in the sculptures *Cremaster I* (1995–96) and *Cremaster V* (1997)—a white, high-heeled Busby Berkeley–style sandal on top of a white plastic tiered plinth, and a sleek acrylic, nylon, and velvet cushion and pouch, both enclosing videodiscs—appear as fetishized abstractions of the body in the films' complex themes: in *Cremaster I*, the camp Miss Goodyear, around whom the film revolves, and in *Cremaster V*, the baroque Queen of Chain, and the satyrlike knight, Barney. As always, both sets of objects present a symbolic orifice that invites penetration—the placing of fingers into the hole at the center of the cushion or the inserting of a foot into the shoe.

The shoe in *Cremaster I* and the cushion and pouch in *Cremaster V*, evoking the courtly possessions of a knight and queen, make oblique allusion, in sculptural terms, to the narrative of each accompanying film. The complex iconography and sexual ambiguity of Barney's work situate him at the center of a postmodern American world at the end of the twentieth century, in which identity is defined by Hollywood fantasy, corporate control, science fiction, and an uncertain sexual morality. In his personal universe, film, video, sculpture, drawing, and performance are fused into a single, mannerist *Gesamtkunstwerk*, in which suffering, anxiety, and endurance are transformed into a disturbing theater of high artifice.

1. HANSMARTIN SIEGRIST, "Barney in the Motion Picture," in *Cremaster I: Matthew Barney* (Basel: Museum für Gegenwartskunst, 1998), 26. This important essay includes a revealing analysis of the influence of Hollywood, in particular Kubrick's films, on Barney's *Cremaster* series.
2. Ibid., 31 n. 2.
3. Cronenberg's use of similar imagery in *Dead Ringers* provided the strongest influence, however.
4. See THEODORA VISCHER, "A Different Story of Gender and Generation," in *Cremaster I*, 21.
5. JAMES LINGWOOD, essay in exhibition brochure for *Matthew Barney: Cremaster IV* (London: Artangel; New York: Barbara Gladstone Gallery; Paris: Fondation Cartier pour l'Art Contemporain, 1995), unpaginated.
6. RICHARD FLOOD, "Notes on Digestion and Film," in *Matthew Barney: Pace Car for the Hubris Pill*, ed. Matthew Barney and Gracia Lebbink (Rotterdam: Museum Boymans van Beuningen, 1995), quoted by Siegrist, "Barney in the Motion Picture," 31 n. 14.

Plate 92
MATTHEW BARNEY,
Cremaster IV,
1994–95, video still.

Overleaf:

Plates 93–94
MATTHEW BARNEY,
Cremaster I,
1995–96, video stills (details).

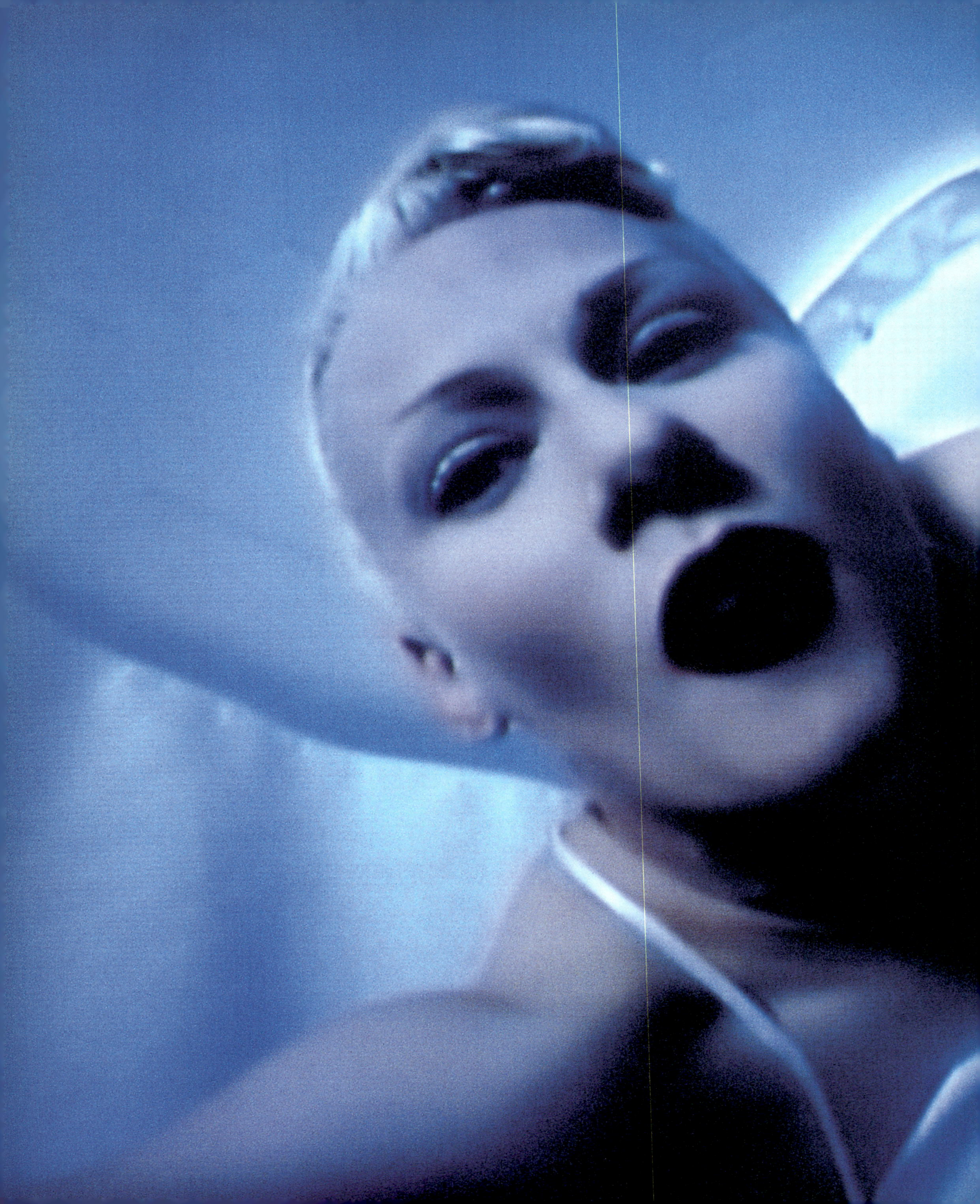

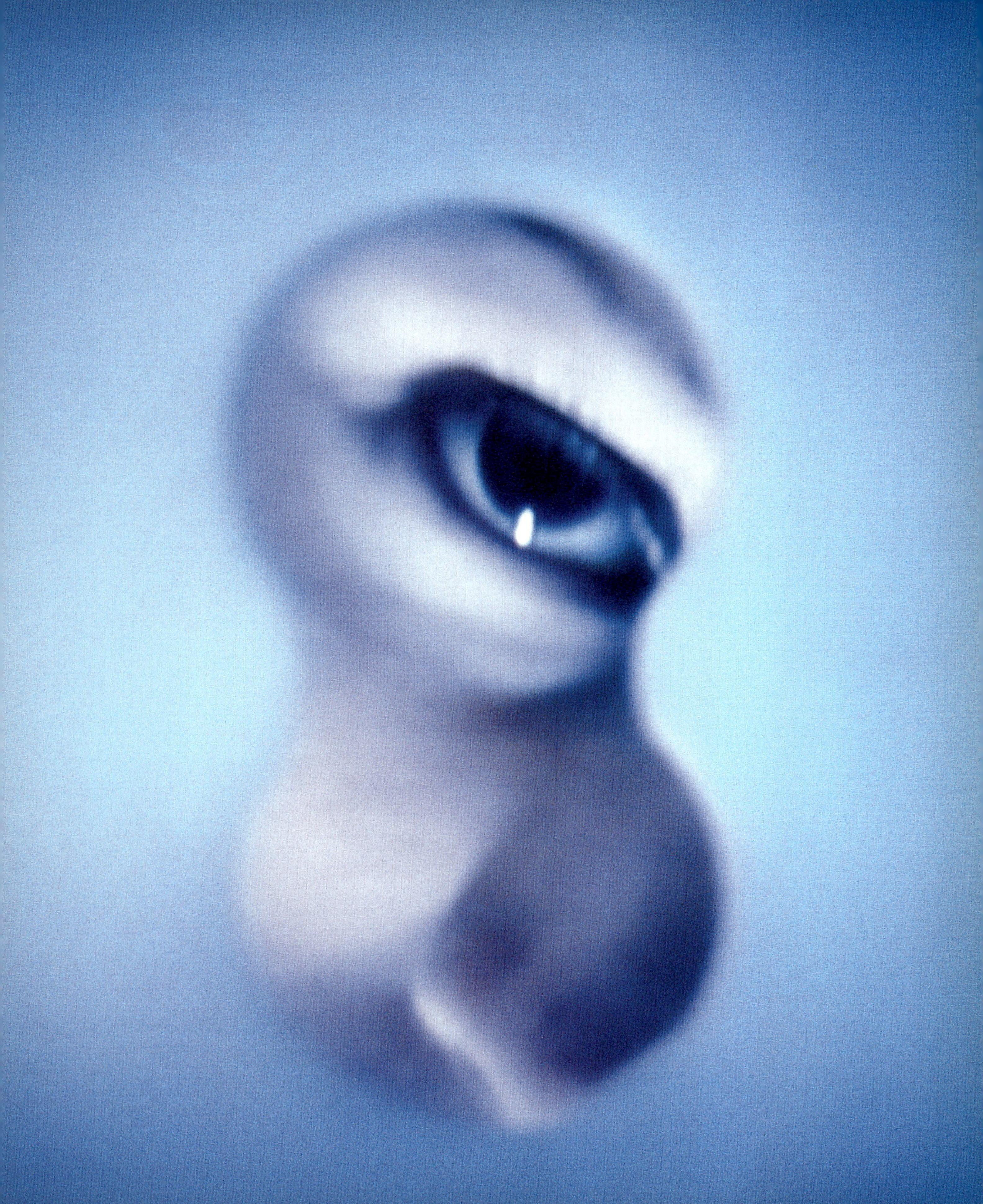

NOTES ON THE FORMATION AND EVOLUTION OF A COLLECTION

THEA WESTREICH

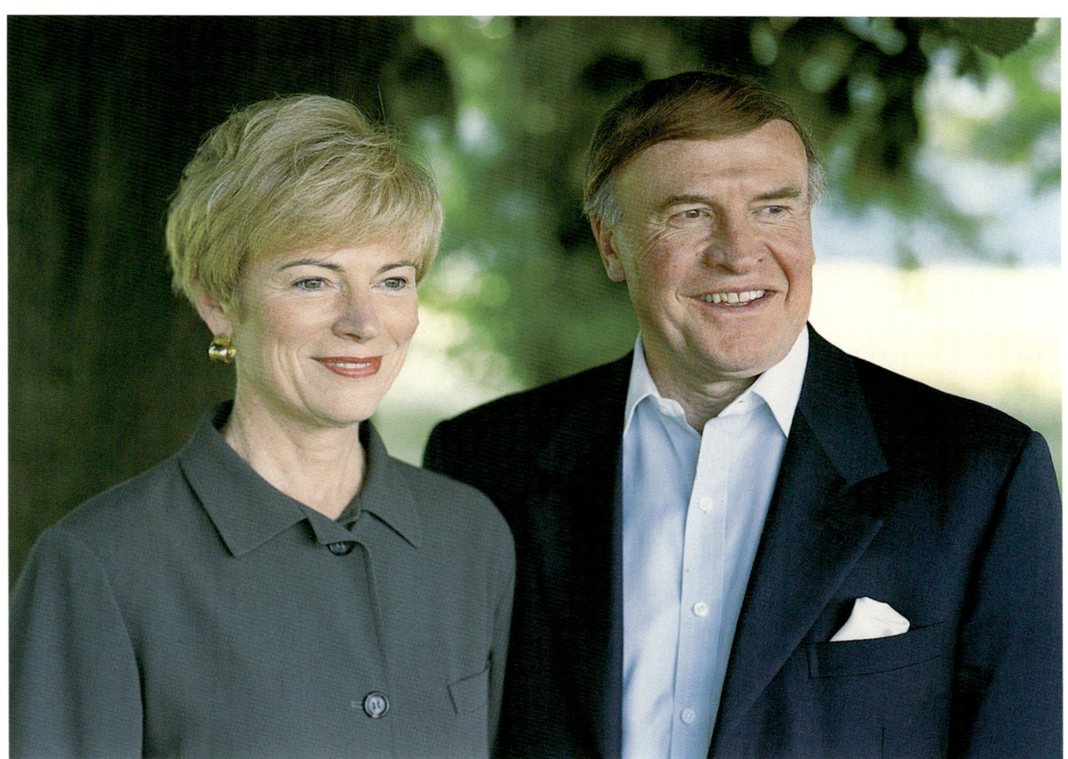

Figure 18
Photograph of Pamela and Richard Kramlich by Thomas Struth, courtesy Marian Goodman Gallery.

Ten years ago, when the concept for the collection of Pamela and Richard Kramlich took root, the notion of collecting primarily video, new media, and time-based works seemed more a theoretical curiosity than a realizable end. For the Kramlichs, however, it became a plan of action. In the years since, a groundbreaking collection has been assembled, and it seems fitting that now, a decade later, highlights of the collection are being exhibited at the San Francisco Museum of Modern Art as a millennial show, setting the stage for the twenty-first century.

As forward-looking as it is, the collection does have a history. When John Caldwell, the San Francisco Museum of Modern Art's former curator of painting and sculpture, came to the museum under the directorship of Jack Lane, he had an immediate and enormous influence on both established and nascent collectors. Under his tutelage and fueled by his enthusiasm, collectors were beginning to travel internationally to exhibitions, collections, art fairs, and artists' studios. Among those who admired John's enthusiasm, scholarship, and commitment to the art of his time—and there were many—were the Kramlichs.

Several years earlier I, too, had come to know John Caldwell. We soon developed a strong personal and professional relationship and spoke on an almost daily basis about what we were seeing and learning. It was through John that the Kramlichs were introduced to me and my advisory service. At first, the Kramlichs and I spent our time together looking at art and talking about what they could do to further engage their intellects and make a contribution to the museum and their community. It was out of this process that the idea of a video collection arose. The concept seemed fitting in light of Dick's professional activities as a successful venture capitalist in the field of new technologies. It also appealed to Pam's sense of adventure and curiosity and her belief, inspired in part by Dick's business ventures, in the importance of technology as an expressive tool for the artist.

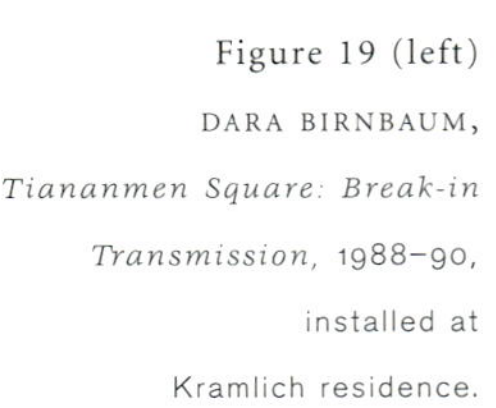

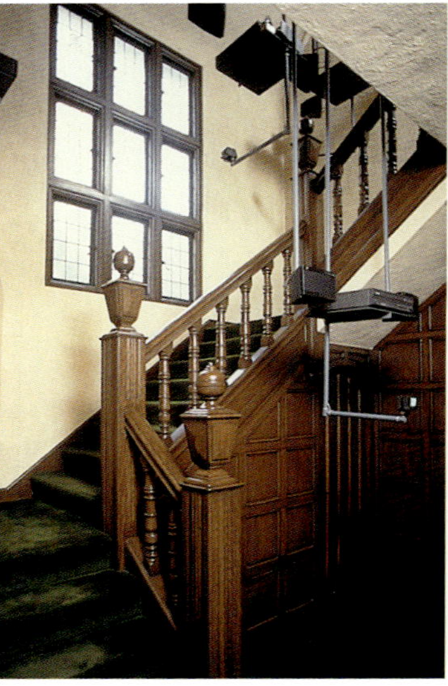

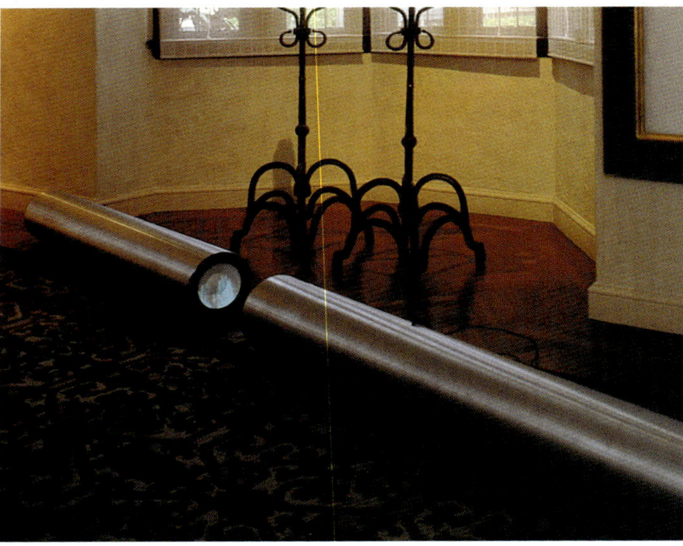

Figure 19 (left)
DARA BIRNBAUM, *Tiananmen Square: Break-in Transmission*, 1988–90, installed at Kramlich residence.

Figure 20 (right)
GARY HILL, *Cut Pipe*, 1992, installed at Kramlich residence.

As the idea for the collection evolved, we initiated numerous discussions with artists and curators, as well as spending hours upon hours viewing videotapes to help establish the history of the medium. John Hanhardt, then curator of film and video at the Whitney Museum of American Art and now at the Solomon R. Guggenheim Museum, gave several talks on this history for the Kramlichs. These were of great importance at this early stage, helping to provide a framework and context for the selection process that was to take place. Stephen Vitello at Electronic Arts Intermix regularly set up video viewings and recommended tapes. Throughout, John Caldwell and Jack Lane continued to offer support and encouragement, and later, but no less importantly, Bob Riley, who joined the San Francisco Museum of Modern Art as curator of media arts in 1988, began to contribute his erudition and expertise.

By March 1992 we were able to concretize what we had been thinking about and discussing for several years, and a philosophy of the collection was committed to paper. The goals, as formulated then, were as follows:

1 To assemble a significant and carefully curated collection of video art with two distinct components: (a) historical/scholarly/archival videotapes [and] (b) discrete objects, installations, and artworks that make use of video technology in the creation of art.

2 To actualize the collectors as leaders in their endeavor and to use their acquisition activities to serve the community both through the museum [SFMOMA] and in arranging events/performances/symposia at the collectors' residence.

The emphasis was to be on art, not technology for its own sake. The plan went on to describe in detail the proposed collection, its procedures, and its protocols. It is interesting to note that those words, written seven years ago, still provide a framework for our activity today.

Like many innovative collections, the Kramlich collection did not get under way in an entirely accepting atmosphere. There were those who were unconvinced of the importance of the medium and naysayers who were suspicious of an art form that could be so effortlessly copied. Still others were skeptical as to whether these artworks could be installed and integrated in a private home.

By the time we all visited *Documenta 9* in the summer of 1992, however, the Kramlichs had become fully committed to moving forward, and it was clear that artists represented in that exhibition—such as Matthew Barney, Dara Birnbaum, James Coleman, Stan Douglas, Gary Hill, and Bruce Nauman—were of compelling interest to them. The 1992 *Documenta* was the first of hundreds of exhibitions around the world that offered both stimulation and education and served as a catalyst for discussions with artists, gallerists, curators, collectors, museum directors, and writers.

As the Kramlichs learned more, it became clear that contemporary video art had a richly textured, if brief, history. They realized that the wealth and breadth of this history needed to be represented in the collection if they were to fully engage in a dialogue with the medium. To this end, the compilation of an extensive single-channel video reference library was undertaken. The reference library is intended to supplement the collection, amplifying its scope and providing a valuable counterpoint to the more personal and critical selection of artworks and curated installations.

The tapes in the library are used to trace important trends and approaches in the medium. The earliest of them represent a period in which the primary use of video by artists was as a record of their performances. The early works of Vito Acconci, Joan Jonas, Bruce Nauman, and William Wegman, dating from 1968 to approximately 1974, exemplify the fascination with the body as a vehicle for artistic expression. Many of these works did not derive from an impulse to create "objects" as such and were not editioned in the tradition of printmaking or cast sculpture. They were created using rudimentary technology that was attractive for its immediacy and ability to capture the event as it unfolded. Most historical single-channel video works were distributed in unlimited numbers and have never been accessible in any other format. Thus, the history of the medium could, by and large, be "collected" and viewed only through the creation of the reference library. The video library, then, serves as a touchstone for evaluating the material being received from or viewed at galleries, exhibitions, and fairs. It was by constantly refocusing this map of the historical and the personal that the acquisition process began, and continues today.

Works by Matthew Barney, Dara Birnbaum, and Gary Hill were among the Kramlichs' first acquisitions, indicating the diversity of expression and range of personal sensibilities that would be characteristic of their collection. The search was not geared toward works whose content was easily understandable or that were necessarily compatible with a living environment. Whether narrative or iconic, all the works possessed an ineffable, abstract criticality. What defined the Kramlichs' approach to collecting was the willingness, simply put, to employ the same criteria used to judge any work of art.

The Kramlichs recognized that their assessment of a work's importance should be guided by the highest standards of scholarship and connoisseurship and that they should not be seduced by mere technological wizardry. In many ways, this curatorial approach resembled Dick's business program in the field of emerging technologies. It was not the technology itself that was important, but its application: how effectively the developer—or artist—had exploited its capability to process and transmit content. While there are certain indicators that one can use to compare the relative value of start-up companies—or emerging artists (and certainly there are aspects of art that can be measured objectively)—in the end the decision must be based on a highly intuitive qualitative judgment.

Each artwork in the Kramlich collection stands on its own as an expression whose form is seamlessly integrated with its meaning. Form and signification reinforce each other whether the artist is confronting the individual's role in society, issues of identity, or the creation of structures of meaning through art. Indeed, new media are pervasive in our culture, but the media artworks in this collection hold a significance that transcends the specificity of the medium. They bear a relationship to the periods in which they were produced, but it is their content and the way it is expressed by each artist that render the works significant to the Kramlichs, and this significance must be renewable for them over time. In many ways, the relatively new medium of video captured their interest not because it was new, but because, at its best, it was relevant. It has changed the way we perceive and understand things, and its messages are timeless.

It did not take long before it became palpably clear that the activity of collecting was of moment for the Kramlichs, that it was of abiding interest, that it was emotionally engaging and intellectually stimulating. But it was, after all, a personal collection, and at some point it needed to have a place in their home. It was when Dara Birnbaum came to San Francisco at Pam's invitation to install *Tiananmen Square: Break-in Transmission* (1981–90; fig. 19) that the video collection became part of the Kramlichs' everyday life. The piece was installed in the center stairwell of their Tudor-style home, and the moving images and haunting soundtrack began to animate the residence. As each new work became a part of their environment, the Kramlichs' passion grew, and the meaning of each work became more fully realized. The collection had become a living thing—both audible and visible—and an undeniably central part of their lives.

But it did not end there. Throughout the process the Kramlichs have acted as catalysts for discussion and discourse, generously hosting events—not only for those in the art world but for those in business and other communities as well. Pam has sought out, engaged, and convened a diverse group of people, and Dick is

Figure 21
MATTHEW BARNEY, *Cremaster IV*, 1994–95, installed at Kramlich residence (also on the mantle: Christopher Wool, *Untitled*, 1990).

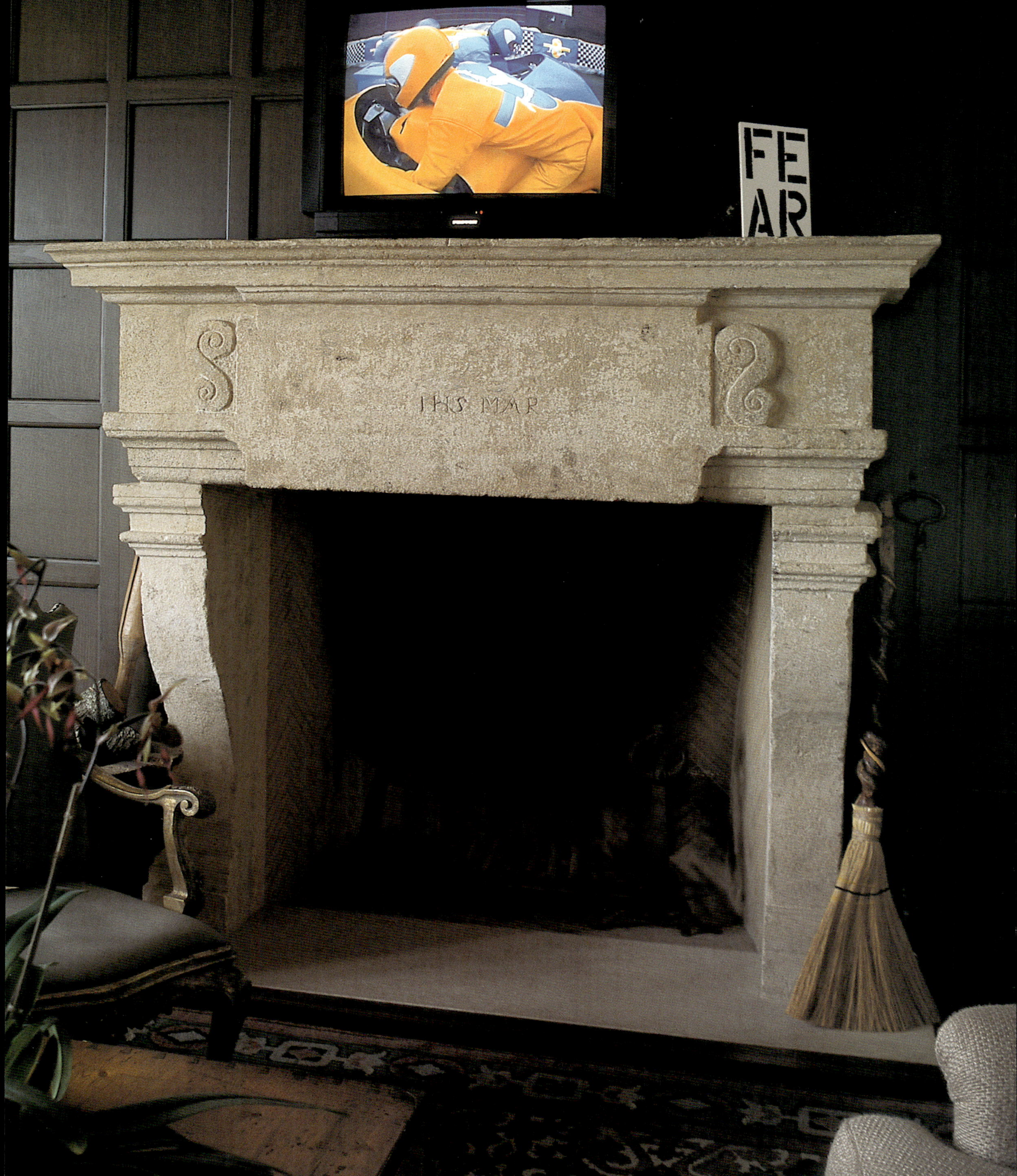
FE
AR
IHS MAR

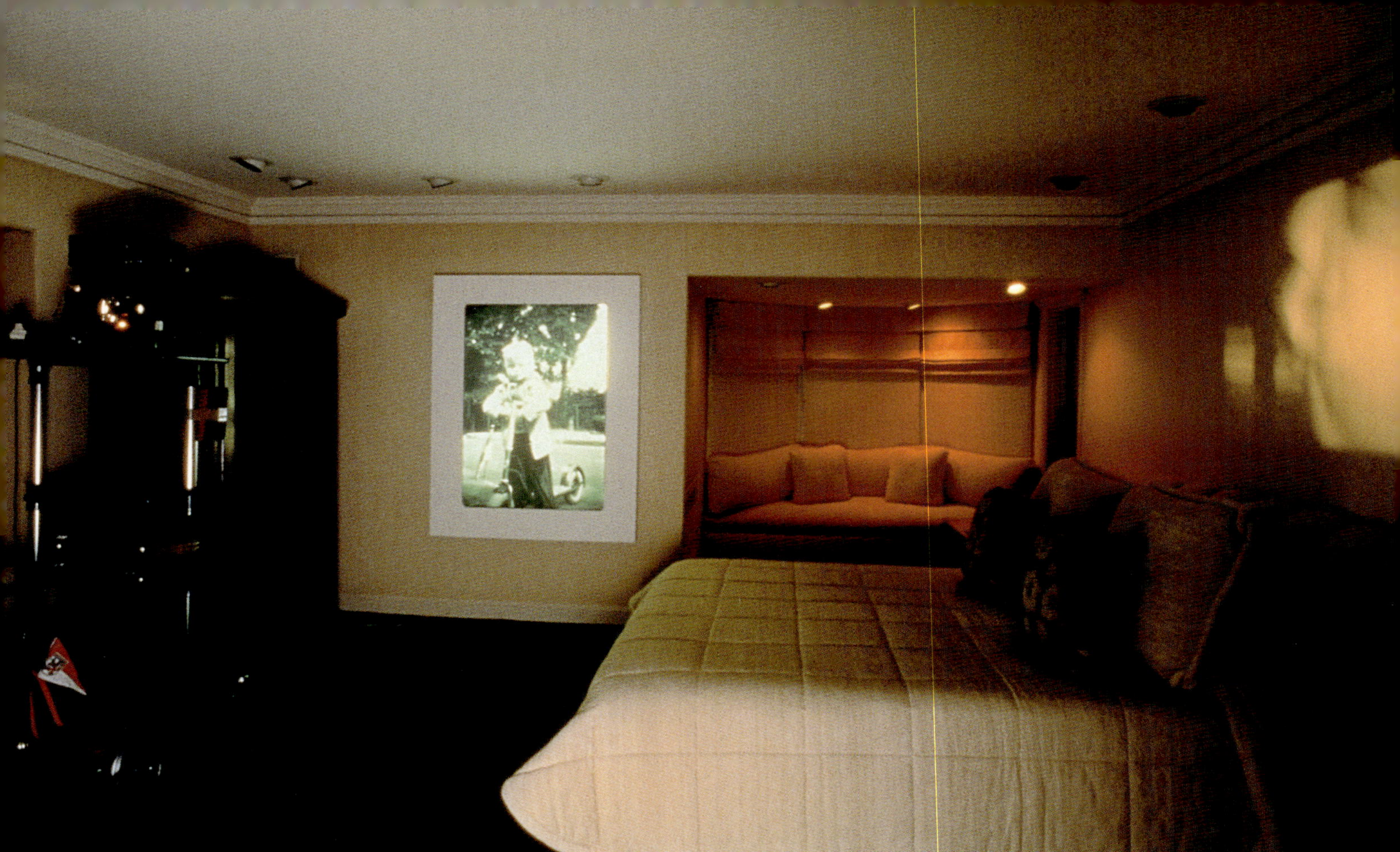

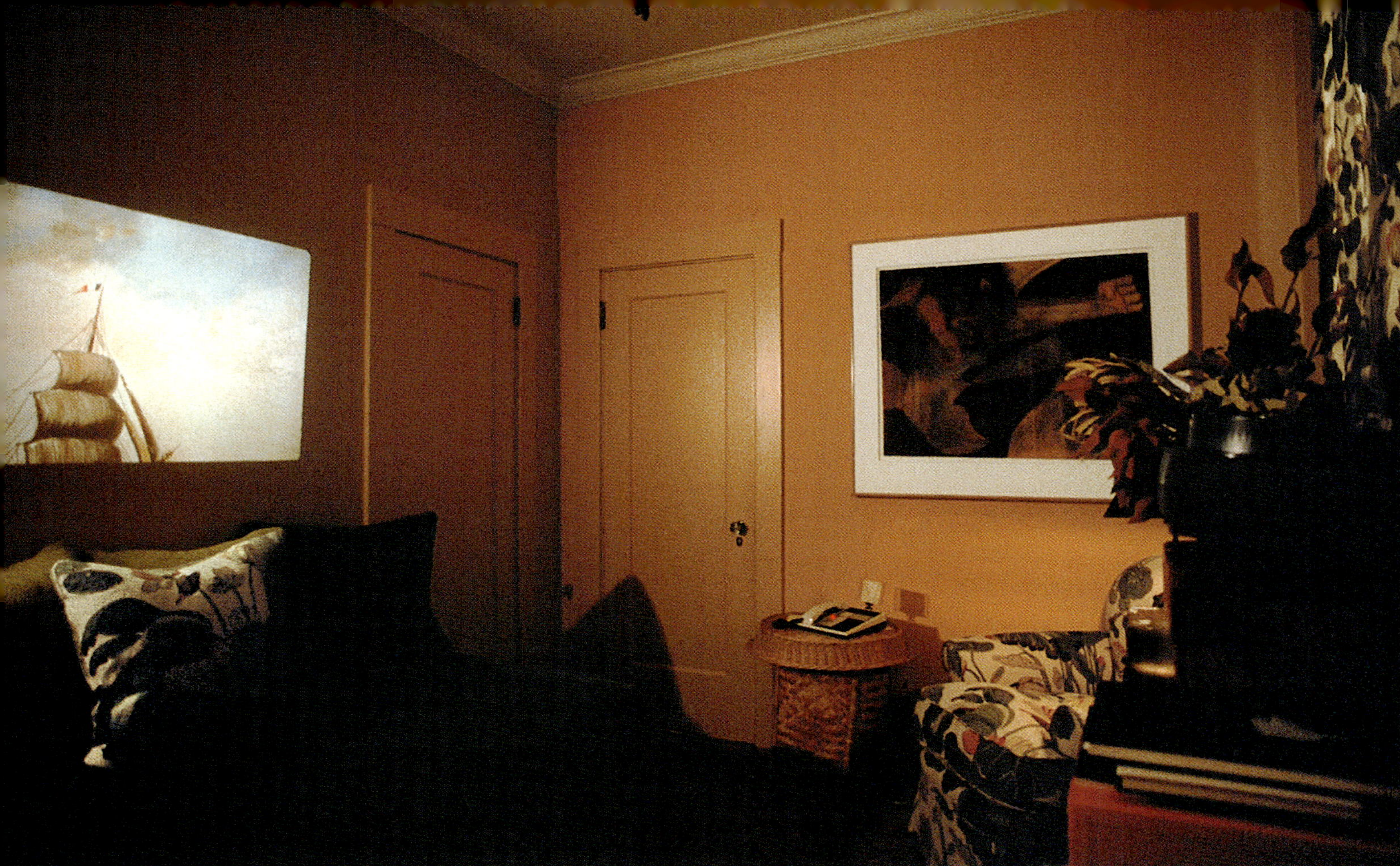

perhaps legendary for his skill in encouraging his guests, however reluctant they may sometimes be, to speak up and share ideas. These efforts have added to the already varied ways in which the collection can intrigue, incite, and inspire.

Certainly one of the great challenges going forward is meeting the demands of managing this unique collection. New databases and systems for cataloguing have had to be developed as well as a lexicon to describe the material, with its new and ever-changing formats. The Kramlichs have cast a wide net. Experts in the field are continually consulted and encouraged to consider carefully the questions that arise about key issues such as conservation and preservation. And people from all specialties, including museum personnel, have in turn sought information and guidance from the Kramlichs. For all involved in new media, framing the questions is perhaps now the priority.

There are countless individuals who have been helpful over the years and who continue to collaborate with the Kramlichs and me in this arena. They include, in addition to those already mentioned, Callie Angel, Rena Bransten, Christopher Eamon, Sallie Jo Fifer, Barbara Gladstone, Marian Goodman, Chrissie Iles, Anthony d'Offay and Robin Vousden, Anthony Reynolds, Caroline Schneider, Barbara Wise, and Donald Young, to name only a very few. As we continue to encounter new people, the list grows, and it is to the Kramlichs' credit that the doors are always open to those with ideas and talent—be they artists, curators, advisers, critics, gallerists, writers, or anyone else who shares their passion.

Figure 22 (left)
REINHARD MUCHA,
Auto Reverse, 1994–95,
installed at
Kramlich residence.

Figure 23 (above)
MARCEL BROODTHAERS,
Bateau tableau, 1973,
installed at
Kramlich residence.

CATALOGUE OF THE EXHIBITION

Unless otherwise noted, all works are Collection of Pamela and Richard Kramlich, courtesy of Thea Westreich Art Advisory Services.

VITO ACCONCI

American, b. 1940

1. *Pornography in the Classroom*, 1975
   Plates 74–77
   Video and projected image installation with sound; plan
   Dimensions variable; video: 21:58 min., projected image: 35:28 min.
   Media: eighty 35mm slide transparencies, two BetaSP videotapes authored to DVD (digital versatile disc) (original Super-8 film remastered to BetaSP video)
   Equipment: one Kodak Ektagraphic III AMT slide projector, one slide carousel, two Pioneer DVD-V7200 DVD players, one Sony PVM 2030 20-inch video monitor, one Sony 1041Q CRT (cathode ray tube) projector, two Sony SS-X7 monitor speakers

EIJA-LIISA AHTILA

Finnish, b. 1959

2. *Anne, Aki, and God*, 1998
   Plates 68–69
   Seven-channel video installation with sound; plan
   Dimensions variable (approx. 23 x 46 ft.); 30:00 min.
   Media: seven BetaSP PAL videotapes authored to DVD (digital versatile disc)
   Equipment: five Sony PVM 20N2U 20-inch video monitors, one Technovision seven-channel DVD sync unit, two Boxlight ProColor 2001 LCD (liquid crystal display) projectors, seven Philips 170 DVD players, one 79-by-59-inch rear projection screen, one 71-by-47-inch front projection screen, two Acoustic Research Powered Partners loudspeakers
   Materials: wooden structure, curtains, bed, table, armchair, lamps, text panels
   Collection Pamela and Richard Kramlich; courtesy Thea Westreich Art Advisory Services and Klemens Gasser & Tanja Grunert, Inc., New York

DARREN ALMOND

English, b. 1971

3. *H.M.P. Pentonville*, 1997
   Plates 49–50
   Single-channel video projection with sound; plan
   20 x 20 ft.; 60:00 min.
   Media: one 3/4-inch videotape authored to DVD, one audio CD
   Equipment: one Barco CRT (cathode ray tube) projector, one Sony CDP500 compact disc player, one Philips 170 DVD player, two JBL Control-5 loudspeakers, one Samson Servo 120 amplifier

MATTHEW BARNEY

American, b. 1967

4. *Scabaction*, 1988
   Plates 83–88
   Single-channel video with drawing installation; plan
   Dimensions variable; 9:54 min.
   Media: one laser disc, twelve mixed-media drawings
   Equipment: one Pioneer LD-V8000 laser disc player, one Mitsubishi CS2710RA 27-inch video monitor
   Materials: graphite, ink, steel, petroleum jelly on paper, prosthetic plastic, foam, self-lubricating plastic, nylon binding straps
5. *Cremaster IV: MANANNAN*, 1994
   Plate 91
   Three Cibachrome prints with self-lubricating plastic frames
   20 x 30 in., 28 x 40 in., 20 x 30 in.
6. *Cremaster IV*, 1994–95
   Plate 90
   Objects and vitrine
   41 x 48 x 36 in.
   Materials: one silk-screened laser disc in onionskin sleeve, prosthetic plastic, one satin bridal sash, one Manx tartan, one custom self-lubricating plastic vitrine with Plexiglas cover
7. Video installation: *Cremaster IV*, 1994–95, and *Cremaster I*, 1995–96
   Plates 89, 92–94
   Video monitor and overhead mount; plan
   Dimensions variable; *Cremaster IV*: 42:00 min., *Cremaster I*: 40:00 min.
   Media: one laser disc
   Equipment: one Pioneer LD-V2600 laser disc player, one Sony PVM 2530 video monitor, one prosthetic plastic ceiling mount, two JBL Control-1 loudspeakers
8. *Cremaster I*, 1995–96
   Objects and vitrine
   48 x 48 x 36 in.
   Materials: one silk-screened laser disc, cast polyester, self-lubricating plastic, prosthetic plastic, patent vinyl, one custom self-lubricating plastic vitrine with Plexiglas cover

9. *Cremaster V*, 1997
Objects and vitrine
37 x 48 x 36 in.
Materials: one silk-screened laser disc, one cast polyester and acrylic laser disc box, one custom self-lubricating plastic vitrine with Plexiglas cover

LOTHAR BAUMGARTEN

German, b. 1944

10. *"Da gefällt's mir besser als in Westfalen" Eldorado 1968–1976* ("I like it better there than in Westphalia" El Dorado 1968–1976), 1968–76
Plates 30–32
Projected-image installation with sound; plan
Dimensions variable; 36:52 min.
Media: 187 35mm slide transparencies, one audio CD (compact disc)
Equipment: three Kodak Ektagraphic III+ slide projectors, three slide carousels, three 85–210mm lenses, one Audio Visual Laboratories Dove X2 control unit, one Tascam CD-301 compact disc player, one Samson Servo 120 amplifier, four JBL Control-5 loudspeakers, one Alesis M-EQ 230 stereo equalizer

DARA BIRNBAUM

American, b. 1946

11. *Tiananmen Square: Break-in Transmission*, 1988–90
Plates 45–48
Multichannel video installation with sound; plan
Dimensions variable; duration continuous
Media: four laser discs
Equipment: four Pioneer LD-V2000 laser disc players, four Sony FDM-330 Watchmans, four Sony Watchman 3305 mounting systems, four Sony Watchman AC-D4L power transformers, one NEC PM 2571-A color monitor, one Panasonic WJ-525 sequential switcher, eight Acoustic Research Powered Partners Teledyne loudspeakers

MARCEL BROODTHAERS

Belgian, 1924–1976

12. *Fig. 0, Fig. 1, Fig. 2, Fig. A*, (Example G), 1971
Plates 1–10
16mm film projection on hand-painted screen; plan
Dimensions variable; 37:00 min.
Media: five 16mm film prints: *Une discussion inaugurale* (1968), *Un voyage à Waterloo (Napoléon 1769–1969)* (1969), *Charlie als Filmstar* (1971), *Brüssel Teil II* (1971), and *Belga Vox-Mode-20th Century Fox* (1971)
Equipment: one Eiki SSL-1 16mm film projector, one RFS LT-45 16mm film looping system, one 62-by-81-inch hand-painted screen

13. *Bateau tableau* (Boat tableau), 1973
Plates 11–12
Projected-image installation; plan
Dimensions variable; 33:45-min. cycle
Media: eighty 35mm slide transparencies
Equipment: one Kodak Ektagraphic III AMT projector, one slide carousel, one Schneider ProLux 70–120mm *f*2.8 lens

LARRY CLARK

American, b. 1943

14. *Nate, G-Street Live*, 1992
Plates 70–73
Single-channel video with sound
18:00 min.
Media: one 3/4-inch videotape authored to DVD (digital versatile disc)
Equipment: one Pioneer DVD-V7200 DVD player, one Sony PVM 2530 monitor, two Sony SS-X7A loudspeakers
Collection Pamela and Richard Kramlich; courtesy Thea Westreich Art Advisory Services and the artist

JAMES COLEMAN

Irish, b. 1941

15. *I N I T I A L S*, 1993–94
Plate 55
Projected-image installation with sound; plan
25 x 50 ft.; 18:00 min.
Media: ninety-five 35mm slide transparencies, one audio CD (compact disc)
Equipment: three Kodak Ektagraphic III+ slide projectors, three Schneider ProLux 85–210mm *f*2.8 lenses, three slide carousels, one Audio Visual Laboratories Dove X2 control unit, one Sony CDP500 compact disc player, four JBL Control-5 loudspeakers, one Samson Servo 120 amplifier, one Alesis M-EQ 230 stereo equalizer

STAN DOUGLAS

Canadian, b. 1960

16. *Television Spots*, 1987–88
Plates 39–41
Single-channel video with sound and photo installation
Dimensions variable; 4:32 min.
Media: one laser disc, twelve black-and-white gelatin silver prints framed with text plates
Equipment: one Sony PVM 2030 20-inch video monitor, one Pioneer LD-V2400 laser disc player

17. *Monodramas*, 1991
Plates 42–44
Single-channel video with sound and photo installation
Dimensions variable; 8:30 min.
Media: one laser disc, ten black-and-white gelatin silver prints framed with text plates
Equipment: one Sony PVM 2030 20-inch video monitor, one Pioneer LD-V2400 laser disc player

GILBERT & GEORGE

Gilbert: Italian, b. 1943; George: English, b. 1942

18. *The Nature of Our Looking*, 1970
Plates 13–16, 21
16mm film projection with sound
Dimensions variable; 18:00 min.
Media: one 16mm film print
Equipment: one Eiki SSL-1 16mm film projector, one RFS LT-20 16mm film looping system

19. *A Portrait of the Artists as Young Men*, 1972
Plates 17–20
Single-channel video with sound
8:00 min.
Media: one BetaSP videotape authored to DVD (digital versatile disc)
Equipment: one Philips 170 DVD player, one Sony 1910Q video monitor

DAN GRAHAM

American, b. 1942

20. *Body Press*, 1970–72
Plate 24
16mm film installation; plan
Dimensions variable; 8:00-min. cycle
Media: two 16mm film prints (polyester base)
Equipment: two 16mm Thomson projectors, two Xenon power supplies, two lenses, two loop cabinets, one interlock projector synchronizer

GARY HILL

American, b. 1951

21. *Cut Pipe*, 1992
Plates 62–63
Video installation with sound
Approx. 6 x 12 ft.; 5:00 min.
Media: one laser disc
Equipment: one laser disc player, one custom 5-inch black-and-white monitor, one TV projection lens, one program controller, three 8-inch loudspeakers, one stereo amplifier
Materials: two 60-inch aluminum pipe sections

22. *Circular Breathing*, 1994
Plates 60–61
Video installation with sound
40 x 40 ft.; duration continuous
Media: one D2 videotape copied to laser disc for exhibition
Equipment: one Pioneer LD-V4400 laser disc player, five Eiki LC300 LCD (liquid crystal display) video projectors, one custom digital video switcher, two Tannoy PBM8 loudspeakers, one Stewart Electronics PA-50B amplifier, one DOD 430 Series II equalizer
Computer software and hardware: custom DOS program on floppy disk, MS-DOS-based laptop computer
The Whitney Museum of American Art, Promised gift of Pamela and Richard Kramlich

STEVE MCQUEEN

English, b. 1969

23. *Deadpan*, 1997
Plates 66–67
Single-channel video projection (silent); plan
Approx. 13 x 20 ft.; 4:35 min.
Media: one laser disc
Equipment: one Pioneer LD-V2400 laser disc player, one Sony 1041Q CRT (cathode ray tube) projector

MARIKO MORI

Japanese, b. 1967

24. *Miko no inori* (The shaman girl's prayer), 1996
Plates 64–65
Single-channel video with sound
Dimensions variable; 29:23 min.
Media: one videotape authored to DVD (digital versatile disc)
Equipment: one Pioneer DVD-V7200 DVD player, one video monitor
Materials: one 1-inch glass ball in glass case

REINHARD MUCHA

German, b. 1950

25. *Auto Reverse*, 1994–95
Plates 51–52
16mm film and image installation with sound; plan
Approx. 20 x 25 ft.; duration continuous
Media: one 16mm film print, one audiotape, one mounted photo transparency
Equipment: one Eiki NT-2 16mm projector, one Eiki loop box, one Technics TR474 cassette deck, one Technics A800 MKII amplifier, two Bose 101 loudspeakers
Materials: two scooters, two glass wall panels, one Unicol stand with shelves

BRUCE NAUMAN

American, b. 1941

26. *Raw Material—OK, OK, OK*, 1990
Plates 56–59
Two-channel video installation with sound; plan
Approx. 14 x 20 x 12 ft.; duration continuous
Media: two 3/4-inch videotapes authored to DVD (digital versatile disc)
Equipment: two Pioneer DVD-V7200 DVD players, two 20-inch Sony PVM 2030 video monitors, two Sony SS-X7A loudspeakers, one Sony 1041Q CRT (cathode ray tube) video projector, one Technovision PC/2 two-channel sync unit
San Francisco Museum of Modern Art, Fractional gift of Pamela and Richard Kramlich; courtesy Thea Westreich Art Advisory Services

STEPHANIE SMITH AND EDWARD STEWART

Smith: English, b. 1968; Stewart: Irish, b. 1961

27. *Intercourse,* 1993

Plates 78–79

Two-channel video installation with sound; plan

Dimensions variable (image: 9 x 12 ft.); 60:00 min.

Media: two 3/4-inch videotapes authored to DVD (digital versatile disc)

Equipment: two Philips 170 DVD players, two Sony VPLX 1000U LCD (liquid crystal display) video projectors, one Technovision PC/2 two-channel sync unit, two JBL 4410 loudspeakers, two Samson Servo 120 amplifiers

28. *Sustain,* 1995

Plates 80–82

Two-channel video installation with sound; plan

Dimensions variable; 60:00 min.

Media: two 3/4-inch videotapes authored to DVD (digital versatile disc)

Equipment: two Philips 170 DVD players, two Sony PVM 2530 monitors, one Technovision PC/2 two-channel sync unit, four Sony SS-X7A loudspeakers

THOMAS STRUTH

German, b. 1954

29. *Louvre 1,* 1989

Plate 33

Cibachrome print

73 1/4 x 94 1/4 in.

THOMAS STRUTH AND KLAUS VOM BRUCH

Struth: German, b. 1954; vom Bruch: German, b. 1951

30. *Berlin-Project,* 1997

Plates 34–38

Four-channel video installation with sound; plan

23 x 23 ft.; 80:00 min.

Media: four BetaSP PAL videotapes authored to DVD (digital versatile disc)

Equipment: four Philips 170 DVD players, four Sony VPLX 1000U LCD (liquid crystal display) projectors, one Technovision PC/2 four-channel sync unit, two JBL Control-5 loudspeakers, one Samson Servo 120 amplifier

KEITH TYSON

English, b. 1969

31. *Artmachine Iteration AMCHII-XLII: Angelmaker Part II Quadruped,* 1995

Plates 27–29

Multimedia installation with sound; plan

Dimensions variable (approx. 16 x 20 x 26 ft.); duration continuous

Media: four BetaSP videotapes authored to DVD (digital versatile disc): *Untitled Limb (Titanic); Quake, Burn, and Quench; Bacterial Endotoxin; Automatic Oxygen Debt*

Equipment: four Philips 170 DVD players, one Sanyo PLC 9000N LCD (liquid crystal display) projector, one Sony VPLX 1000U LCD projector, one Panasonic DT 2730MS 27-inch monitor, five electronic sync and effects boxes, two digital counters, two projection screens, four JBL Control-5 loudspeakers, two JBL 4410 loudspeakers, three Samson Servo 120 amplifiers, motion sensors, custom electronics

Materials: porthole, light boxes, periscope, colored lightbulbs, glass screen, mirror, smoke machine, linoleum floor tiles, wooden door, construction materials

BILL VIOLA

American, b. 1951

32. *The Greeting,* 1995

Plates 53–54

Single-channel video projection with sound; plan

21 ft. 6 in. x 25 ft. 6 in.; 10:00 min.

Media: one laser disc

Equipment: one Pioneer LD-V8000 laser disc player, one Sony VPH 1252Q projector, two JBL 4408 studio monitors, one Panasonic TR990C black-and-white monitor, one Stewart 111-by-95-inch Video Tek 130 screen, one Rane ME 15 equalizer, one QSC 1200 power amplifier

JEFF WALL

Canadian, b. 1946

33. *The Quarrel,* 1988

Plate 25

Cibachrome transparency and light box

52 1/2 x 74 in.

34. *Untangling,* 1994

Plate 26

Cibachrome transparency and light box

74 1/2 x 88 in.

JANE AND LOUISE WILSON

English, b. 1967

35. *Stasi City,* 1997

Plates 22–23

Four-channel video installation with sound; plan

Dimensions variable (image: 10 x 12 ft.); 29:00 min.

Media: four laser discs

Equipment: four Pioneer LD-V2600 laser disc players, four Sony VPLX 1000U LCD (liquid crystal display) projectors, one Technovision PC/2 four-channel sync unit, four JBL Control-5 loudspeakers, two Samson Servo 120 amplifiers, one subwoofer

DEDICATED TO THE MEMORY
OF JOHN CALDWELL (1941–1993)